Children and The Law

Essays in Honour of Professor H. K. Bevan

Hull University Press

Professor H. K. Bevan

Children and The Law

Essays in Honour of
Professor H. K. Bevan

Edited by

David Freestone
The Law School
University of Hull

HULL UNIVERSITY PRESS
1990

© Hull University Press

British Library Cataloguing in Publication Data

Children and The Law
    1. Children. Law
    I. Freestone, D. A. C. (David A. C.)   II. Bevan, H.K.
    (Hugh Keith) *1922-*
    342.087

ISBN 0-85958-496-8

Phototypeset in 11 on 12 pt Times and printed by Fretwells, Hull.

Contents

Foreword

The Right Honourable Sir Stephen Brown
The President of the Family Division
of the High Court

The Law relating to Children is in a state of rapid development. Its paramount importance in our society is now widely recognised by academic and practising lawyers alike. The essays in this volume illustrate the wide scope of the subject and something of its intricacies. They range over a number of the more important topical and controversial issues involving children and the law. Each essay is the product of impressive scholarship directed to vitally important practical problems. All concerned with this area of the law will find them both stimulating and informative. They deserve a wide circulation. It is a privilege to commend them to all concerned with this vital area of our law. They constitute a worthy tribute to a splendid career.

Acknowledgements

The Editor would like to acknowledge the assistance of a number of individuals in the preparation of this volume, in particular Dr Joyce Bellamy for her careful copy editing, Wendy Mann for preparing the tables and index, and Jean Smith and the staff of the Central Print Unit for their swift and efficient processing of the text. Acknowledgement must also be given to the Law School, and in particular the Dean, Raymond Smith, for support and encouragement of the project.

The Contributors

P. M. Bromley	Emeritus Professor of Law, University of Manchester.
I. Boruta	Lecturer in Law, University of Wodz, Poland.
J. R. Carby-Hall	Senior Lecturer, Law School, University of Hull.
S. M. Cretney	Professor of Law, University of Bristol.
J. S. Davidson	Senior Lecturer, School of Law, University of Canterbury, Christchurch, New Zealand. Formerly Lecturer, Law School, University of Hull.
D. Dixon	Lecturer, Law School, University of Hull. Currently Visiting Research Fellow, Faculty of Law, University of New South Wales, Sydney, Australia.
M. D. A. Freeman	Professor Law, University College, London.
D. Freestone	Senior Lecturer, Law School, University of Hull.
M. Gould	Lecturer, Law Faculty, University of Bristol. Formerly Lecturer, Law School, University of Hull.
J. C. Hall	Fellow of St John's College, Cambridge.
W. N. R. Lucy	Lecturer, Law School, University of Hull.
His Excellency Sir Roy Marshall	Barbados High Commissioner to London. Formerly Vice-Chancellor of the University of Hull.
M. L. Parry	Senior Lecturer, Law School, University of Hull.
P. R. H. Webb	Emeritus Professor, University of Auckland, New Zealand.

Table of Cases

English Courts

New Zealand

Table of Legislation

United Kingdom

Table of
European Community Legislation

Table of Treaties

Table of Reports and Papers

Hugh Bevan: An Appreciation

Hugh Bevan: An Appreciation

His Excellency Sir Roy Marshall CBE

The forty years of Hugh Bevan's academic career coincide in general terms with the development of University law teaching in the post-war era and in particular with the teaching of law at the University of Hull to which he has devoted himself.

Hugh was appointed to the Law Department of the University College of Hull (as it then was) in January 1950 as an Assistant Lecturer. The Head of Department was the late Professor (then Mr) F. W. Taylor, other colleagues were J. E. Hall Williams (later Professor at the LSE), J. D. Newton (subsequently Senior Lecturer at the University of Liverpool and practitioner at the Chancery Bar on the Northern Circuit) and A. H. Hudson (now Professor at the University of Liverpool).

Like most of his generation, Hugh's education had been interrupted by the war. From Neath Grammar School he went up, in 1941, to the University College of Wales, Aberystwyth to read Classics. However his study of the classics was prematurely ended by military service. He joined the Royal Artillery Signals in 1943, serving first in North Africa and then with the Kenyan African Rifles in East Africa where he first demonstrated a talent for teaching, being appointed Principal Lecturer in Ki-Swahili.

In 1946 he returned to Aberystwyth, this time to study law in the Department led by Professor Llewelfryn-Davies. He graduated with a First Class Honours LLB in 1949, and moved to take up his post at the University College of Hull in the New Year of 1950, when Hull was still teaching students for the University of London External LLB. It was a time when University teachers did not have a large number of students, but were expected to teach a wide spread of subjects. In his first years Hugh taught Roman Law, Legal History, Constitutional Law, Private International Law, and English Legal System, to which he later added Contract and Administrative Law.

In 1954 the University College became the University of Hull under a Royal Charter which empowered it to award its own degrees. In recognition of this development, a number of existing Heads of Department, including Law, received chairs. Fred Taylor, whose efforts to sustain law teaching at Hull during the war and immediate post-war years had ensured the survival of the Department, became the University's first Professor of Law. With characteristic foresight, energy and skill, Hugh Bevan put to good use the freedom which the Department now enjoyed to develop its own curriculum. As a result, Hull was among the first to offer Family Law as a final year optional subject, and it soon achieved the popularity among students which it has maintained to the present.

The first edition of Bromley's *Family Law*[1] in 1957 firmly established it as a University subject and it began to occupy the majority of Hugh's academic efforts. His first article appeared in the *Law Quarterly Review* in 1957;[2] he was called to the Bar of the Middle Temple in 1959, and was awarded the degree of LLM by the University of Wales in 1966 for a dissertation on Matrimonial Causes.[3] By that time Hugh had established himself as an authority on Family Law, through a series of articles and the publication in 1964 (with P. R. H. Webb, then of the University of Nottingham) of the highly acclaimed *Source Book of Family Law*.[4] In recognition of his standing as a scholar the University promoted him to a Senior Lectureship in 1961 and appointed him to the newly created second Chair in Law in 1969. He immediately became Head of Department.

---

1   P. M. Bromley, *Family Law* (London: Butterworths, 1957).
2   'Belief in the Other Spouse's Adultery' (1957) 73 *Law Quarterly Review* 225.
3   The external examiner was J. C. Hall of St John's College, Cambridge.
4   P. R. H. Webb and H. K. Bevan, *Source Book of Family Law* (London: Butterworths, 1964) lii + 673 pp.

He gave his inaugural lecture on *Child Protection and the Law* on 5 March 1970.[5]

The creation of a second chair reflected the increasing size and reputation of the Department, over both of which Hugh Bevan had considerable and, at times, a decisive influence. By 1970, the Hull Law Department, like similar departments at Universities around the country, had grown from some 16 students and 3 staff in 1950 to 175 students and 15 staff.

With the benefit of hindsight it is possible to envisage the Department in 1970 poised to expand to accommodate the unprecedented rise in student numbers in Law during the following decade, but at that time trends in University legal education were still uncertain. Hugh was a very steady hand on the helm during those days. He had, early on, set himself the aim of Faculty status for the growing Department, and did a great deal at a personal level to ensure that research played an important part in the activities of the Department, despite the pressures of growing student numbers. His own commitment to research and his now national reputation were evidenced by the award from the Home Office in 1972 of a major grant to investigate the legal process in the Juvenile Court in the light of the 1969 Children and Young Persons Act, as well as by the publication in 1973 of *The Law Relating to Children*.[6]

Hugh spent the academic year 1973-4 as a Visiting Fellow at Emmanuel College, Cambridge, from which he paid flying visits to Hull to oversee the progress of the research project and to argue for the grant of Faculty status to the Law Department. In this busy period he was appointed a JP in Hull and enlisted by Dr David Owen to assist with the development and drafting of his private member's Children Bill. After the 1974 election, Dr Owen became Minister of State at the DHSS and the Labour Administration took over the project. A number of the original features of the Owen Private Member's Bill were retained in the 1975 Children Act, but to Hugh's disappointment the extended concept of guardianship which he had

5   *Child Protection and the Law*, Inaugural Lecture in the University of Hull, 5 March, 1970. (Hull: University Press, 1970) 25 pp.
6   *The Law Relating to Children*, (London: Butterworths, 1973) lix + 522 pp.

favoured was dropped and replaced by the new hybrid notion of 'custodianship'.[7]

In 1974 the Law Department achieved Faculty status, to stand with Science, Arts and Social Sciences, with Hugh as its first Dean. The retirement of Professor F. W. Taylor and the appointment of his successor in 1974 allowed Hugh the opportunity to alternate the role of Head of Department and Dean of the Faculty and thus to find time to work (with his younger colleague Martin Parry) on his commentary on the 1975 Children Act.[8] This appeared in 1978 to a very warm welcome. Both authors then became closely involved in the establishment and writing of the major Family Law Encyclopaedia *Butterworths Family Law Service* which was first published in 1983 under the General Editorship of Professor Bromley.[9]

Despite continued pressure for a second edition of his 1973 work, Hugh took the view that the developments in child law were so fundamental that a longer term, more comprehensive, work was called for and thus was born the book which in 1989 became *Child Law*[10] hailed typically by a recent reviewer as 'a scholarly survey of English child law which will be an invaluable resource for practitioner and academic alike.'[11] However it must be said that Hugh's decision to embark on a long term rather than short term project was in part pragmatic, for his duties in the University which had always been onerous were further added to in 1979 when he was appointed a Pro-Vice-Chancellor of the University. It was in this role that he received the news of the July 1981 University Grants Committee letter which imposed major financial cuts on the University and resulted in the immediate freezing and subsequent loss of the third Chair in Law for which he had argued long and hard.

---

7   For an elaboration of the new notion of 'guardianship' (involving a development of existing concepts of care and control) which he proposed, see H. K. Bevan and M. L. Parry, *Children Act, 1975* (London: Butterworths, 1978) p. 114.

8   H. K. Bevan and M. L. Parry, *Children Act, 1975* (London: Butterworths, 1978) xviii + 307 pp.

9   *Butterworths Family Law Service* (London: Butterworths, 1983 -) vols 1, 2 and 3.

10 *Child Law* (London: Butterworths, 1989) lxxviii + 856 pp.

11 Review [1990] Fam Law 150.

The following years were hard for all in the University sector. Major restructuring of the administration of the University led to the abolition of Faculties and the division of teaching departments into fourteen Schools. The Law School - one of the largest single-subject schools - was born in October 1988, the same month that Hugh's term of office as President of the Society of Public Teachers of Law expired. Hugh has always been an enthusiastic supporter of the SPTL and it was fitting that in September 1988, when Hull hosted the annual SPTL Conference for the second time in its short history, it should be with Hugh as its President. The theme, chosen by Hugh, was 'The Commonwealth'. Typically his Presidential address was devoted to the problems of funding legal research.[12]

Throughout this period Hugh maintained a practice at the Bar, based in chambers in Hull, although in later years through pressure of other commitments he restricted himself to Chancery work. His work as a JP on the Juvenile and Domestic Panels resulted in his appointment as Chairman of the Justices in 1985, a post he held until this year. He was also Chairman of the Hull Citizens Advice Bureau and since 1982 he has been a Legal Chairman of the Yorkshire Rent Assessment Committee. He has also served for many years on the Policy and Purposes Committee of the National Children's Bureau, and is currently Chairman of the Hull and North Humberside Family Conciliation Service.

1990 has been a memorable year for Hugh. He has been elected to a Fellowship at Wolfson College, Cambridge where, following his retirement from Hull, he had been spending the 1989-90 session as a Visiting Fellow. He has received the Honorary Degree of LLD from the University of Hull, which has also established the H. K. Bevan Chair of Law in his honour with the support of contributions from colleagues, former pupils, friends and well-wishers. And, finding it impossible to give up teaching and research to which he has devoted his entire working life, he has become the part-time director of training and research for a firm of Cambridge solicitors.

Throughout his career Hugh has had an interest in international affairs. His wartime experiences in East Africa gave him the feel of that vast continent and the large number of students

---

12   Published in the *SPTL Newsletter* [1989] Summer, pp. 1-10.

from West Africa and the West Indies, whom he taught at Hull in the post-war years before the establishment of systems of legal education in their own countries, became his friends and enlarged his Commonwealth connections. More recently these have been enhanced by lecturing tours to Cyprus and Hong Kong. Not surprisingly, therefore, he made a point of emphasising Commonwealth issues in the agenda of the SPTL Annual Conference in 1988, the year of his Presidency. He invited Professor K. W. Patchett, the founding Dean of the Faculty of Law of the University of the West Indies to deliver the feature address and myself to chair a panel discussion on student mobility and higher education co-operation within the Commonwealth.

Hugh has also been active in establishing and strengthening relationships between the University of Hull and European Institutions of higher education. He has encouraged the development of courses in European Community law and has lectured in Poland at the University of Lodz.

Of all the honours bestowed and to be bestowed upon him, I am sure that Hugh will rank none higher that this *Festschrift*. It is a fitting tribute to a man whose steadfastness, integrity, selflessness, sense of values and concern for his family, his colleagues, his pupils and his friends are manifest as much in his everyday life as in his work and his writings. He has set examples which few are likely to equal and even fewer surpass.

1

The Legal Aspects of Surrogacy Agreements

P. M. Bromley

Surrogacy agreements can take a number of forms, but all have one element in common: one woman (known as 'the surrogate mother') agrees to bear a child which, after it is born, is to be handed over to another woman (variously referred to as 'the commissioning mother', 'the commissioning wife' or 'the commissioning woman') to be brought up as her own. The purpose of this paper is to examine the legal effects of surrogacy agreements and the difficulties they may give rise to.

Types of surrogacy agreements

As a degree of secrecy surrounds the making of most surrogacy agreements, it is impossible to speak with any confidence of what current practices are. It would seem that the vast majority of commissioning women enter into surrogacy agreements because they cannot bear a child of their own or, occasionally, because there is a risk of their passing on a genetically transmitted disease (for example, haemophilia) or of bearing a handicapped child. Consequently it is usually agreed that the commissioning woman's husband is to be the father and that the child is to be conceived either as the result of adultery[1] or, probably more usually, by artificial insemination.[2] This, like AID, will enable the couple to bring up a child that is biologically the child of one of them but not of both. If the commissioning woman produces fertile ova but cannot bear a child (for example, because of a malformed uterus or a previous hysterectomy) the agreement may contemplate the child's conception by *in vitro* fertilisation (or IVF) of the commissioning mother's ovum by her husband's semen and the implanting of the resulting embryo in the surrogate mother's uterus. Such an agreement might also be entered into by a woman who is perfectly capable of bearing children herself but fears pregnancy or wishes to avoid the inconvenience and hardship of pregnancy and childbirth or the possible loss of income and career prospects that might result. The increase in the number of people who enter into a stable union outside marriage also means that a surrogacy agreement may be entered into by a couple who are not married to each other.

Other possible variations should be noted. The commissioning mother's husband or partner may himself be sterile so that the father of the child will be another man who may be known to the commissioning woman or the surrogate mother or, if the child is conceived as the result of AID or IVF, may be known to neither of them. Similar arrangements may be made by others who wish to have a child, for example a sterile woman who is unmarried and has no permanent partner, a sterile lesbian or a homosexual man. Although such arrangements cannot be ignored, they are likely to be rare: consequently their legal effects will be considered separately towards the end of this paper.

The surrogate mother may be a friend or relation, for example the sister of one of the commissioning parents.[3] She will then

1   As in *Re Adoption Application (payment for adoption)* [1987] Fam 81 where Latey J referred to a 'physical congress with the sole purpose of procreating a child' (at p. 83).

2   As in *A v C* [1985] FLR 445; *Re C (a minor) (wardship: surrogacy)* [1985] FLR 846; and *Re P (minors) (wardship: surrogacy)* [1987] 2 FLR 421.

3   Her husband may also be the father. See the cases cited by Wright, 'Surrogacy and Adoption: Problems and Possibilities' [1986] Fam Law 109, 110, and Morgan, 'Surrogacy: Giving it an Understood Name' [1988] JSWL 216, 227-32.

probably act gratuitously, but surrogacy agreements usually contemplate payment to the surrogate mother. Some act generously to help a childless couple and the payment may be intended merely to compensate the recipient for the inconvenience and discomfort she suffers, expenses in connection with the pregnancy and birth, and any loss of earnings.[4] In other cases the surrogate mother may seek to exploit the situation for her own financial gain and some very large sums are believed to have been paid.[5]

The status of the child at birth

If the surrogate mother and the commissioning man are the genetic parents, *prima facie* the child will be their illegitimate child. In this case the Births and Deaths Registration Act 1953 requires the name of the mother to be entered in the register of births: presumably the father will normally be anxious to have his name registered as well, but this can be done only if the surrogate mother agrees.[6] There is one case, however, where the commissioning father will not be regarded in law as the child's father. If the surrogate mother is married[7] and the child was conceived by artificial insemination, section 27(1) of the Family Law Reform Act 1987 provides that her husband, and not the donor, is to be treated as the father unless it can

4   As in *Re Adoption Application*, (above, n. 1)
5   In *Re C* (above n. 2), £6500 was to be paid to the surrogate mother and a further £6500 to the agency: see 15 Fam Law 71.
6   His name may be registered at the joint request of both parents (in which case both must sign the register) or at the request of either of them (in which case the parent registering the birth must make a declaration on the prescribed form that the man is the child's father and the other must make a statutory declaration to the same effect): Births and Deaths Registration Act 1953, s. 10 (as substituted by the Family Law Reform Act 1987, s. 24). Hence the mother may prevent the father from registering his name by refusing to provide the statutory declaration. If the mother's name alone has been registered, the Registrar General may permit the birth to be re-registered by adding the father's name provided that the same conditions are satisfied: ibid., s. 10A (as substituted by the Family Law Reform Act 1987, s. 25).
7   Apparently in the USA most surrogate mothers are married women with children because this indicates their ability to bear healthy children.

be shown that he did not consent to the insemination.[8] It does not seem that he can give a conditional consent, namely that he is not to be treated as the father, because that would undermine the whole purpose of the section. Parties who act without full legal advice may be ignorant of these provisions and startled and dismayed when they learn of them, not least the husband who has to be registered as the child's father and remains liable to maintain him. The section was passed to meet an entirely different situation - that of the childless couple who resort to artificial insemination because the husband is sterile and who intend to keep the child born as a result[9] - and its application to surrogacy agreements is wholly inappropriate.

These principles are not affected by the proposals contained in the Human Fertilisation and Embryology Bill (henceforth referred to as 'the Bill').[10] They do not apply at all if the child is conceived by adultery. Clause 27 preserves the principle contained in section 27 of the Family Law Reform Act if the surrogate mother is married and the child is conceived by artificial insemination;[11] in other cases it provides that a man whose sperm is used for the purpose of treatment services is not to be treated as the father of any child conceived if his consent is required by Schedule 3. 'Treatment services' include any medical services provided to assist women to carry children[12] and thus must include artificial insemination, but the clause does not apply in the situation under consideration because consent will not be required if the sperm is to be used for treatment services of the donor and another together.[13]

In vitro fertilisation of the commissioning mother's ovum followed by embryo transfer or the placing of her ovum in the

8   The section has no application if the birth occurred before 4 April 1988 or
        at any time outside England and Wales. The mother is regarded as married
        if the marriage is voidable or void provided that in the latter case either or
        both of the spouses reasonably believed it to be valid at the time of the
        insemination: s. 27(2).

9   See the Law Commission's two reports on Illegitimacy (Law Com. No.
        118, paras 12.1-12.27, and Law Com. No. 157, para. 3.20).

10   The clause numbers are those in the Bill as introduced in the House of
        Lords (22 Nov. 1989).

11   If the surrogate mother is inseminated after clause 27 comes into operation,
        it will apply wherever the birth takes place.

12   Clause 2(1).

13   Sched. 3, para. 5.

surrogate mother gives rise to a much more difficult problem of status. Is the child to be regarded in law as the child of the surrogate mother or the commissioning mother? The writer has argued elsewhere that common sense dictates that a court should recognise the carrying mother as the legal mother.[14] This will be given statutory effect by clause 26 of the Bill.

The legal position if the child is handed over to the commissioning parents

Custody

A clause in a surrogacy agreement that the surrogate mother is to hand the child over to the commissioning parents is not enforceable.[15] Even though her doing so voluntarily would appear to amount to a tacit agreement between them that she should surrender all parental rights and duties to them, this is equally of no legal effect.[16] Consequently if the commissioning parents wish to

---

14   See 'Aided Conception' in P. Bean (Ed.) *Adoption: Essays in Social Policy, Law and Sociology* (London: Tavistock, 1984) pp. 189-90.

15   See below.

16   Although it is generally assumed that s. 1(2) of the Guardianship Act 1973 (as substituted by section 3 of the Family Law Reform Act 1987) enables the unmarried parents of a child to agree that one shall have exclusive custody (see e.g. H. K. Bevan, *Child Law* (London: Butterworths, 1989) paras. 1.68 and 2.15; P.M. Bromley, *Family Law*, (London: Butterworths, 7th Edn., 1987) p. 266), it is not clear that this is so. The subsection refers to an agreement as to the *exercise* (as distinct from the transfer) of parental rights and duties. This appears to limit its operation to the exercise of rights and duties that the parent already has and would not enable the mother to agree to the father's exercising a right he does not already possess. (Cf. section 3(3A) of the Act (added by section 5 of the Family Law Reform Act 1987) which provides that, if a child's parents are not married to each other, neither of them may apply for the direction of the court if they disagree on a question affecting the child's welfare unless an order is in force giving the father all legal rights and duties, or legal or actual custody, or care and control. This suggests that the father can acquire no rights or duties by agreement.) The point will be put beyond doubt when s. 2(9) of the Children Act 1989 comes into force because this expressly provides that a person who has parental responsibility for a child may not surrender or transfer any part of it to another.

strengthen their legal position, they must obtain a court order. If the commissioning father is regarded in law as the child's father, he should apply for custody under section 9 of the Guardianship of Minors Act 1971[17] rather than a parental rights and duties order under section 4 of the Family Law Reform Act 1987[18] because he would wish the surrogate mother's rights to be terminated. His wife or unmarried partner could similarly apply for a custodianship order under section 33 of the Children Act 1975 (as he himself could if he were not in law the father).[19] Because of the difficult problems that may arise, however, the most appropriate procedure to determine care and control in all cases is to make the child a ward of court. The most effective way of gaining permanent security, of course, is for the commissioning parents to adopt the child: this will prevent any possible application for custody by the surrogate mother in the future and place the child in the position of the applicants' legal child with respect to any claim relating to parental rights and duties and property.

Wardship

A court deciding who is to have care and control of a ward of court must regard the child's welfare as the first and paramount

---

17   As substituted by the Family Law Reform Act 1987, s. 10. This will be replaced by a residence order and a prohibited steps order when s. 8 of the Children Act 1989 comes into force.

18   To be replaced by a similar order under s. 4 of the Children Act 1989.

19   If the commissioning father is to be regarded in law as the child's father, he cannot apply for a custodianship order. If the commissioning parents are married, the child will have to have had his home with the wife for a period of at least three months before she can apply for a custodianship order. If they are not married, the period is twelve months: Children Act 1975, s. 33(3), (4) and (9A). Custodianship orders will disappear when the Children Act 1989 comes into force. The commissioning mother will then have to obtain the leave of the court to obtain a section 8 order: ibid., s. 10(2).

consideration,[20] and the fact that it was conceived and born as the result of a surrogacy agreement is relevant only if this indicates that the claimants' willingness to enter into the agreement 'would reflect upon their moral outlook so adversely as to disqualify them as potential custodians'.[21] There have been only two reported cases involving a child who has been handed over to the commissioning parents by the surrogate mother, and in each of them Latey J had no hesitation in leaving the child with the former.

In *Re C (a minor) (wardship: surrogacy)*[22] the commissioning parents lived in the USA.   The wife was unable to have children so the father entered into an agreement with an agency in America as a result of which a surrogate mother was found in England.   A child was conceived by artificial insemination with the commissioning father's semen.   The commissioning parents came to this country in anticipation of the birth and the mother left the baby in the hospital a few hours after this occurred.   On the same day the social services department of the local authority (presumably alerted by the hospital authorities) obtained a place of safety order[23] - an action which the judge commended as they knew nothing about the commissioning parents, although, he added, with hindsight they

20   Guardianship of Minors Act 1971, s. 1.   'The golden thread which runs through the whole of this court's jurisdiction - the welfare of the child, which is considered in this court first, last and all the time' (*per* Dunn J in *Re D (justices' decision: review)* [1977] Fam 158, 163).   '[The court's] paramount concern is the welfare of its ward' (*per* Lord Scarman in *Re E (SA) (a minor) (wardship: court's duty)* [1984] 1 WLR 156, 159). 'First and foremost, and at the heart of the prerogative jurisdiction in wardship, is what is best for the child or children concerned.   That and nothing else' (*per* Latey J. in *Re C (a minor) (wardship: surrogacy)* [1985] FLR 846, 847).

21   Per Sir John Arnold P. in *Re P (minors) (wardship: surrogacy)* [1987] 2 FLR 421, 425.   'The fact that . . . generation of a child has been achieved by . . . AID . . . can have no effect upon the duty of a court to try to afford that child such a life as will best promote the child's welfare' (per Cumming-Bruce LJ in *A v C* [1985] FLR 445, 458).   See also Latey J in *Re C* (above) at pp. 847-8.

22   [1985] FLR 846.   The case attracted a great deal of popular attention before the child was warded and became known as 'The Baby Cotton Case'.

23   Presumably on the ground that the baby's health was being avoidably neglected.

might have done better to ward the child immediately in view of the unusual and complex nature of the case. The father then warded the child himself. Latey J committed the care and control of the child to the commissioning parents and gave them leave to take her out of the jurisdiction. In two paragraphs which lie at the heart of his judgment he said:[24]

> So, what is best for this baby? Her natural mother does not ask for her. Should she go into Mr and Mrs A's [the commissioning parents'] care and be brought up by them? Or should some other arrangement be made for her, such as long-term fostering with or without adoption as an end? ...
>
> Mr A is the baby's father and he wants her, as does his wife. The baby's mother does not want her. Mr and Mrs A are a couple in their 30s. They are devoted to each other. They are both professional people, highly qualified ... Materially they can give the baby a very good upbringing. But, far more importantly, they are both excellently equipped to meet the baby's emotional needs. They are most warm, caring, sensible people, as well as highly intelligent ... Looking at this child's well-being, physical and emotional, who better to have her care? No one.

Latey J reached a similar conclusion in the second of the two cases, *Re Adoption Application (payment for adoption)*,[25] which was concerned not with wardship but with the adoption of a child now aged two years whom the surrogate mother had left with the commissioning parents when it was nine days old. Indeed, in all cases where the mother has voluntarily parted with the child to the commissioning parents, the test the judge formulated in *Re C* is bound to lead the court to give care and control to the latter unless they are unfit for some other reason. If they are unmarried, they may

24　　At p. 848.
25　　[1987] Fam 81. See further below.

face a more difficult hurdle because the court may wish to be assured that they are sufficiently committed to each other to make it desirable to give them care and control of a ward.   It could only be in rare cases that their having entered into a surrogacy agreement would in itself show such a degree of irresponsibility as to disqualify them.[26]

There has been no reported case in which the mother has attempted to recover a child after she has surrendered it to the commissioning parents.   The court must resolve the dispute as it would any other dispute between a parent and others who have actual custody of a child.   If it has been away from her for only a short period of time, the court might well restore the child to her if she were otherwise a fit person to have care and control because it would doubtless be greatly influenced by the natural bonding between mother and child and probably little troubled by her vacillation in the circumstances.   The longer the separation has lasted, the more difficult she may find it to succeed: if the child is settled in a loving and caring family, evidence of the mother's lack of commitment may well outweigh any natural claim she has.[27]

Adoption

Commissioning parents wishing to adopt the child face a number of obstacles.[28]

(1) Section 11 of the Adoption Act 1976 makes it an offence for a person other than an adoption agency to make arrangements for the adoption of a child, or to place a child for adoption, unless the proposed adopter is a relative of the child, or he is acting in pursuance

---

26   For a case where the court might have taken this view, see *A* v *C* (above, n. 21), discussed further below.

27   'There is really no argument which is in favour of the child remaining with the petitioner except that the petitioner is her mother.   That is undoubtedly an important factor, but its force in the present case is greatly reduced by the petitioner's conduct in abandoning her child at the age of seven months and leaving her with her father for the next $2^1/_4$ years' (*per* Wood J delivering the judgment of the Court of Appeal in *Stephenson* v *Stephenson* [1985] FLR 1140, 1148-9).   See generally *J* v *C* [1970] AC 668.

28   They will also have to satisfy the conditions relating to age and domicile: Adoption Act 1976, ss 14 and 15.

of an order of the High Court. It is also an offence to receive a child placed in contravention of the section. A person is deemed to make arrangements for the adoption of a child if

> he enters into or makes any agreement or arrangement for, or for facilitating, the adoption of the child by any other person, whether the adoption is effected, or is intended to be effected, in Great Britain or elsewhere . . .[29]

No offence will be committed if the commissioning father is to be regarded as the child's unmarried father because he will then be a relative for the purpose of the Act.[30] In other cases this provision raises a number of questions. The first is whether the parties' acts bring them within the definition of 'an arrangement or placing for adoption'. The test must be whether they contemplated that the commissioning parents would apply for an adoption order after they had received the child.[31] If this was an express term of the surrogacy agreement or if, when the child was handed over, the parties all knew that this was the commissioning parents' intention, an offence is clearly committed. Conversely, no offence is committed if no thought was given to adoption until after the commissioning parents received the child[32] or, perhaps, if they merely contemplated that they *might* seek adoption in the future.[33] If this was their intention all along but the mother was unaware of it and did not hand over the child with a view to adoption, none of them commits an offence: the mother does not make arrangements for the adoption of the child or place it for adoption and consequently the commissioning parents do not receive it in contravention of the section.[34]

29   Adoption Act 1976, s. 72(3).
30   Ibid., s. 72(1).
31   See *Gatehouse* v *R* [1986] 1 WLR 18.
32   Cf. *Re Adoption Application (payment for adoption)* [1987] Fam 81 (discussed below).
33   In which case the commissioning parents become subject to the provisions of the Foster Children Act 1980 and must give notice to the local authority that they have received the child. (To be replaced by the Children Act 1989, Schedule 8, para. 7.)
34   *Gatehouse* v *R*, (above n. 31).

　　　The court is not expressly forbidden to make an adoption order if there has been a contravention of section 11.[35]　This is in marked contrast to the express prohibition contained in section 24(2) if there has been an unauthorised payment.[36]　Nevertheless in both the reported cases in which the point has been raised it has been assumed that no order should be made unless the High Court exercises its dispensing power.　In neither case, however, did counsel apparently base a submission on the difference in wording between the two sections.　In *Re S (arrangements for adoption)*[37] the county court judge hearing an adoption application concluded that there had been an unauthorised placement and ordered that the proceedings be stayed pending an application to a judge of the High Court.　An appeal against that order was dismissed.　This was followed in *Re A (adoption: placement)*[38,] where Anthony Lincoln J, having authorised the placement, remitted the case to the county court.　Until a body of case law relating to the adoption of children born as the result of surrogacy agreements has been established, it is no doubt desirable that such applications should be heard in the High Court.　Once that has been done, is there any reason why the application should not be dealt with in a county court even though the parties face prosecution?

　　　In each of the cases mentioned it was assumed that the High Court can authorise a placement retrospectively.　This accords with the decision of Latey J in *Re Adoption Application (payment for adoption)*[39,] where he considered the court's corresponding power to authorise payment for adoption.　The learned judge pointed out that there is nothing in the ordinary definition of the word to suggest that an authorisation may only be given prospectively and the consequences of holding otherwise would be draconian, barring an adoption however much the welfare of the child demanded it and however modest the payment.　The curious effect of these decisions

35　　Although in exceptional circumstances it may make a supervision order (which implies that the child will remain with the applicants) or commit the child to the care of a local authority:　Adoption Act 1976, ss 11(5) and 26.
36　　See below.
37　　[1985] FLR 579.
38　　[1988] 1 WLR 229.
39　　[1987] Fam 81.　*Re S* was not cited in argument and *Re Adoption Application* was not cited in *Re A*. For unauthorised payments, see further below.

is that the court can legalise a criminal offence *ex post facto* even, apparently, after the participants have been prosecuted.

The purpose of the restriction is to prevent unsatisfactory or even irresponsible placements with or by acquaintances rather than by adoption agencies' trained social workers.[40] Adoption of a child born as the result of a surrogacy agreement is *sui generis* and outside the mischief the Act seeks to remedy. The child needs the security of adoption by the commissioning parents: consequently it is submitted that the court should always authorise the placement unless the applicants would be unsatisfactory adoptive parents, in which case the order should not be made on this ground.

(2) No order can be made unless the surrogate mother agrees to the adoption or her agreement is dispensed with. (If the child is the legitimate child of the mother and her husband, his agreement will also be required.)[41] She is most likely to withhold her agreement if she wishes to recover custody and the correct procedure in this event would be to ward the child so that the question of custody could be resolved first. If the court leaves custody with the commissioning parents or if the mother refuses to agree for some other reason, the court should normally dispense with her agreement (and *a fortiori* her husband's) on the ground that it is unreasonably withheld because no reasonable parent would disregard the substantial benefit the child would derive from adoption or be wilfully indifferent to its welfare which demands an adoption order.[42]

If the surrogate mother is prepared to agree to the adoption only if she has continuing access to the child, it is inconceivable that the court would make an order with a condition attached to this effect without the applicants' consent.[43] Access could cause great confusion to the child and undermine the security that adoption should give; consequently it should be entirely at the commissioning

---

40   See the *Report of the Departmental Committee on the Adoption of Children* (the Houghton (or Stockdale) Report) 1972, Cmnd 5107, paras 81-92.

41   Adoption Act 1976, s 16.

42   *Cf. Re W (an infant)* [1971] AC 682, particularly *per* Lord Hailsham LC, Lord MacDermott and Lord Hodson at pp. 700, 709 and 719 respectively.

43   See Re H *(a minor) (adoption)* [1985] FLR 519;   Re M *(a minor)* *(adoption order: access)* [1986] 1 FLR 51;   Re C *(a minor) (adoption order: conditions)* [1989] AC 1.

parents' discretion.   If they refuse to countenance it, the court should either dispense with the mother's agreement or refuse to make the order.

(3) We have already noted that commissioning parents may - and probably usually do - make the surrogate mother a payment which may range from bare compensation for medical expenses, loss of earnings, etc. to a substantial sum.   This could lead to a *prima facie* breach of the provisions of section 57 of the Adoption Act. Subject to certain exceptions, this section (which is designed to prevent commercial trafficking in children for adoption) makes it an offence to give or receive (or to agree to give or receive) any payment or reward in consideration of (a) the transfer of a child for the purpose of adoption or (b) the giving of an agreement to adoption, unless the payment or reward is authorised by the court.   The particular significance of this is that section 24(2) provides that a court shall not make an adoption order unless it is satisfied that the applicants have not contravened section 57.

The impact of these two sections on surrogacy agreements was considered by Latey J in *Re Adoption Application (payment for adoption)*.[44]   The surrogate mother, a married woman with two children of her own, was anxious to help a childless couple.   With her husband's support she placed an advertisement in a magazine as a result of which she agreed with the commissioning parents that she would conceive a child by sexual intercourse with the husband and that she would hand the child over to them after its birth.   She was to be paid £10,000 which represented her 'loss of earnings, expenses in connection with the pregnancy, and emotional and physical factors'. The child was duly handed over and the mother was paid £5000; she refused to take the remaining £5000 because she had made money out of the publication of a book describing her experiences.   On the commissioning parents' application for an adoption order the question arose whether section 57 had been contravened.

Latey J found as a fact that there was no commercial element in the agreement.   The mother had not been primarily motivated by any financial consideration and it was only after the payments had been made and the baby was born that any of the parties turned their

44   [1987] Fam 81.

14 *Children and The Law*

minds in any real sense to adoption and regulating the legal position. He therefore concluded that there had been no breach of the provisions. It is submitted that the test to be applied is that proposed in relation to unauthorised placements: did the commissioning parents contemplate that they would apply for an adoption order when they made the payment? If they had given no thought to the question at that time (as in *Re Adoption Application*) or perhaps if they only contemplated adoption as a possibility in the future, no illegal payment will have been made.

Latey J went on to hold that, if he were wrong on that point, the Act enabled him to authorise the payment retrospectively[45] and that in the circumstances he would have no hesitation in doing so. But it must be emphasised that this agreement did not envisage any sort of commercial profit. How would a court exercise its discretion in a case like *A* v *C*?[46] The facts were extraordinary. The commissioning mother, unable to have a child of her own, decided to find a surrogate mother by attending Bow Street magistrates' court and selecting a prostitute from among those being prosecuted for soliciting. The woman chosen declined the offer but introduced her to a girl of 19 who, if not herself a prostitute, was involved in the world of prostitution. She agreed to act for a sum of £3000 and the use of a flat during her pregnancy. The question of adoption did not arise because the girl refused to hand over the baby when it was born and the court was concerned with whether the father should have access to the child. One must, however, contrast the judges' description of the transaction with the benign view that Latey J took of the agreement in *Re Adoption Application*. Comyn J referred to 'a purported contract for the sale and purchase of a child . . . a pernicious agreement';[47] Ormrod LJ spoke of 'this extraordinary and irresponsible arrangement' and 'a sordid commercial bargain';[48] Cumming-Bruce LJ castigated the whole agreement as 'a kind of baby-farming operation of a wholly distasteful and lamentable kind',

45   See above. It should be noted that the payment may be authorised by the court hearing the application for adoption and not (as in the case of an unauthorised placement) merely by the High Court.
46   [1985] FLR 445 (Comyn J and CA). The case was decided in 1978. See further above.
47   At p. 449.
48   At pp. 454 and 457.

'a guilty bargain which should never have been made' and 'a lamentable commercial transaction';[49] Stamp LJ confined himself to describing the case as 'an ugly little drama'.[50] It is difficult to believe that either Comyn J or the Court of Appeal would have been prepared to authorise the payment if this had been the issue before them. Nevertheless one may question whether refusing to make an adoption order would have been the right course in the circumstances. However pernicious the agreement, the court would be faced with the fact that the child had been born and handed over to the commissioning parents and that it needed the security of adoption as much as the child in *Re Adoption Application*.[51] The difficulty is that section 24(2) prohibits the court from making an order if there has been any contravention of section 57 and the only power it has under the latter section is to authorise the payment. In contrast to its powers when dealing with unauthorised placements,[52] the court has no dispensing power. Consequently it must either condone the payment or refuse to make an order: it is urged that the law should be changed so that the court is not faced with this dilemma.

If the court concludes that the applicants' irresponsible conduct in entering into the agreement makes them undesirable adoptive parents, it should refuse to make an order specifically on this ground rather than decline to authorise a payment which, once made, cannot further affect the child's future.

(4) If the commissioning parents are not married to each other, they cannot jointly apply for adoption.[53] Whichever of them makes the application,[54] he or she runs the risk that it will be refused on the ground that the parties' domestic circumstances make the applicant an unsuitable adoptive parent.

---

49   At pp. 459 and 460.
50   At p. 461.
51   See Latey J's judgment, [1987] Fam at p. 87.
52   Under s. 11(1). See above.
53   Adoption Act 1976, s. 14(1).
54   If the commissioning mother were to make the application, the child would have to live with her for 12 months before an order could be made (instead of 13 weeks if the applicant is a relative, including the child's unmarried father): ibid., s. 13.

If the mother refuses to hand over the child

This was the issue that faced Sir John Arnold P in *Re P (minors) (wardship: surrogacy)*.[55]   There is of course no question of the commissioning parents obtaining specific performance of the contract.   As Sir John Arnold pointed out:[56]

> The existence of the agreement is relevant to this extent, that plainly one of the factors which has to be taken into account in determining where the welfare of the children lies, is the factor of the character of the rival custodians who were put forward for consideration and it might be that the willingness of those persons to enter into a surrogacy agreement would reflect upon their moral outlook so adversely as to disqualify them as potential custodians at all.

In this case the surrogate mother offered her services to the commissioning parents for payment.   The father was motivated by a desire to have a child to complement his strong marriage;   the mother had a genuine conviction that she could help the commissioning parents and she also wished to acquire some financial security for the benefit of her existing seven-year-old son.   As a result of artificial insemination with the husband's semen, she bore twins whom she then refused to hand over.   Both she and the father independently approached the local authority who applied to have the children made wards of court.   In weighing the merits of the claimants for care and control, Sir John Arnold P left out of account the fact that they had entered into the agreement because in his opinion there was nothing so shameful or disreputable in the conduct of either of them as to make them unfit to have custody.   What was relevant was that, on the one hand, the commissioning parents could offer the children financial and material advantages and an intellectual stimulus which they would lack with their mother;   moreover, they bore traces of the father's Asiatic origin and the resulting problems might be better

55   [1987] 2 FLR 421.
56   At p. 425.

understood, discussed and reconciled in his family. Against that, the twins had been looked after by their mother for five months and there must have been some bonding with her. In the circumstances Sir John Arnold P concluded that this outweighed all the advantages the commissioning parents could offer them and he accordingly awarded care and control to her.

The only other reported case of a surrogate mother's refusing to hand over the child is *A* v *C*,[57] the facts of which have already been given. The father reluctantly abandoned his claim for care and control before Comyn J but continued to seek access which the judge awarded him. The Court of Appeal unanimously allowed the mother's appeal against this order. The views of the agreement held by Comyn J and the members of the Court of Appeal have already been noted, but these only partly affected their decision. Comyn J was much more critical of the commissioning parents than of the mother in view of the discrepancy between their ages, social position and education; in Ormrod LJ's opinion the whole proceeding showed grave defects in the characters of all the participants. The significance of these findings can be seen in the following passage of Ormrod LJ's judgment:[58]

> The judge took the view - no doubt quite rightly - that it is almost inconceivable that this child should ever be handed over to the care of the father and his present wife, given the characters which the judge found them to have. So what is the good of keeping this wholly artificial, painful tie going? My answer is: No good will be done whatever . . . To my mind, to permit access to continue in the circumstances of this case is to perpetuate the most artificial situation that one can possibly imagine.

> Unless care and control are to be denied to the mother for

---

57   [1985] FLR 445 (decided in 1978).
58   At p. 457. Cumming-Bruce LJ similarly took the view that the father's visits could have nothing but a disruptive effect upon the mother which would be bound to have an adverse effect on the child (at p. 460). Stamp LJ agreed with Ormrod LJ's reasons.

some other reason (for example, because of defects in her character or
the surroundings in which the child would be brought up) it is highly
unlikely that a court would take the child from her.   The
commissioning father will then, of course, be liable to contribute to
its maintenance.[59]   If the child were not to remain with the mother, in
most cases it would almost certainly be in its interest for the court to
give care and control to the commissioning parents (unless they were
themselves disqualified) rather than place it in the care of the local
authority.

If the commissioning parents refuse to take the child

There has been no reported case in which the commissioning parents
have refused to take the child, but one can envisage a number of
circumstances in which this might occur quite apart from a newly
found reluctance to assume the duties of parenthood.   Death or
illness of one of them might lead the other to conclude that he or she
could not rear the child single-handed.   They might refuse to take
over a child born physically or mentally handicapped.   They could
face a further dilemma if the conception resulted in twins, as in *Re P.*

If the mother is prepared to keep the child, no immediate
problem arises, although the circumstances of the birth may affect the
relationship of mother and child.   If she does not want to keep it,
there can be no question of forcing it upon the other parties (although
the commissioning father will remain liable to maintain it).   Unless
another relative (for example, the maternal grandmother) is prepared
to look after the child, it will almost certainly find its way into local
authority care sooner or later;   if, as in *Re C*, it is left in the maternity
hospital a matter of hours after its birth, the authority will have no
alternative to obtaining an immediate place of safety order.   The
possibility of the commissioning parents' reneguing on the agreement
may not occur to a potential surrogate mother when she undertakes to
act. She overlooks it at her, and - what is worse - the child's, peril.

---

59   Guardianship of Minors Act 1971, s. 11B (added by the Family Law
        Reform Act 1987, s. 12).   (To be replaced by Schedule 1 to the Children
        Act 1989.)

Other forms of surrogacy agreements

We have up to now been considering what might be termed the 'normal' surrogacy agreement where the commissioning father is also the genetic father. There are, however, other possible forms of agreement.

If the commissioning man is sterile

If both the commissioning couple are sterile (or anxious not to pass on a genetically transmissible disease), the child will have to be conceived (usually by artificial insemination) using the semen of another man ('the donor') who could, of course, be the surrogate mother's husband. The legal position will then differ in the following ways.

(1) If the surrogate mother is married and the child is conceived by artificial insemination with her husband's consent or her husband is the father, it will be their legitimate child. In other cases the child will at present be the illegitimate child of the surrogate mother and the donor; by clause 27(4) of the Bill, however, it will be regarded as fatherless.[60] If the normal practice in AID of preserving the parties' anonymity were followed, neither the surrogate mother nor the commissioning couple would know the donor's identity and he would be unaware of the birth of the child.

(2) If the surrogate mother hands over the child, the commissioning parents would normally be granted care and control if the child were warded, as they would if the husband were the father.[61] They face further complications, however, if they seek to adopt it. An offence is bound to be committed under section 11 of the Adoption Act 1976[62] because the commissioning man will not be the child's father, and no adoption order can be made until the child has

60   Because the purpose of the insemination would not be to provide treatment services for the donor.

61   By analogy with *A v C* [1985] FLR 445 (above) it seems inconceivable that a court would give the donor parental rights or access even if he knew of the child's existence and wanted contact with it.

62   For s. 11 see above.

had his home with the applicants for a continuous period of 12 months.[63]

(3) If the surrogate mother refuses to hand the child over, the commissioning parents' claim will be even weaker than it is if the commissioning man is the father.

Surrogacy agreements made by homosexual commissioning parents

There have been cases of surrogacy agreements made by sterile lesbians wishing to rear a child.   As a lesbian will presumably have no male partner, the child will be conceived by AID and its status will be the same as that of the child considered in the last section. Similarly homosexual men wishing to father and bring up their own children are said to have entered into agreements by which surrogate mothers are artificially inseminated with their semen.   The child will then be either the illegitimate child of the commissioning father and the surrogate mother or, if she is married and her husband consents, the legitimate child of her and her husband.

The commissioning parent's sexual tendencies may raise insuperable problems when it comes to the care and control or adoption of the child.   The question has arisen in connection with dispensing with a parent's agreement to adoption.   In *Re D (an infant) (adoption: parent's consent)*[64] members of the House of Lords were at pains to point out that the fact that a parent is homosexual is not of itself a reason for dispensing with agreement on the ground that it is unreasonably withheld,[65] but they held that the county court judge was justified on the facts in doing so in that case. The father did not merely engage in isolated acts of homosexual conduct but had had a series of associations with young men; further contact between him and his son would inevitably bring the latter into the society of other actively homosexual men so that a reasonable father in his circumstances would say 'I must protect my

63   Adoption Act 1976, s. 13.   If one of the applicants is a parent or relative, the period is 13 weeks and the child must be at least 19 weeks old.
64   [1977] AC 602.
65   At pp. 629, 640, 642 and 647.

boy . . . so that he can be free from this danger'. This argument is even stronger if the applicant is homosexual, particularly if a man is the sole applicant. Moreover if he or she were living in a homosexual relationship, the court might well take the view that an order would not be for the welfare of the child because of the possibility that the family might be ostracised on account of the couple's sexual orientation. Hence if a judge were to refuse to make an order, it is inconceivable that any appellate court would disturb the decision. If neither the surrogate mother nor any relative wishes to have actual custody of the child, it must necessarily go into the care of the local authority.

The legal control of surrogacy agreements

The Surrogacy Arrangements Act 1985

The Warnock Committee in its report in 1984 expressed alarm at the prospect that agencies designed to recruit surrogate mothers, which were already operating in America, would become active in this country, and they recommended that it should be a criminal offence to establish or operate them here.[66] Only a few months later the 'Baby Cotton' case[67] brought to light the operations of such an agency. In a hurried response to public concern Parliament passed the Surrogacy Arrangements Act designed to ban commercial agencies. Under the Act it is an offence for anyone other than the surrogate mother or commissioning parents to negotiate or make a surrogacy agreement on a commercial basis. It is also an offence (for which the surrogate mother and commissioning parents can be convicted) to publish any advertisement (a) containing an indication that any person is or may be willing to enter into or negotiate a surrogacy arrangement, or (b) seeking a woman willing to become a surrogate mother or persons wanting a surrogate mother.[68]

---

66   Cmnd 9314, para. 8.18. All members agreed that agencies acting for profit should be forbidden; the majority also recommended that this should extend to non-profit making bodies.

67   *Re C* [1985] FLR 846. See above.

68   For details, see the Act.

The legality of surrogacy agreements at common law

We have already seen that the legality of the agreement is irrelevant when the court is considering the question of the care and control or adoption of the child. It will be of importance, however, if either the surrogate mother or the commissioning parents sue on the contract. This could occur in a number of situations.

(a)   A woman, having undertaken to become a surrogate mother, refuses to undergo artificial insemination or, having become pregant, has an abortion.

(b)   The surrogate mother hands over the child but the commissioning parents fail to pay her the agreed sum.

(c)   The surrogate mother refuses to hand over the child or to repay any money she has received from the commissioning parents.

(d)   The commissioning parents refuse to take the child.

Even though the agreement is not specifically enforceable, if it is lawful then an action for damages for breach of contract or to recover the sum agreed will lie, as will an action to recover money paid for a consideration that has totally failed. Conversely, if the contract is illegal, no action will lie for breach of it or for the recovery of money paid.[69]

It is generally accepted that contracts affecting the due discharge of parental duties are contrary to public policy,[70] and in the nineteenth and early twentieth centuries this was certainly true of any

69   Money paid would be recoverable if the contract were still wholly (or perhaps substantially) executory and the payer genuinely repented of having entered into it: see *Alexander* v *Rayson* [1936] 1 KB 169, 190; *Bigos* v *Bousted* [1951] 1 All ER 92.

70   W. R. Anson, *Law of Contract* (Oxford: Clarendon Press, 26th Edn., by A. G. Guest, 1984) 317; G. H. Treitel, *Law of Contract* (London: Stevens 7th edn., 1987) 336; Chitty, *Contracts* (London: Sweet and Maxwell, 25th edn., by A. G. Guest, 1983) vol i, 582.

agreement by a parent to divest himself or herself of custody or parental rights. In *Vansittart* v *Vansittart*,[71] for example, a wife brought an action for specific performance of articles of separation. They provided *inter alia* that she should have custody of two of the parties' four children and should bring them up as Protestants. The Court of Appeal in Chancery held that, as a father is given parental rights for the benefit of his children, he has a duty to exercise them and consequently the agreement was contrary to public policy. As the consideration was not severable, the whole agreement failed and no action would lie. The courts' view of public policy, however, may change with changing social conditions.[72] Whether or not contracts contemplating the transfer of parental rights and duties would still generally be regarded as illegal at common law, it is submitted that the old rule should still apply to surrogacy agreements at least. Undoubtedly they are beneficial in some circumstances in that they offer some couples the only prospect of having a child which is genetically the offspring of one of them. Against this, however, must be measured the damage they are capable of doing. At least six major objections can be raised against them.[73]

(1) The introduction of a surrogate mother undermines the institution of marriage. Whatever individuals' views of the institution may be, it remains the basis of English social life and should be supported, not weakened, by judicial decisions.

(2) Many criticisms may be made of the commercialisation of reproduction. The surrogate mother may be exploited, particularly if she is undertaking the role purely for financial gain, when the

---

71   (1858) 2 De G & J 249. See also *Hope* v *Hope* (1854) 8 De GM & G 731; *Walrond* v *Walrond* (1858) John 18; *Humphrys* v *Polak* [1901] 2 KB 385 (illegitimate child).

72   *Rodriguez* v *Speyer Bros.* [1919] AC 59, 79 (*per* Viscount Haldane); *Nordenfelt* v *Maxim Nordenfelt Guns & Ammunition Co. Ltd* [1894] AC 535, 553 (*per* Lord Watson); *Nagle* v *Fielden* [1966] 2 QB 633, 650 (*per* Danckwerts LJ).

73   See also the Warnock Report, chapter 8; Harding, 'The Debate on Surrogate Motherhood' [1987] JSWL 37; de Cruz, 'Surrogacy, Adoption and Custody: A Case-study' [1988] Fam Law 100.

agreement may be likened to a form of prostitution.[74]   Conversely, the surrogate mother may exploit the commissioning parents by demanding a further sum to hand the child over after it has been born. A surrogacy agreement can be seen as a form of baby selling;   if, on the other hand, it is regarded as 'womb renting', it contemplates a commercial use of a human organ prohibited in the case of commercial transplantation by the Human Organ Transplants Act 1989.

(3) Parliament has seen fit to make payment in consideration of adoption a criminal offence.   *A fortiori* an agreement contemplating payment for the conception, birth and handing over of a child should be illegal.

(4) We have already noted some of the emotional problems that surrogacy agreements can create.   During the surrogate mother's pregnancy the commissioning parents live in constant anxiety that she will change her mind and refuse to hand the child over when it is born, and if their fears are realised, the consequences to them can be devastating.[75]   If she does hand it over, the consequences to her may be equally grave, as they may also be to any other children she already has.

(5) A surrogacy agreement is potentially damaging to the child.   If the agreement is carried out, it deprives the child of the mother who has carried it and with whom it will have bonded.[76] Conversely, if the commissioning parents refuse to take it, it is likely to be brought up by a mother who does not want it or finish up in the care of the local authority.

---

74   If the agreement is arranged through a commercial agency, there is the further danger that the agency will have a financial interest in accepting all applicants without screening out unsuitable ones and in seeing that all parties carry out the terms of the agreement.

75   See the remarks of the solicitor for the surrogate mother in *Re P*: [1987] Fam Law 395.

76   Although the extent of this bonding is controversial: see Harding, above, n. 73, 56-7.

(6) It is scarcely in the child's interests that his conception and birth should be surrounded by secrecy. If he is adopted, he may feel the need to exercise his statutory right to obtain information about his birth[77] and thus seek out his mother, with the possibility of even graver emotional damage to himself, the surrogate mother and her family than in the usual case of adoption.

If surrogacy agreements are illegal, either the surrogate mother or the commissioning parents could suffer a substantial financial loss. Nevertheless it is submitted that the social evils they could give rise to require them to be classed as contrary to public policy.

Whether money paid to a commercial agency by the surrogate mother or the commissioning parents could be recovered is less clear. Although neither of them commits an offence under the Surrogacy Arrangements Act, the payer would know (or be presumed to know) that the receipt of the money would constitute an offence by the payee. *Prima facie* this would preclude recovery. It could be argued that the parties were not *in pari delicto* because the Act was passed to protect the payer from the activities of the agency. In the absence of an express statutory power, however, it would seem that payment could be recovered only if the statute was passed to prevent the exploitation of a class of persons of which the plaintiff is a member.[78] A court is more likely to conclude that the purpose of the Surrogacy Arrangements Act is to prevent commercial surrogacy in the interests of society generally rather than to prevent exploitation of potential surrogate mothers and commissioning parents,[79] so that the agency would not be obliged to refund the payments.

---

77   Under s. 51 of the Adoption Act 1976.

78   See *Kiri Cotton Co. Ltd* v *Dewani* [1960] AC 192 (tenant who has paid an illegal premium in consideration of the granting of a lease is entitled to recover it).

79   Cf. *Green* v *Portsmouth Stadium Ltd* [1953] 2 QB 190, where it was held that a bookmaker could not recover an illegal charge made to give him entry to a racecourse because the statute was passed to regulate racecourses and not to protect bookmakers.

The Human Fertilisation and Embryology Bill

Apart from the clauses dealing with the status of children born as a result of AID or embryo transfer, the only provision in the Bill which directly affects surrogacy agreements is the following proposed amendment to the Surrogacy Arrangements Act: 'No surrogacy arrangement is enforceable by or against any of the persons making it.'[80] If the agreement is contrary to public policy at common law, it is not clear whether the effect of this wording is merely to restate the common law position or whether it converts the contract into one which is unenforceable in the technical sense, and not void. In either case no action for damages will lie, but the distinction is important for, if one party repudiates an unenforceable contract, the other may sue for services rendered on a *quantum meruit*[81] or recover money paid for a consideration that has totally failed.[82] Hence the surrogate mother could sue for the value of services rendered at the request of the commissioning parents if they refused to pay her, and they could recover any money paid if she refused to hand over the child. If the contract is contrary to public policy, it is submitted that clearer wording than that contained in the Bill is needed to remove illegality.

Possible reforms

We must accept that, whatever problems surrogacy agreements pose, they will continue to be made. The advance of artificial reproductive techniques, coupled with the drying up of the conventional sources of children placed for adoption, will force some to resort to surrogacy as the only method open to them of overcoming the emotional and mental problems of what is frequently perceived as the stigma of infertility.

Nevertheless the problems presented by surrogacy agreements indicate that some change in the law is necessary. This could take a number of forms: the recognition and specific enforcement of agreements; control over their formation and terms;

---

80 Clause 32(1).
81 *Scarisbrick* v *Parkinson* (1869) 20 L T 175; *Pullbrook* v *Lawes* (1876) 1 QBD 284.
82 See *Gosbell* v *Archer* (1835) 2 Ad & E 500; *Pullbrook* v *Lawes* (above) at pp. 289 (*per* Blackburn J) and 290 (*per* Lush J).

or their complete banning. If control is desirable, it can be effected either by giving positive encouragement to comply with restrictions imposed by statute or by penalising those who fail to observe them.[83]

Neither extreme view is satisfactory. The first has been recommended by the Ontario Law Reform Commission,[84] which has proposed a regulatory system under which an agreement approved by the court would be specifically enforceable, if necessary by the seizure of the child. The court would be required to approve and assess the parties' suitability and to agree to any payments, and the contract would have to contain terms relating *inter alia* to the arrangements if one or both of the commissioning parents die or they cease to live together before the child's birth. The specific performance of a surrogacy agreement precludes any exercise of discretion if there is a dispute over custody and thus runs wholly counter to the fundamental principle that the welfare of the child must remain an English court's first concern. Hence the adoption in this country of the Canadian proposal would be impossible.

The other extreme, which would involve making the entry into any surrogacy agreement a criminal offence, is equally unacceptable. Given that people will continue to use surrogacy and the ease with which artificial insemination can be carried out without the need of expert medical help (assuming the child is not conceived by normal sexual intercourse), criminal sanctions would tend to drive the practice underground and thus remove any desirable control which might otherwise be imposed.[85]

The compromise is some limited form of control. It is possible to identify three distinct problems to which surrogacy agreements give rise: the future of the child; the financial exploitation of the parties; and the need to counsel all those taking part and to screen potential surrogate mothers. The future of the individual child can only be decided, as it is now, by the intervention of the court. Whether the agreement is unenforceable or illegal, no

---

83 See Dickens, 'Surrogate Motherhood: Legal and Legislative Issues', *Genetics and the Law III*, 3-5; Morgan (1986) 49 MLR 358.

84 *Report on Human Artificial Reproduction* (1985), paras 233 *et seq*.

85 And what would be an appropriate sentence if a surrogate mother or commissioning parent were convicted?

help is afforded at present to parties seeking to exploit the situation. Even if it is contrary to public policy, justice to the surrogate mother dictates that, if the parties agree that she should be paid, she should be able to recover a reasonable sum (not to exceed the agreed amount) for expenses, loss of earnings, inconvenience, and the like. Limiting the claim to a reasonable sum would prevent either side from benefiting from a commercial transaction. The proposal would require legislation, and some thought might also be given, by analogy with the law of adoption, to making it an offence for anyone (including the commissioning parents and the surrogate mother) to give or receive any payment or reward for entering into a surrogacy agreement in excess of reasonable compensation.[86]

This leaves the third question: in what ways could counselling and screening be encouraged? The present Government has indicated that it does not propose to introduce legislation covering non-commercial surrogacy services except for the clause in the Bill making agreements unenforceable.[87] The Bill will, however, indirectly affect some agreements. It proposes the establishment of a Human Fertilisation and Embryology Authority whose duties will include *inter alia* the granting of licences authorising the provision of treatment services and the provision of advice and information to those providing and receiving these services.[88] A person must not give a gamete and a woman must not receive an embryo unless he or she, and, in the case of embryo-transfer, the man with whom the woman is being treated, are given an opportunity of being counselled. But the donor and the recipient need not be offered counselling before artificial insemination is carried out if they are receiving treatment together.[89] This is sensible if the donor is the woman's husband or unmarried partner, but not if their purpose is surrogacy. The licensing scheme will ensure the normal high standard of medical screening before embryo-transfer or (provided it is carried out by a medical practitioner) artificial insemination. The weakness of the proposed

86   In Victoria *all* payments and rewards are illegal: Infertility (Medical Procedures) Act 1984, s. 30.

87   See *Human Fertilisation and Embryology: A Framework for Legislation,* Cm. 259 (1987), paras 73-5.

88   Clauses 11(1)(a) and 8(c).

89   Sched. 3, paras 3 and 5. The proposals are not clear because the wording of the Bill appears defective. The references in clause 13(5) to paras 1 and 3 of Sched. 3 should apparently be to paras 5 and 7.

legislation in its application to surrogacy agreements is that counselling need not be offered at all to the commissioning mother (unless she provides the ovum) or to any of the parties in most cases of artificial insemination. It is strongly urged that the advice issued by the Authority should require a practitioner to offer counselling to all concerned if he discovers that those seeking treatment services are parties to a surrogacy agreement.

Although the Authority is to be asked to report on surrogacy, and its activities could be extended to cover surrogacy agreements,[90] it is regrettable that the opportunity has not been seized in the Bill to make it mandatory to offer counselling to all those contemplating entering into an agreement. A carrot might be held out by enacting that the surrogate mother should be able to recover reasonable expenses only if the child had been conceived by a procedure conducted by a person licensed to provide treatment services. (Money paid for a consideration that has failed would be recoverable in the same circumstances.) This could be seen as a fair compromise and it would at least be a step towards providing guidance for those who are intent on pursuing a course which, whatever its consequences, will inevitably be followed.

90   Cm 259, paras 74-5. See clause 8(d) of the Bill.

2

The Contractual Position
of Minors and the Prohibition
on Employment

J. R. Carby-Hall and I. Boruta

In this work we propose to examine (a) the contractual effects upon the minor of below the age of eighteen who enters into a contract of employment, (b) the contractual effects upon a minor who has reached the minimum age of sixteen and who is unlawfully employed, and (c) the contractual effects of the minor who has not reached the minimum age of sixteen and who is lawfully employed, for example, by reason of the exceptions provided by the legislation. Since there exists virtually no English case law on the contractual effects of aspects (b) and (c) above, these will be treated by implication.

In order to carry out this examination, we propose first to make certain preliminary observations relating to the divergence which exists in English Law between the minimum age, namely sixteen, and the age of capacity, namely eighteen.

Second, we propose to examine the contractual relationship and its effects between the parties, when one is a minor. In this connection we shall treat the nullity or otherwise of the contract of employment. An examination of an alternative to the notion of nullity of the contract of employment will then take place, to be followed by some conclusions. It will readily be noticed that we propose to treat the implications of the capacity of minors to contract only in connection with the contract of employment and related contracts. Similarly, we will consider in a contractual setting only, the laws which ratify the ILO Convention[1] and which prohibit or restrict the employment of minors in various occupations.[2]

The statutory prohibition of, or restrictions on, the employment of children and young persons respectively, all of which carry criminal penalties, supplement the common law. The thrust of this essay is directed at the common law, namely the capacity of the minor to enter into a contract of employment. For the sake of simplicity, we will use throughout this essay the term 'minor' to cover all age groups below eighteen, as the terms 'children' and 'young persons' may lead to confusion.

For a more complete appreciation of the problem we propose to examine not only the English system but also those of two other European countries, namely France (as a representative country in Western Europe albeit with a different type of jurisdiction) and Poland (as a representative country in Eastern Europe). Occasional references to other European countries' laws, by way of illustration only, are not, however, precluded.

A number of countries in the world,[3] including the United Kingdom, recognise the minimum age for work set by the International Labour Organisation (ILO).[4] Article 2(3) of the ILO

1   The Employment of Women, Young Persons and Children Act 1920 s. 1(1) and s. 1(3); Children and Young Persons Act 1933 s. 18; Education (Work Experience Act 1973; Young Persons (Employment) Act 1938; Young Persons (Employment) Order 1938; Shops Act 1950 ss 24-36; The Employment Act 1989 repeals (see below) the provisions relating to young persons (and not children) while still complying with international and European Community requirements.

2   E.g. industrial undertakings.

3   As at 1 Jan 1989, 38 countries had ratified the ILO Convention No. 138, 'Convention concerning minimum age for admission to employment of 26 June 1973. (M. Bowman and D. Harris, *Multilateral Treaties: Index and Current Status*). (London and Nottingham: Butterworths and University of Nottingham Treaty Centre, 6th suppl., 1990). For text see Cmnd 5829, 1015 UNTS 297.

4   See also Recommendation No. 146 of the International Labour Organisation (1973) relating to minimum age of employment.

Convention No. 138 of 1973 relating to minimum age provides: 'The minimum age specified . . . shall not be less than the age of completion of compulsory schooling and, in any case, shall not be less than 15 years.'

In England the age 'of completion of compulsory schooling' is set by the Raising of the School Leaving Age Order 1972[5] at sixteen years. Children (which in this context means those persons under the school-leaving age of sixteen) may not be employed at all if they are under thirteen years of age. Nor may children be employed in any industrial undertaking.[6] Furthermore children may not be employed before the end of school hours on a day on which they are required to go to school, or if employed, they must not be so employed for more than two hours of a school day, before seven in the morning and after seven in the evening, or lift or carry anything which is so heavy as to be likely to cause them injury.[7]

Under the Education (Work Experience) Act 1973, where a person under sixteen whilst in his *last year at school* has entered into an approved work experience scheme, the above restrictions do not apply. At the time of writing, 'young persons' (defined as persons between sixteen and eighteen) may not work *at night* in an industrial undertaking,[8] though there exist some exceptions in connection with certain circumstances or some processes, for example emergencies, sugar manufacturing, paper manufacture, steel, iron and glass. Until 1990 restrictions applied to young persons of between sixteen and eighteen employed in certain jobs as to the *permissible hours of work*. These jobs were: the running of errands, the receipt and dispatch of goods and their collecting and delivery, hotels, entertainment, lift operators, etc. Records had to be kept and notices of permissible hours posted.[9] Similar provisions applicable to young persons existed under the Shops Act 1950[10] and the employer could choose which of the Acts he wished to be bound by. Special provisions relating to the

---

5   S I, 1972, No. 444.
6   Employment of Women, Young Persons and Children Act 1920, s. 1(1).
7   Children and Young Persons Act 1933, s. 18.
8   Employment of Women, Young Persons and Children Act 1920 s. 1(3).
9   Young Persons (Employment) Act 1938; Young Persons (Employment) Order 1938, S.R.O., 1938 No. 1501.
10   ss 24 to 36.

employment of young persons in factories and other premises were also to be found in other legislation.[11] The Employment Act 1989 repeals the provisions on young persons discussed briefly above, though not those relating to children.[12] By s. 10 of the Employment Act 1989 legislation on hours of work of young persons and certain other restrictions on their employment are repealed and amendments made to other provisions regulating the employment of young persons. The Secretary of State is given power to make orders amending or repealing legislation for these purposes. This provision came into force immediately upon the passing of the Act (s. 10(3) - (6)). The remaining parts of s. 10 took effect on 16 January 1990, except for the provisions on night work of young persons and the requirement for employers to notify the careers office when they employ young persons. A subsequent commencement order will treat these matters.

Subject to the above restrictions, the minimum age at which a person in England is enabled to work in an industrial undertaking is therefore sixteen; however, it should be noticed that a person under eighteen years of age[13] does not normally have the necessary capacity to contract.[14] The case law which has come before the English courts has not examined the effects of the minimum age on the contract of employment; rather the courts have concentrated on the notion of the

---

11   E.g. Factories Act 1961, ss 86-94

12   In response to the Government's consultative document, *Restrictions on the Employment of Young Persons and the Removal of Sex Discrimination in Legislation*, the Health and Safety Executive generally agreed that there should continue to be statutory limitations on the employment of young persons, but that the system should be simplified. See 1988 *Employment Gazette* 261.

13   Family Law Reform Act 1969, ss 1, 9.

14   As far as a contract of employment is concerned, a minor has contractual capacity and may always enforce such a contract, but the general rule is that he is only bound by the contract of employment if it is on the whole beneficial to him.

capacity of minors[15] to contract. This means that the English courts have not directed their minds *per se* to the contractual situation of a minor below the statutory minimum age who is unlawfully employed.

Preliminary observations on the divergence between the ages

It will be recalled that the age of majority in England is provided for by statute and fixed at the age of eighteen years.[16] The law regards that age as the minimum age whereby a person has the capacity to enter into a valid contract.[17]

The fact that there exists the age of capacity, namely eighteen, and a statutory minimum age, namely sixteen, begs certain observations to be made. First, the minimum age has the effect of lowering the capacity of the person in England to enter into a contract of employment. The minimum age (i.e. sixteen) has two values: the first is that there is a prohibition on the employment of a person under that age, the second is that it is lawful to employ a person over the minimum age. Such an observation may equally be made in the case of France[18] and Poland[19] upon examination of their respective

15   The English law terminology of 'minor' is used throughout this essay, although when discussing common law and statute the term 'infant' will be used for purposes of authenticity in the appropriate case. Under English law a minor is a person below the age of eighteen, but in other countries the minimum age may vary. In England, persons of under the age of twenty-one were in law considered as 'infants' prior to 1 January 1970. As from that date the Family Law Reform Act 1969, s. 1 reduced the age of majority to eighteen. Thus a person '. . . who is not of full age may be described as a minor instead of as an infant'. (s. 12). Section 1 of the 1969 Act gives effect to one of the recommendations of the *Latey Committee Report* [*Report of the Committee on the Age of Majority*, Cmnd 3342 (1967)], the only recommendation concerned with contracts of minors which has been implemented by legislation.

16   Family Law Reform Act 1969, s. 1. s. 9 provides that a person attains 18 '. . . at the commencement of the [18th] anniversary of his birth'.

17   On capacity to contract see A. L. Smith LJ in *Clements v London and North Western Railway Co.* [1984] 2 QB 482 (CA) at pp. 494-5: 'There can be no doubt that *prima facie* an infant is incapable of contracting'.

18   See *Code du travail*, Art. L211-6 (the minimum age in France is 16 years).

19   See *Kodeks pracy*, Art. 190 para. 1. (the minimum age in Poland being 15 years).

Labour Codes. When one examines the common law in England during the past century, it becomes apparent that the age at which a person has the capacity to conclude a contract of employment is that of reaching his majority, namely eighteen (or twenty-one, as it was prior to 1970). The judgments within the various cases dating from 1920 onwards do not generally treat, or even consider, the minimum age.[20] Thus although the minimum age operates in England, the courts do not seem to have taken this into consideration in *a contractual setting*.

Second, when there are two ages - in this case the minimum age and the age of capacity - this constitutes an illogicality. Two different ages impose two different results. If there were only one age of capacity (of eighteen years), the courts in England would have to assess simply whether the contract was valid because it was beneficial[21] to the minor, or void because it was not. The existence of a separate *minimum* age of employment of sixteen poses a problem. The implication is that a contract of employment of a minor of between sixteen and eighteen years of age is valid *per se* since after the age of sixteen, employment is not prohibited. These two notions cannot co-exist comfortably. This illogicality had presented itself in France and in Poland, but these countries have succeeded in eliminating it by using the rule of interpretation *lex specialis derogat legi generali*.[22] Consequently, if the law provides for a minimum age at which a person may enter into a contract of employment (in France sixteen and in Poland fifteen), the law relating to capacity to contract (eighteen in both these countries) is superseded by the former law. In England, despite the fact that there exists the illogicality provided by the two ages, namely sixteen and eighteen, the courts have not considered this contradiction, presumably because the age of capacity is eighteen and the courts have applied the law of contract for the additional protection of the minor. It follows therefore that in France

---

20   The first ILO Convention on the minimum age was Convention No.5 in 1919. It should be noted that Great Britain ratified the 1919 Convention in 1920.

21   The notion of 'beneficial contract of employment' is discussed *below*, at p. 44 *et seq*.

22   This maxim means that if there is legislation concerning the contract of employment, that legislation has priority over legislation which deals with the law of obligations generally.

and Poland there is only one minimum age whereas in England there are two such ages.

Third, in England we submit that the exception makes the rule, whereas in Poland and France the equilibrium between the rule and the exception is not violated. This needs explanation. In England the court bases its judgment on two notions. First, it has to apply the law of contract as to capacity - this being the rule. Second, it has to determine whether the contract of employment entered into by the minor is beneficial to him - this being the exception.[23] If it is beneficial to the minor, then, the contract is binding on him; if not, it is not binding. This 'beneficial' notion opens the door for, *inter alia*, minors between the ages of sixteen and eighteen to enter into valid contracts. It is clear that a significant number of persons in that age group do in fact work or are serving apprenticeships.[24] It is thus noticeable that in England the exception replaces the rule. On the other hand, in Poland and France the reality that minors do enter into contracts of employment or apprenticeship is accepted within the legal system itself and therefore such a contract entered into after the minimum age has been reached, is valid. It is only where there is an exception[25] that the contract is terminated by a court.

Four specific conclusions can therefore be made from the previous observations. (a) The consequence of the notion of the minimum age constitutes a *de facto* lowering of the age of capacity. (b) When there are two such ages, these have the effect of providing a contradictory function. (c) The notion of the 'beneficial contract of employment' which is used in England is in fact the exception to the rule which makes valid an otherwise void contract of employment of a minor. (d) The two minimum ages do not make for a coherent system and can be a cause of uncertainty in the law itself. Uncertainty arises from the fact that it is the court which has to decide whether or not the contract of a person between the ages of sixteen

---

23   Fry LJ in *De Francesco* v *Barnum* [1890] 45 Ch D 430 talked of '. . . one exception as to the incapacity of an infant to bind himself relates to a contract for his good teaching'. He talked of another exception, 'based on the desirableness of infants employing themselves in labour'. (pp. 438-9).

24   See some examples provided by the case law discussed below.

25   E.g. Where the parents prove to the court that the minor's health will be seriously affected as a result of his employment; this being outside the normal health and safety legislation.

and eighteen is beneficial and therefore valid; if the minimum age were the norm, that would to a great extent remove the source of the existing uncertainty.

The fact that the Employment Act 1989 abolishes most restrictions relating to young persons, shows a general tendency and points a finger towards the elimination of restrictions concerning the employment of minors of over the age of sixteen. Although this legislation does not have anything to do with the contract of employment, it could have an influence on this latter by eventually eliminating the uncertainty which currently exists as a result of the two ages.

Contractual relationship and its effects

In this part, we propose to examine how judicial systems - whether through case law or legislation - have taken into account the reality of the situation in connection with the employment of a minor. This reality is that, despite the prohibition by the ILO Convention and the fact that contracts with minors are considered as void in a number of European countries, nevertheless minors do enter into contracts of employment.[26]

The nullity of the contract of employment

Under the respective codes of virtually all European civil law countries a contract of employment to which a minor is a party is null and void.[27] This results from two fundamental juridical notions. The

26 In the *industrialised* countries of the world there are one and a half million minors in employment. In the *developing* countries there are fifty-three million minors in employment. (Source: *International Labour Conference*, 67th Session, 1981).

27 E.g. The French Labour Code (*Code du travail*) Art. L211-1, the French Civil Code (*Code Civil*) Art. 1108, the Polish Labour Code (*Kodeks Pracy*) Art. 190, para. 2 and the Polish Civil Code (*Kodeks Cywilny*) Art. 14, para. 1.

first, that such a contract is against public policy;[28] the second, that a minor does not possess the necessary capacity to enter into a valid contract of employment.[29]

In England, despite the (now repealed) Infants' Relief Act, 1874, contracts of employment and contracts of apprenticeship which are of *benefit* to the minor are, and have always been, fully binding on him at common law.[30] If the employment or apprenticeship contract is *not* beneficial to him, the contract is wholly void[31] and the minor

28   See e.g. L 211-1 of the French Labour Code and Art. 6 of the French Civil Code; Art. 170, para. 2 of the Polish Labour Code and Art. 58 of the Polish Civil Code. Although Fry LJ in *De Francesco* did not talk directly of public policy in his judgment, in finding that the contract was not beneficial to the infant, he did take into consideration, by implication, the notion of public policy. See also Sinclair-Fox for Mrs Parnell in the *De Francesco* case who pleaded that the provisions of the *Deed* were against public policy because (1) they were in restraint of trade, (2) they were in restraint of matrimony, (3) they derogated from the rights of the parent, and (4) the plaintiff was given the power to take the infants out of the jurisdiction.

29   See Art. 1108 of the French Civil Code and Art.14 of the Polish Civil Code. This has been stated judically in numerous cases in England. See also G. H. Trietel, *The Law of Contract* (London: Stevens, 7th edn, 1987) pp. 416-35. Cheshire and Fifoot, *Law of Contract* (London: Butterworths, 10th edn, by M. P. Furmston, 1981) 379 *et seq.*

30.   Contracts for 'necessaries' are also fully binding on the minor. Other contracts *were* voidable at the option of the infant. Two types of voidable contracts existed: (a) contracts under which the infant was bound until he avoided them during the period of his minority or within a reasonable period after attaining his majority; and (b) contracts which were not binding unless they were ratified by the infant after he reached his majority. Section 1 of The Infants' Relief Act 1874 made certain contracts 'absolutely void' and s. 2 made unenforceable any subsequent ratification (i.e. upon attaining his majority) by an infant of a contract entered by him while he was an infant. The 1874 legislation has been repealed by the Minors' Contracts Act 1987; thus as from June 1987 the capacity of a minor to enter into contracts rests upon the common law.

31   See *De Francesco* v *Barnum* [1890] 45 Ch D 430 at p. 436. See also *Corn* v *Matthews* [1890] 1 QB 310 (CA) where Lord Esher MR said (at p. 314):
> The mere fact that some conditions in the deed being against the apprentice does not enable the Court on that ground only to say that the agreement is void. It is impossible to frame a deed . . . in which some of the stipulations are not in favour of the one and some in favour of the other. But if we find a stipulation in the deed which is of such a kind that it makes the whole contract an unfair one, then that makes the whole contract void . . .

See also Lord Esher MR at p. 315, and Kay LJ in *Clements* v *London and North Western Railway Co.* [1894] 2 QB 482 (CA) at p. 494.

will not be bound by it. It was so found in *Corn* v *Matthews*[32] where *one* stipulation in the deed of apprenticeship was of such a kind that it made the *whole* contract an unfair one and therefore void. The stipulation was to the effect that the employer reserved the right, in certain circumstances, not to pay wages to the apprentice, yet at the same time he was bound to work for the employer provided he could not, and did not, get employment from other employers. Lord Esher MR[33] found '. . . that that is so unfair to the infant, so solely in favour of the master that it vitiates the whole contract and makes that contract void.'

A similar decision was reached in *Olsen and Another* v *Corry and the Gravesend Aviation Ltd* [34] where an apprenticeship contract with a minor was held void as not being beneficial to him. One of the contractual terms relieved the employers from *all* liability in negligence. Greaves LJ held that:

> Taking into consideration every suggested advantage that may still accrue to the plaintiff ... the deed is so wide in the extent to which it purports to relieve the defendants that it is not for the benefit of the plaintiff and is therefore void.[35]

Whereas in France and Poland the legislation specifically provides that a minor's contract of employment is void by reason, *inter alia* of public policy, in England it is in the case law that *dicta* will be found which raises issues of public policy. In the unreported case of *Davies* v *Larkham and Excess Insurance Co. Ltd,*[36] Cauldfield J, talking about a minor of ten years old being employed illegally within the meaning of the Children and Young Persons Act 1933

32   [1893] 1 QB 310 (CA).
33   Ibid. at p. 315. See also *R* v *Lord* 12 QB 757 where the contract with a minor was vitiated because the employer was able to refuse paying wages and insist that the apprentice be bound to serve him, cf. *Leslie* v *Fitzpatrick* (1877) 3 QBD 229 where the contract of employment with a minor '. . . was to be terminated by the employer'. This is unlike *Corn's* case where the contract was not to be terminated but the minor was to be bound to continue his services, no matter how onerous the stipulations.
34   [1936] KBD 241.
35   Ibid. at p. 249.
36   88/NJ/4518, Queen's Bench Division, 21 Apr. 1989.

ss 18(1) and 30 and the Employment of Women, Young Persons and Childrens Act 1920, said'. . . he was employed illegally, which is against public policy.'

In England, it is the common law which regulates, and which has always regulated,[37] the contractual relationship between the employer and the apprentice or employee who is a minor. The common law rule that the contract of employment is not void if it is *on the whole* beneficial to the minor does not apply to a minor who is below the statutory minimum age, since statute prohibits such employment.[38] In these circumstances the contract is void because it is prohibited by law. Similarly it is void in France and Poland because legislation expressly so provides.[39] It is also void in these countries because the minor lacks the necessary capacity to enter into a contract.[40]

The consequent nullity of the contract of employment entered into by a minor means, *prima facie*, that, despite the appearance of the existence of a valid contract of employment productive of rights and obligations, the contract has no juridical effects. Or does it?

How null is null? The approach taken by the courts

Under the laws of the various European countries which prohibit the employment of persons below the minimum age, the nullity of the contract of employment to which a minor is a party has not always been upheld by the courts. Despite the statutory provisions on nullity which exist in France and Poland, the courts have sought to protect the minor who has been employed in contravention of the respective laws. In England this phenomenon has not occurred in connection with nullity by reason of the statutory prohibition of employment of persons below the minimum age. This situation must be distinguished from the common law in England in connection with beneficial contracts of employment which has no equivalent in France and Poland and which will be discussed later.

37   The Infants' Relief Act 1874 did not apply to contracts of employment.
38   Employment of Women, Young Persons and Children Act 1920 s. 1(1).
39   See e.g. Art. 170 of the Polish Labour Code (on prohibition) and Polish Civil Code, Art. 58 (on nullity).
40   See e.g. Art. 14 of the Polish Civil Code (on capacity to contract).

Anxious to provide such protection, the courts in the countries under discussion have held, *inter alia,* that contracts of employment entered into by minors are not entirely stripped of their juridical effects. Though the contract of employment is void, the courts have allowed certain juridical consequences to flow from it. One of the consequences relates to the unjust enrichment of the employer by the benefits he has received from the services rendered by the minor employee.[41] An action *in rem verso* is used in such cases to guarantee payment for the work already performed or partly performed by the minor and which remains unpaid.[42] Another consequence is that damages have to be paid by the employer for the prejudice which the minor has suffered by reason of this latter having been unlawfully employed.[43]

Another direction, taken principally by the French courts to protect the minor who has been employed in contravention of the statutory prohibition, has been to hold the contract of employment valid, despite the fact that the law says that such contract is void. A number of diverse judicial arguments have been presented with invocations being made, *inter alia,* to equity, without consideration being given to the irregularity of the employment itself.[44]

41 See G. Lyon-Caen and J. Pélissier, *Les grands arrêts de droit du Travail* (Paris: Sirey, 2nd edn. 1980) pp. 253 *et seq.*
42 Problems have, however, presented themselves. One such problem relates to the evaluation of such payment. Some courts have held that the payment should be calculated independently of the agreed wages in the contract: see e.g. in France, Arrêt du 16 juillet 1963, Soc 16 juillet 1963, *Bull IV* No. 593 p. 492; cf. Soc 1 mars 1961 *Droit Social* 1961 p. 483, observation by J. Savatier. Other courts have held that a more equitable solution would be to enforce the contractual wages since this corresponds to the value placed upon the work to be performed and agreed to by the parties. See for example in France. Note F. D. Sous, Soc 27 octobre 1959 JCP; 60 II 11603; Soc. 8 avril 1957; D 1958 221, note Ph. Malaurie; Soc 1 mars 1961 *Droit Social* 1961 p. 483 (observation by J. Savatier). The weakness of an action *in rem verso* has been pointed out by various authors. See e.g. in France, Ch. Freyria, 'Nullité du droit de travail et relation de travail', *Droit Social* (1960) p. 613 and s. No. 9; A. Brun et H. O. Galland, *Bilan de cinq années* (Paris: Sirey, 1962) p. 42.
43 See Lyon-Caen and Pélissier, *Les grands arrêts,* pp. 253 *et seq*; A. Brun, *La jurisprudence en droit du travail* (Paris: Sirey, 1967) pp. 169-70; Soc 15 fevrier 1978: D 1970 TR 388 (observation by J. Pélissier).
44 A. Brun, ibid, p. 167.

It should be noticed that the reference made to equity above shows a loose link with the concept of a *contrat de fait* developed under the influence of the French and Polish sociological schools of law. Certain factual situations ('the social contact') produce the same juridical effects as a contract does.[45]

Another notion which has been suggested is the 'enterprise concept'. Despite the nullity of the contract of employment entered into by a minor, the fact remains that in reality the employee had belonged to, and had formed part of, the enterprise. This constitutes a factual and a real link with the enterprise; this link being independent of the ordinary contractual relationship. Such a link appears to be sufficient to explain the justification for remuneration being paid to the minor.[46] Finally, it has been suggested that such a contract is a *putative* contract.[47]

It is interesting to note that the majority of the opinions expressed above have been presented for the purpose of finding a juridical basis upon which to guarantee to the minor a form of payment.[48] Thus far, remuneration and the legality in certain circumstances of the contract of employment have featured. Other matters either incidental, or related, to the notion of the existence of a valid contract of employment have also been considered by the French courts. These include: matters which are accessory to wages,[49] the giving of testimonials certifying that work had been

45   This notion has been criticised as being against the rules of legality. See e.g. W. Szubert, *Zarys Prawa Pracy* (Warsaw, 1976) p. 117; T. Liszcz, *Niewaznosc Czynnosci Prawnych W Umownych Stosunkach Pracy* (Warsaw, 1977) pp. 198-9; Brun, *Droit de travail*, p. 167. See also S. Grzybowski, *System Prawa Cywilnego Czesc Ogolna* (Warsaw, 1974) pp. 557 *et seq.*

46   This concept is French in origin and may be traced back to P. Durand who developed the analysis of the concept of the 'link with the enterprise' by calling the institutional theories developed by Horion and Renard. See P. Durand, *Traité de droit du Travail* (Paris: Dalloz, 1947) pp. 151 *et seq.*

47   i.e. that there is the presumption of a contract. See Malaurie Soc 27 octobre 1959, D 1960 p. 109.

48   27 octobre 1959, D 1960 p. 109; 1 mars 1961 *Droit Social* 1961 p. 483 (note by J. Savatier); 16 July 1963 *Bulletin Civile IV*, No. 593; J. Savatier, 'Les sanctions civiles de l'emploi des travailleurs étrangers en situation irrégulière' (1986) *Droit Social* p. 429 *et seq.*

49   In this sense see e.g. French judgment of 8 avril 1957, Civ Sect, Soc 8 avril; 2 février 1961 p. 236.

performed satisfactorily or otherwise, tax returns made by the employer,[50] paid holidays, damages for wrongful dismissal,[51] other indemnities flowing from the employer-employee relationship,[52] and guarantees relating to social security and accidents at work.[53]

Furthermore, it should be noticed that legislative provisions in some countries reject, in certain circumstances, the notion of nullity of the contract of employment entered into by minors. For example, the Belgian law of 16 March 1971[54] which relates to employment, provides that the contract of employment entered into by minors cannot be detrimental to them.[55] Granted that a contract of employment entered into by a minor is *prima facie* void by reason of the legislative provisions in France and Poland, the above discussion shows that such contracts are far from being void where certain circumstances exist.

If one were to examine the same situation in England, namely that of a minor under the minimum age of sixteen employed in contravention of the statutory provision, the contract would be null and void. But would such a person be able to recover any monies due to him as a result of the work he performed? To the best of these authors' knowledge there is no case law in England similar to the case law gymnastics which have taken place in France (and outlined above) which deals with this situation. Presumably this is because the question has not been legally tested in a court in England. Should a case arise in the future before an English court, it might be useful for it to examine the reasoning behind the solutions provided by the French case law. It should equally not be forgotten that the remedy of *quantum meruit* is available in England, where the parties think that they have entered into a contract although in fact they have not. In

---

50   J. Camarlynk and G. Lyon-Caen, *Précis de Droit du Travail* (Paris: Dalloz, 1969) at pp. 135-6.
51   Lyon-Caen and Pélissier, *Les grands arrêts*, p. 255.
52   Ibid.
53   Camarlynk and Lyon-Caen, *Précis*, at p. 136.
54   Art. 5, para.1.
55   See M. Jamoulle, *Le contrat du travail*, Tome I (Faculté de Droit, d'Economie et de Sciences Sociales de Liège, 1982) p. 363. Cf. the common law in England.

these circumstances the plaintiff cannot bring an action for breach of contract since there is no contract, but he will be able to succeed on a *quantum meruit* basis through his services to the defendant and the defendant's implied acceptance of them.[56]

It will be recalled that contracts of employment entered into in France and Poland by minors of sixteen and fifteen years of age respectively are legally binding upon them despite the fact that they do not have the necessary contractual capacity, before they attain the age of eighteen, to enter into any other type of contract. Therefore few problems arise in connection with these age groups. In England however, *beneficial* contracts of employment entered into by persons of below eighteen years of age are fully binding on them. It should be noted that this applies to contracts entered into by minors who are above the minimum age as well as to those minors who are below it but whose contracts of employment are not prohibited by statute, for example, light work within certain age groups, or work within certain hours. It is proposed to examine briefly some case law which treats this aspect.

In England the notions used by the courts to avoid the total nullity of a contract of employment to which a minor is a party have been different from those of other European countries. The courts have examined whether or not the contract of apprenticeship or of employment is on the *whole* to the *benefit* of the minor.

---

56   See Treitel, *The Law of Contract* at pp. 814-15 and Denning (1955) LQR 54. See also *Craven-Ellis* v *Canons Ltd* [1936] 2 KB 403 (CA) where the contract of employment of a managing director was void and consequently he could not recover his salary. The Court of Appeal held that he was entitled to a *quantum meruit*. In this case Greer LJ said (at p. 410) that payment of *quantum meruit* . . . is an inference which a rule of law imposes on the parties where work has been done or goods have been delivered under what purports to be a binding contract but is not so in fact. Cf. *Lawford* v *Billericay RDC* [1903] 1 KB 722 but note that this case has been made obsolete by reason of the Corporate Bodies Contracts Act 1960.

Fry LJ in *De Francesco* v *Barnum*,[57] summed up the situation as follows:

> Is there or is there not in this case a valid contract between the infants and Signor De Francesco? Now, from a very early date it has been held that one exception as to the incapacity of an infant to bind himself relates to a contract for his good teaching or instruction whereby he may profit himself afterwards, to use Lord Coke's language. There is another exception, which is based on the desirableness of infants employing themselves in labour; therefore, when you get a contract for labour and you have a remuneration of wages, that contract, I think, must be taken to be, *prima facie*, binding upon the infant.

Contracts of apprenticeship and contracts of employment if they are beneficial to the minor are, therefore, binding and constitute an exception to the rule relating to incapacity.

In such contracts, the case law has addressed itself to the question as to whether or not the particular contract is *on the whole* of benefit to the minor. In *De Francesco*, Fry LJ thought the relevant question to be: 'Is the contract [on the whole] for the benefit of the infant? Not, is any one particular stipulation for the benefit of the infant?' That latter question is not pertinent because both contracts of employment and of apprenticeship - as indeed any contract - contain some stipulations for the benefit of one of the contracting parties, and some for the benefit of the other. Fry LJ [58]

---

57   [1890] 45 Ch D 430 (CA).
58   Ibid. at p. 439. See Lord Hansworth MR in *Doyle* v *White City Stadium Ltd* [1935] 1 KB 110 (CA) at p. 124 where he adopts Fry LJ's dictum in *De Francesco's* case, Slesser LJ at p. 130 and Romer LJ at p. 138. See also Lord Esher MR in *Corn* v *Matthews* [1893] 1 QB 310 (CA) who said that the judgment of Fry LJ 'is one with which one would agree' and confirms the principles laid down by Fry LJ in *De Francesco*. See too

went on to say:

> It is not because you can lay your hand on a particular
> stipulation which you may say is against the infant's
> benefit, that therefore the whole contract is not for the
> benefit of the infant. The Court must look at the
> *whole contract* having regard to the circumstances of
> the case, and determine, subject to any principles of
> law which may be ascertained by the cases, whether
> the contract is or is not beneficial *(emphasis added)*.

In relation to accidents at work the interesting case of
Clements v *London and North Eastern Railway Co*[59] should be noted.
The plaintiff, a minor, was employed as a porter. He was injured at
work while still a minor and brought an action against his employers
claiming damages at common law or under the Employers' Liability

---

Clements v *London & North Western Railway Co* [1894] 2 QB 482 (CA),
particularly Lord Esher's *dictum at* p. 489:
> I am of the opinion that the answer to this proposition depends on
> whether, on the true construction of the contract as a whole, it was for
> his advantage. If it was not so, he can repudiate it; but if it was for
> his advantage it was . . . one binding on him which he had no right to
> repudiate.

See also *Wood* v *Fenwick* [1842] 10 M&W 195. In this case it was held
that a contract of employment for wages was a beneficial contract on the
whole and therefore binding upon a minor, despite the fact that clauses
therein provided for forfeitures for neglect and arbitration where disputes
to arise. See *Olsen* v *Corry and the Gravesend Aviation Ltd* [1936] All
ER 241. It is thought that the origins of beneficial contracts of
employment being binding on minors are to be found in *Coke upon
Littleton* (1st edn) at p. 172a. There he says
> An infant may bind himself to pay for his necessary meat, drink,
> apparel, necessary physicke, and such other necessaries, and likewise
> for his good teaching or instruction, whereby he may profite himselfe
> afterwards.

The course of years has subsequently added the contract of employment.

59   [1894] 2 QB 482 (CA).

Act. At the time when the plaintiff entered into employment he agreed as a term in his contract of employment that if he should sustain injury, whether or not through his employers' negligence, he would be compensated in one of two ways: either by a payment during the time of disablement, or where permanent injury or death occur, by payment of a fixed sum to him or his representatives. Having accepted these terms, the minor undertook that he would not bring an action against his employer for damages. The plaintiff claimed and received compensation under the contractual terms, but subsequently brought an action against the employer for damages. The Court of Appeal had to examine whether the contract *as a whole* was to the plaintiff's advantage. Lord Esher MR, Smith LJ and Kay LJ all agreed that the employers gave to their employees,

> an advantage greater than the law gives because it enables them to obtain compensation even where the injury was not caused by the negligence of the company or of a superior workman under whose control the injured man was working. The compensation fixed may not be so large as the amount that could be obtained from a jury; but there was this advantage that it would be payable in cases where there would be no remedy against the company . . . [60]

The contract *seen as a whole* being beneficial to the minor, he was not entitled to repudiate it. Being bound by it, he could not therefore bring an action for damages.

The above case is to be contrasted with the case of *Olsen and Another* v *Corry and the Gravesend Aviation Ltd*[61] where compensation was awarded *inter alia* for negligence where severe

---

60 Ibid., *per* Kay LJ at pp. 491 and 492. See also A.L. Smith's *dictum* particularly at p. 495 where he enumerates the advantages available to the minor under the contract of employment by avoiding litigation, solicitors' fees and other costs, the uncertainty of a verdict, and the difficulty of establishing a cause of action.
61 [1936] KBD 241.

injury was caused to the plaintiff's arm by an aeroplane propeller, when, as a result of a misunderstanding, the aeroplane's starter was switched to the 'on' position causing the engine to start.

It is interesting to note that the courts have extended the notion of 'benefit', to contracts entered into by minors other than pure contracts of employment, namely to contracts which are

> so nearly concerned with his entering upon a form of employment or occupation . . . that it is within the type of contract which, if found to be for his benefit, the Court ought to hold it not voidable by the infant.[62]

In *Doyle* v *White City Stadium Ltd*[63] the Court of Appeal held, *inter alia*, that the minor's contract with the British Boxing Board of Control was so closely connected with a contract of employment that therefore, the contract being on the whole for his benefit, he was bound by it. Slesser LJ commented:

> If the realities of the present case be looked to and the *dicta* which are to be found scattered in the authorities that the opportunity of an infant to earn his living is one of those matters which may properly be said to be binding when that opportunity has been given to him by a contract, it becomes clear, I think, that as the licence which this infant obtained was the means whereby he was able to enter into a contract of service or performance, whichever it may be, as a boxer, and thereby to earn his living, it was *ancillary* and *incidental* to the contract which he made with the promoter of the fight.[64] (*emphasis added*).

Romer LJ put it more succinctly when he said,

> It appears to me. . . that this contract of membership;

---

62   *Per* Lord Hansworth MR in *Doyle* v *White City Stadium Limited* [1935] 1
      KB 110 (CA) at p. 122. See also Slesser LJ's *dictum* above at p. 131.
63   [1935] 1 KB 110 (CA).
64   Ibid. at pp. 132-3.

being an essential in practice to the plaintiff for obtaining employment as a professional boxer is so *bound up* with those contracts of employment which he hopes to enter into, that it must have applied to it the considerations that are applied to a contract of service in the case of an infant . . .[65] (*emphasis added*).

Prior to *Doyle* the Court of Appeal considered this issue in *Clements* v *London and North Western Railway Co.*[66] The learned judges, in that case thought that the agreement by the minor to become a member of the insurance society, and to be bound by its rules, was a part of his contract of employment as it was sufficiently akin, incidental, or ancillary, to an employment contract as properly to be one where a minor might bind himself. The *Clements* case provides ample authority for saying that where a contract which a minor entered into was so associated with a contract of employment, such contract would be binding if beneficial to him.[67]

---

65 Ibid. at p. 137.
66 [1894] 2 QB 482 (CA).
67 See also *Chaplin* v *Leslie Frewin* (Publishers) [1965] 3 All ER 764 (CA) where a contract with a publisher was found to be *analogous* to a contract of service, which, if found to be to the minor's *benefit*, would be binding on him. In *Chaplin*, Danckwerts LJ (with whom Winn LJ concurred) considered that the agreement was, *at the time when it was made*, beneficial to the minor:

> I find it difficult to sympathise with a person who, for the purpose of gain, has approved of a book which is calculated to denigrate his character and afterwards wishes to change his mind ... it may be that the publicity which the book has now received will increase the sales of the book and thus increase the benefits to the plaintiff which were the object of the contract. The mud may cling, but the profits will be secured. Taste is a matter of opinion. (at p. 773).

Lord Denning thought otherwise:

> I cannot think that a contract is for the benefit of a young man if it is to be a means of purveying scandalous information. Certainly not if it brings shame and disgrace on others; invades the privacy of family life; and exposes him to claims for libel. It is not for his good that he should exploit his discreditable conduct for money no matter how much he is paid for it. (at p. 769).

The issue of severability was discussed in connection with restrictive agreements in *Bromley* v *Smith*[68] where it was held that void stipulations may be severable from the rest of the contract and therefore disregarded; the remaining parts of the contract being binding on the minor. Channel J, found in this case that the restrictive agreement was too wide and went beyond what was necessary for the protection of the employer's business. However, the contract was binding on the minor, although it contained restrictive terms, since the contract seen *as a whole* was beneficial to the minor.

Although not directly concerned with the notion of the contract of employment, this latter was discussed obliquely in *Portsea Island Mutual Co-operative Society Ltd* v *Leyland*. [69] In this case, a milk roundsman employed by the appellants himself employed a boy of ten years old (*without* their knowledge and contrary to their instructions) to help him deliver milk. The appellants were charged with two offences of employing a child contrary to certain byelaws. The magistrates convicted the appellant for the unlawful act of their milk roundsman because he was acting within the course of his employment and his act in employing the boy was to the benefit of the applicants. A fine of £5 for each offence was imposed and the appellants had to pay costs amounting to £20. On appeal, the Queen's Bench Division did not agree with the magistrates and found the appellants not liable. The appellants would have been liable as employers of the minor if it was shown that they, or an authorised person, had employed the boy. Since the boy was employed by the milk roundsman *without* the employers' knowledge and *contrary* to their instructions, the appellants were *not* the boy's employers and were held not liable for the unauthorised act of their milk roundsman.

Talbot J, giving the leading judgment (with whom Widgery CJ and Watkins J concurred), said that,

> the master can only be made liable for contravention of the section . . . if either he employed the child and there is clear evidence of that, or if an agent of his, such as a personnel manager . . . who is engaged to

---

68   [1909] 2 KB 235.
69   [1978] ICR 1195; [1978] Crim LR 554.

take persons into employment of the master, does in fact make a contract of employment with a child in breach of the byelaw. But where the actual taking on of the child - the employment of the child - is done by an employee of the master . . . who has no authority other than to sell and deliver milk, and who has no authority to take on staff or to employ a child, then it cannot be said in the light of these authorities that the master becomes responsible.

The roundsman's actions did not therefore result in a contract of employment between the appellants and the minor.

This case, and others,[70] demonstrate that, despite the fact that a minor of below the minimum age is employed, the law as interpreted by the courts is not effective in actually preventing such a person from entering employment. This is another way - albeit a different way to the approach taken by the French courts already examined above - by which the law, which aims at protecting persons of below the minimum age, is not effective.

From the above discussion, it may be concluded, therefore, that so far as minors who fall *between* the minimum age and the age of capacity to contract are concerned, they are reasonably well protected in France and Poland since they have full capacity (with certain restrictions for their protection) to enter into contracts of employment. In England, despite the problems which have arisen,

---

[70] See e.g. *Robinson* v *Hill* [1910] 1 KB 94 (a van man employed a child to deliver bread, contrary to the Employment of Children Act 1903). Lord Olvestone CJ said:

There must purport to exist on the facts a contract of employment between the child and the employer. In this case, upon the facts, it is obvious that there is nothing of the kind. The master had no knowledge of any employment of the child in contravention of the section. All he knew was that the child was being employed during permitted hours. There is therefore no evidence of a contract of employment of the child by or on behalf of the master during prohibited hours . . .

See also *Boyle* v *Smith* [1906] 1 KB 432, cf. *Rose* v *Plenty* [1975] ICR 430 (CA) and particularly Lord Denning MR at p. 433; *Burns* v *Schofield* (1922) 128 LT 382 and *Star Cinema (Shepherd's Bush) Ltd* v *Baker* 86 JP 47.

and have been examined above - in connection with what is, and what is not, 'beneficial' to the minor - the case law provides a satisfactory and flexible answer in protecting the minor in connection with employment.

The position relating to minors employed *below* the minimum age is, however, unsatisfactory. We therefore propose to make some interstitial submissions in connection with the legal position of such minors who are employed in contravention of the appropriate legislation.

An alternative to the notion of nullity

Two models

The analysis already made, leads us to suggest two models relating to the contractual status of the minor. The first model leads to the prohibition of all employment, with all the consequences which pertain to the contract of employment including the nullity of such a contract. The second model does not normally prohibit the employment of minors; it is therefore up to the court to decide in any given case if the employment is void, in which case all the consequences will follow which pertain to the contract of employment, including the validity of the contract. This model is similar to the situation which exists in England in connection with beneficial contracts of employment of minors below the capacity to contract. We have the legal basis for these two models in developments which have taken place in the various countries under discussion and which have been examined above.

Of the two models above, the first model is preferable. What leads us to this opinion is the fact that - as we have already seen - minors below the minimum age do in fact enter into employment. This fact justifies the notion that all formal legal measures should be taken to eliminate such employment in order to guarantee the most complete mental and physical development of the minor. The prohibition of employment with all the consequences which follow from this is the most efficient way to ensure the effective abolition of the employment of persons below the minimum age.

It may be that in the future such statutory prohibition will not be necessary in that the technical, economic and social development in a given country will be such as to eliminate the incentive for persons below the minimum age to work. This would mean that there would be no need to have any legislation which prohibits the employment of minors; alternatively a liberalisation of the judicial system towards the second model could take place.

Since we have a preference for the first model - namely the prohibition of employment for minors below the minimum age - such prohibition has an important consequence upon the contract of employment this being, the nullity of the contract. This is already the case in the countries under discussion, but we have seen that the courts in France and Poland have not applied that nullity in all cases which have come before them. For that reason, we have to seek an alternative to nullity of the contract of employment, whilst at the same time preserving the prohibition on the employment of minors below the minimum age.

A reason for abandoning the nullity notion

We have a reason for making our submission of abandoning the nullity of the contract whilst at the same time prohibiting the employment of persons under the minimum age. This reason is that it is not equitable to leave a person who is below the minimum age without any protection, by reason that the contract of employment is null and void. It is for this very reason that the courts in France and Poland have applied the equitable doctrine and that this doctrine has also been mentioned in the English courts. Kay LJ in *Clements* v *London and North Western Railway Co*[71] said that contracts of employment are not contracts to an action on which the plea of majority is a complete defence and '. . . the question has always been, both in law and in equity whether the contract . . . is for the benefit of the minor.'[72] In *De Franceso* v *Barnum*,[73] Fry LJ mentions 'equity' in another context, namely the apprentice being 'sued in equity'.[74]

Both equity and the nullity of the contract of employment have their respective values. The value of nullity is to protect the minor by preventing him from working and thus enforcing the prohibition of work of a person below the minimum age. The value

71   [1894] 2 QB 482 (CA).
72   Ibid. at p. 491
73   [1890] 45 Ch D 430 (CA).
74   Ibid. at p. 437.

of equity is to give to a minor below the minimum age a status akin to, though not the same as, an employee and thus protect him from the rigours of nullity.

It may appear, *prima facie*, that the two values contradict one another. It may be said that, if an equitable value were introduced into the nullity of the contract of employment of a person below the minimum age, that would encourage such person to enter into employment and thus vitiate the nullity. We would argue that this is not in fact so because as we have already seen,[75] the nullity of the contract of employment has not necessarily deterred minors from working. This being the case, we would argue that for the protection of the minor against abuses by an unscrupulous employer, the nullity of the contract should be tempered by the doctrine of equity. The value of equity is surely superior in this context to that of nullity for the protection of the minor. Should the case arise in England, we would thus suggest the use of a judge's equitable powers for a satisfactory and fair resolution in connection with the nullity of the contract of employment of persons of below the minimum age.

Retroactive validity for work performed

We have suggested above that we have to seek an alternative to the notion of nullity of the contract in connection with the employment of minors below the minimum age, while at the same time, preserving the prohibition on the employment of persons below that age. Obviously, the contract of employment in such circumstances cannot be valid since that would defeat the object of prohibiting persons of that age entering employment; nor can the contract of employment be totally null. Our proposal is therefore that statute should modify the nullity of the contract. The contract of employment would have retroactive effect only; in other words it would have effects in terms only of the work performed up to the time of the court hearing. Although the Court of Appeal in *Doyle* v *White City Stadium* (above) did not have to decide upon the issue of retroactivity because it found the contract of the minor beneficial to him, the *dictum* of Romer LJ is significant by parity of reasoning.[76] He said:[77]

75   See p. 40 *et seq*, above
76   Because in *Doyle* the contract related to a minor above the minimum age.
77   [1935] 1 KB 110 (CA) at pp. 138-9.

I therefore come to the conclusion that this contract is binding upon the plaintiff. I am very glad to be able to come to that conclusion, because if this Court came to any other it would follow that at no time during the last three or four years during which . . . the plaintiff has been boxing has he been eligible to take any part in a contest held under the sanction of the British Boxing Board of Control, a conclusion, I should have thought, from which the plaintiff would shrink . . . If the contract were not binding on him, he would not be a member of this association, with the consequences I have just indicated.

Our submission on retroactivity in terms only of the work performed by the minor does not constitute either validity or invalidity as is known in the classical sense of the law of contract. It is because such a submission is not known in the law of contract in England that we suggest that it be enacted by statute. In that way the minor who is below the minimum age would enjoy protection through a guaranteed equitable solution. The submission made immediately above illustrates the need to have specific and tailored solutions to the particular problem (other than the classical contractual ones of validity or nullity), to meet the numerous social problems which arise in labour relations.[78]

---

[78] See also Professor Micheline Jamoulle's observations on the social nature of labour law in *Le contrat de travail*, Tome 1 (Liège: Faculté de Droit, d'Economie et de Sciences Sociales de l'Université de Liège, 1982) at pp. 361 *et seq*. For other more general views on the prohibition of employment of minors presented by the International Labour Organisation see L. Swepston, 'Le travail des enfants: sa réglementation dans les normes de L'OIT et ses législations nationales' (1982) *Revue Internationale du Travail* 5 pp. 615 *et seq*; E Mendelievich, 'Le travail des enfants' (1974) 5 *Revue Internationale du Travail* pp. 591 *et seq*; BIT, '"Age minimum" Etude d'ensemble des rapports concernant la convention No. 138 et la récommandation No. 146 sur l'âge minimum', *Rapport de la Commission d'experts pour l'application des conventions et récommandations, Conférence Internationale du Travail* 67 séssion, 1981, Rapport III (partie B). See also S. Rodgers and G. Standing, 'Les rôles économiques des enfants dans les pays à faibles revenus' (1981) *Revue Internationale du Travail* pp. 35-54.

Conclusions

The various issues raised in connection with the employment of minors lead us to four conclusions.

In the first instance, the notion of the minimum age (with which is tied the nullity of the contract of employment of a minor of below the age of sixteen) takes priority over the English common law relating to the beneficial contract of employment. Where, however, the minimum age has been reached, the common law rules apply thereafter until the minor has reached the age of capacity, namely eighteen. It should also be remembered that the common law rule on beneficial contracts of employment applies to contracts by minors of under sixteen in situations where the statutory provisions are not applicable to their employment.

Secondly, there are in fact two parallel rules which co-exist, namely the common law rule on beneficial contracts of employment and the statutory rule which prohibits employment prior to the age of sixteen. This co-existence implies that after the age of sixteen a minor may enter into a contract of employment. This, in fact, he can do but *only* if it is beneficial to him. However, the minor after reaching sixteen does not have the capacity to contract until he reaches the age of eighteen unless the contract of employment is beneficial to him. It should be noticed that this 'beneficial' element is the exception to the rule regarding capacity to contract, yet it will be recalled that this exception has now become the rule. It has been suggested that the minor should be given contractual capacity after the age of sixteen as is the case in France and Poland (the minimum age there being fifteen) as far as a contract of employment only is concerned. The Employment Act, 1989 provisions point towards this submission.

Thirdly, since the contract of employment has important social implications, specialised specific solutions are necessary in connection with such contract in each of the countries under discussion because the law of contract *per se* does not cover all its needs.

Finally, it has been shown that, from a contractual point of view, a minor of below the statutory minimum age in all countries examined is not protected. We have proposed that, on grounds of equity, the minor of below the minimum age who has entered into employment, albeit unlawfully, should not be subjected to the harshness of nullity of the contract of employment, but that an alternative to the notion of nullity be enacted which we suggest should consist of retroactive validity only for the work performed by the minor. Since this submission involves neither the validity nor the nullity of the contract of employment it would have to be specially enacted in any jurisdiction adopting it.

3

Defining the Limits of State Invervention: The Child and the Courts

S. M. Cretney

The thesis put forward in this essay is that the Children Act 1989 significantly redefines the role both of the state and of the courts in relation to intervention in family life. The law is in retreat from the private realm of family life,[1] and the Act in many ways marks a return to doctrinal purity by clarifying and indeed restricting the proper role of the courts and the law which they administer. Yet at the same time, and possibly inconsistently, the courts have been allocated a number of functions - in relation, for example, to the management of cases and to the provision of detailed supervision of local authority responsibilities - which they have not traditionally exercised; and it remains to be seen whether they can be equipped to do so.

The essay is written from the perspective of a lawyer, which is of course only one of many possible standpoints. Child law is a

---

1   The well-known words of *Prince* v *Massachussetts* (1944) 321 US 158 have recently been echoed by Lord Donaldson of Lymington MR in *Re M and another (minors) (wardship: freedom of publication)* [1990] 1 All ER 285, 208.

vast subject; and perceptions of the significance of legislation depend very much on the observer's professional orientation. Thus, for the social historian the Children Act 1948[2] may be seen primarily as a cornerstone of the welfare state, and as embodying an acceptance of the state's obligation to provide services for children who are at risk of being deprived of a normal home life. For the lawyer in contrast the same legislation may often have been seen as primarily concerned with asserting the principle that a child is not to be removed from the home or family against the parents' wishes without the parent having the right to bring the issue before a court where the parent will have a right to be heard.[3]

In the same way, much lawyers' comment on the Children Act 1989 is naturally concerned with the massive changes to the procedural and substantive law administered by the courts when adjudicating on disputes relating to a child; and the provisions of the Act dealing with local authority support for children, voluntary organisations, children's homes, and child minding and day care, in contrast receive little notice.

It is true that the lawyer's perspective does not give an adequate synoptic view of the impact of Child law, which is indeed concerned with much more than court proceedings. But court proceedings do play a vital part in the administration of the law; and an understanding of the fact that courts deploy the judicial power of the state,[4] and that court orders - perhaps having the effect that a child is removed from the parent as if the child had never been born[5] - may ultimately be enforced by the physical coercion of the unwilling is essential to a proper understanding of the role of the law and of courts in relation to the family. It follows from this fact that courts dealing with family matters are not, and cannot be, primarily therapeutic agencies; and the individuals concerned must accordingly be the subject of rights and duties, and not directly or mainly the objects of

2   Subsequently consolidated as the Child Care Act 1980.
3   See *per* Lord Scarman, *Lewisham LBC* v *Lewisham Juvenile Court Justices* [1980] AC 273, 307.
4   Contempt of Court Act 1981, s. 19; applied most recently in *Pickering* v *Liverpool Daily Post and Echo Newspapers plc and others* [1990] 1 All ER 335, CA (Mental Health Review Tribunal a court within the meaning of this definition).
5   Per Lord Goddard, *Hitchcock* v *WB* [1952] 2 QB 561, 571.

assistance.[6]

However, in a number of respects this perception of the role of the courts has been obscured in recent years. Perhaps the clearest example of this confusion - and also the clearest (if not the most important) example of the determined and radical approach of the framers of the 1989 Act to conventional wisdom - is to be found in section 41 of the Matrimonial Causes Act 1973.[7] The way in which the provisions of that section have been dealt with in the 1989 Act provides as good an introduction as any to the thesis of this essay.

The case of children's appointments

Section 41 in effect imposes on the divorce court the duty of investigating the arrangements proposed for the welfare of children of the spouses' family, and requires the court to declare that it is satisfied that those arrangements are satisfactory or the best that can be devised in the circumstances. The working of the Children's Appointments system, under which a judge would sit to discharge the functions imposed by section 41, has long been known to be unsatisfactory in almost every respect.[8] Improvements of detail could certainly be made in the system; but the reality is that conceptually the legislation is fatally confused. The function which is imposed on the court by section 41 is not an adjudicative one, and indeed - as the Booth Committee noted in 1985 - it smacks of paternalism.[9] Nevertheless, the conventional view was for long that it would be politically impossible to make any change of substance in this area of the law. Law reform, at that time, had to take place by consent or not at all;[10] and there would have been vocal opposition to any change in the law

6   *Report of the [Finer] Committee on One-Parent Families*, 1974, Cmnd 5629, para. 4.285. The Finer Committee's analysis of the role of a Family Court remains unrivalled.

7   Wardship - in which the court's role is in many respects administrative - is an even better example: see below p. 68.

8   See G. Davis, A. MacLeod and M. Murch (1983) 46 MLR 121; M. Dodds [1983] JSWL 228; J. Eekelaar (1982) OJLS 63; M. D. A. Freeman, *The Rights and Wrongs of Children* (London: Frances Pinter, 1983).

9   *Report of the Matrimonial Causes Procedure Committee* (1985) para. 2.24.

10 Lord Hailsham of St Marylebone, 'Obstacles to Law Reform' [1981] CLP 279, 281.

which would certainly have been represented as removing some of the protection which the law afforded to children involved in parental divorce. This is no doubt what the Booth Committee had in mind when it said:

> we think that the matter is of such general importance that we could not consider recommending the repeal of section 41 without proposing the substitution of some practicable alternative. We have not received any suggestion as to what that could be.[11]

Five years later, however, it was found possible to make a fundamental change in the legislation - and indeed, by an astonishing stroke of tactical boldness, to make it in the schedule of 'Minor Amendments' in the Children Act 1989.[12] The reasons for the change in attitude to what was and what was not politically possible would themselves make a subject for an interesting essay; but they certainly include the complete abandonment of any belief that law reform is exclusively a matter for consensus politics - an abandonment even more clearly reflected in the provisions of the Courts and Legal Services Act 1990 - and also the creation of a climate of opinion, fuelled by a series of child care disasters[13] that 'something had to be done' about the legal framework governing such matters even if the reality is that the 'something' will rarely be relevant to the mischiefs exposed by the various much-publicised inquiries.

11 *Report of the Matrimonial Causes Procedure Committee* (1985) para. 2.24.
12 Schedule 12, para. 31.
13 For example the Inquiries chaired by Louis Blom-Cooper QC into the deaths of Jasmine Beckford and Kimberley Carlile, 'A Child in Trust' (1985) and 'A Child in Mind' (1987) respectively. The *Report of the Inquiry into Child Abuse in Cleveland* [the Butler-Sloss Report, Cm. 412, 1987] did not appear until the Law Commission's work on the private law [*Guardianship and Custody*, Law Com. No.172, 1988] and the Review of Child Care undertaken by Government were at an advanced stage; and it is wrong, therefore, to attribute the fact that reform was in issue to the publication of the Butler-Sloss report. But the publication of that Report was no doubt a powerful factor in influencing a decision to legislate, and an even more powerful factor in creating a climate of parliamentary and other opinion in which radical reform seemed appropriate.

Under the 1973 legislation the court had to declare its satisfaction about the arrangements proposed for the children of the family; and it would be difficult to find a provision anywhere in the statute book more clearly embodying the paternalist philosophy that the court is likely to know better than the parents what arrangements would be satisfactory for their children after divorce. Such a view is quite inconsistent with the heavy emphasis on family autonomy and on private responsibility for decision-taking which permeates the 1989 Act; it is totally rejected by the substituted section 41. The court will, it is true, still have a duty to 'consider' the arrangements; but its task is to be subtly - yet crucially - different: the court is to ask whether it should exercise any of its powers under the Act in respect of the children. The court - it is now clear - is not a welfare agency which tells parents whether they are doing the right thing by their children; instead its role is to make coercive orders when (but only when - for as we shall see the presumption is to be against the making of any order) it considers that to do so will positively promote the child's welfare.

The presumption against court action

The new section 41 thus marks a radical and restrictive view of the right of the state to interfere in private arrangements; but the sceptical view of the value of introducing state coercion into family life is even more strikingly evidenced by the general provision[14] applying to all orders under the Act.[15] In most civil litigation, a plaintiff who proves the case is entitled to judgment; and it may be that this attitude encouraged lawyers in divorce cases to regard the making of a custody order as 'part of the package' and was seen by courts as part of their task of approving the arrangements made. Whatever the reason, a tendency was observed to assume that some order about children should always be made whenever divorce or separation cases

---

14   s. 1(5).
15   This limitation may be of some significance, since one of the, as yet unexplored, consequences of the Act is that local authorities are to be encouraged (and in many respects required) to have recourse to the (rather obscure) inherent jurisdiction of the court rather than to the powers conferred by the Act itself.

came to court.[16]

The Children Act emphatically reverses that presumption: the court (it is provided) shall not make any order under the Act 'unless it considers that doing so would be better for the child than making no order at all'.[17] It will thus, in every case, be for a party who wants an order relating to children to prove the benefits which would flow from the making of the order rather than merely leaving matters to be regulated by agreement between the parties. The impact of this decision may, in numerical terms, be most apparent in divorce and related proceedings: in 1988 for example, 11,920 custody orders were expressed to have been made by consent, and no less than 46,792 were 'unopposed but not expressly by consent'; while 13,771 joint custody orders were made.[18] Under the new regime it must be questionable whether the making of an order in many of these cases could be shown to be positively beneficial to the child; and it can be expected that there will be a dramatic fall in the number of orders. It can also be expected that the search for agreement and settlement will be intensified: counsellors, conciliators and the proponents of informal justice seem likely to find in the Act parliamentary endorsement of their own approach to the resolution of disputes; and the conciliation industry - however inadequately funded - seems certain to wish to deliver more mediated settlements.

The new 'hands off' approach may thus have an important effect on the extent to which the state seeks to impose its view on divorcing parents about their children's future; but it may well be that the new no-order presumption will be conceptually most important in care proceedings. For the principle will now be that - even if the local authority has successfully made out the threshold condition[19] - no order should be made unless the authority can satisfy the court, as a separate matter, that the making of an order would be better for the child than making no order. Hence, the court will have to assess the child's future as it would be if the court declined to make an order; and it must then compare that outcome with the child's future as it would be if a care or supervision order were to be made. It is difficult

16   Law Com. No.172 (1988) para. 3.2.
17   Children Act 1989, s. 1(5).
18   Civil Judicial Statistics 1988, Table 5.8.
19   s. 31(2); see below.

to see how a court could properly carry out such a balancing exercise without having before it full evidence about the range of facilities and services which the Local Authority will be able to make available for the child; and without hearing evidence about the Authority's plans for the child if a care order were to be made. It is true that under the present law contained in the Children and Young Persons Act 1969 there is a discretion not to make an order even if the relevant conditions have been satisfied; but the Children Act, by requiring positive proof that the exercise of the judicial power of the state will be beneficial to the child, goes very much further.

Parental agreement paramount?

Another, at first sight rather curious, indication of a desire to confine the court's involvement in family issues to the strictly adjudicatory can be detected in the provisions giving effect to the principle that the child's welfare should be the paramount consideration in determining questions relating to the child's upbringing or the administration of the child's property.[20] In order to assist the courts, the parties, and their advisers, the Act follows the Law Commission's recommendation[21] that the legislation should contain a statutory 'checklist' indicating factors - such as the child's wishes, physical and emotional needs, age, sex and background - to which the court should have particular regard in deciding that issue. But the checklist as enacted contains two significant changes from that put forward by the Law Commission.

20   Children Act 1989, s. 1(2). The Act does not follow the Law
      Commission's bold proposal [Law Com. No. 172 (1988) para. 3.14] that the
      welfare of any child likely to be affected should be the 'only' factor. The
      Act thus seems to accept the principle recently articulated by the courts that
      parents have rights in custody disputes to the extent at least that the parent's
      claim to take decisions for a child is only to be displaced if it can be
      affirmatively proved that the child's welfare requires such interference: see
      Re K(a minor) (ward: care and control) [1990] 1 WLR 431, CA applying
      Lord Templeman's robust dictum Re KD (a minor) (access: principles)
      [1988] 2 FLR 139, 141 that the 'best person to bring up a child is the
      natural parent. It matters not whether the parent is wise or foolish, rich or
      poor, educated or illiterate, provided the child's moral and physical health
      are not endangered.'
21   Law Com. No. 172 (1988) para. 3.18.

First, there is included[22] amongst the specified matters a reference to the 'range of powers available to the court under this Act in the proceedings in question'; which might possibly be taken as a tacit warning that too much should not be expected of court intervention. Secondly - and of much greater significance - is the fact that the checklist only comes into play in specified circumstances,[23] that is, where the court is considering an order in care proceedings or an *opposed* application in other proceedings (such as divorce).[24] It is not easy to see why care proceedings should be singled out in this way; but in the case of private law proceedings the message does seem to be clear. It is (it would seem) that the court is not to embark on an inquiry as to the factors which the parties have taken into account in reaching an agreement on the child's future. In particular, there is no counterpart to the requirement in applications for agreed financial relief orders that the court be supplied with prescribed information[25] before it has jurisdiction to make the order the parties seek. Thus, in relation to children, private agreement is to rule, at least in the absence of some patent indication that the order would be inconsistent with the child's welfare. Of course, in divorce cases, the court has the vestigial inquisitorial role under section 41 referred to above; but in any other proceedings - for example, a father's application for contact with his child - it seems that the court will rarely be in a position to deny the parties the relief sought in the pleadings. All this seems a world away from the concern expressed by the Law Commission in its 1982 Report on Illegitimacy about the vulnerability of many single mothers, and about the need to protect them from harassment or blackmail by the child's father.[26] But then the Act is prepared to contemplate that a private agreement between the mother and father of an illegitimate child should be effective to vest parental authority in them jointly - the (surely unworkable) proposal that such an agreement would have to be 'checked' by a County Court 'to ensure that both parents understand the importance

---

22   s. 1(3) (g).
23   s. 1(3).
24   s. 1(4).
25   Matrimonial Causes Act 1973, s. 33A; as inserted by Matrimonial and Family Proceedings Act 1984.
26   Law Com. No.118 (1982) para. 4.26.

and effects of their agreement'[27] having been dropped during the Bill's passage through Parliament. The result is a striking illustration of the fact that the courts no longer have a primary protective role in relation to children.

Parental responsibility - more than draftsman's rhetoric?

If the courts' role is to be diminished, the role of parents is emphasised. Indeed, it is said that 'parental responsibility' is the key concept in the Act; and the official introductory guide to the Act[28] states that this choice of words 'emphasises that the duty to care for the child and to raise him to moral, physical and emotional health is the fundamental task of parenthood and the only justification for the authority it confers'. No doubt the phrase has overtones of self-sufficiency and obligation - 'the world does not owe you a living', and other once popular saws and maxims - which give it a certain appeal; but the lawyer is at first glance likely to regard this as yet another example of the deplorable modern fashion for using the statute book as a vehicle for political rhetoric rather than precise meaning.

This scepticism arises because the Act[29] defines the phrase as meaning: 'all the rights, duties, powers, responsibilities and authority which by law a parent of a child has in relation to a child and his property'; and all the rights of a guardian of the child's estate; and it is difficult to see how this differs from the formula employed in the Children Act 1975 to define the, now deeply unfashionable, concept of 'parental rights and duties'.[30] Even worse (it may be thought) the term is likely in some ways to be dangerously misleading to the lay person. For example, a person (such as the father of an illegitimate child) who has no 'parental responsibility' may nevertheless still be

---

27   Law Com. No.172 (1988) para. 2.18.
28   HMSO, *Introduction to the Children Act 1989*, para. 1.4.
29   s. 3(1).
30   Children Act 1975, s. 85(1): the 'parental rights and duties' means 'all the rights and duties which by law the mother and father have in relation to a legitimate child and his property.'

responsible for the child's maintenance.[31] It may be difficult to explain to such a person how it is that he has no parental responsibility, yet is still to be responsible for providing for the child's maintenance.

But in fact such scepticism would be unjustified. It is true that the change of terminology by itself achieves little if anything; but the detailed provisions of the Act create a scheme which does give effect to a coherent general philosophy much more consistent with a 'responsibility' based framework than with 'rights' based notions. Perhaps the most significant indication of this approach is that the making of a court order does not of itself affect parental responsibility: 'once a parent, always a parent'. Thus, although the court may make an order settling the arrangements to be made as to the person with whom a child is to live, and the person in whose favour such a residence order is made will then have parental responsibility for the child,[32] yet the making of such an order does not deprive anyone else of parental responsibility.[33] Hence a person who has parental responsibility may continue to exercise it (by himself or herself),[34] without any obligation to consult others with such responsibility, provided only that the terms of a court order are not infringed.[35]

Once more, therefore, the courts are to withdraw; and parents are to understand that the state will not relieve them of their responsibilities. Put in this way, the legislation seems to embody a version of what is sometimes called - by academic writers usually pejoratively - Thatcherism;[36] and it is indeed not inconsistent with

31 See Social Security Act 1986, s. 26(3) as preserved by Children Act 1989 s. 3(4) (a).
32 s. 12(2).
33 s. 2(6).
34 s. 2(7).
35 s. 2(8).
36 See notably B. Campbell, *Unofficial Secrets* (London: Virago Press, 1988): 'Child torture came to haunt Thatcherism during the 1980s . . . It all seemed to vindicate Thatcherism's scorn for the busy-body welfare state. But not quite: these children [Jasmine Beckford, Tyra Henry and Kimberley Carlile] died within the family, the institution sanctified by Thatcherism. The state had sinned by omission, not commission - families were kept intact, and children were killed.' [pp. 118-19].

other manifestations of that political stance. But scepticism about what can sensibly be expected of the courts is not the monopoly of a political party; and indeed the most obvious official source for many of the ideas to which the 1989 Act gives effect is in fact the Report of the Matrimonial Causes Procedure Committee under the chairmanship of the Hon. Dame Margaret Booth.[37] It is significant that it was the Booth Committee which emphasised[38] that the primary responsibility for deciding what should happen to a divorcing couple's children, property and marriage should rest with the parties, and that they should be involved at an early stage in seeking to formulate appropriate arrangements in an attempt to 'emphasise their continuing joint responsibility'.[39] The Children Act 1989 gives effect to that view in relation to children; and it is reasonable to suppose that other aspects of family law - such as the dissolution of marriage - will be privatized in the same way in the years ahead.

Care proceedings

But what of the impact of the Children Act in relation to the public law - the system which (in an extreme view) allowed doctors and social workers to conspire to attack family life in Cleveland?[40] Curiously enough, it is much more difficult to detect any consistent philosophy in the - very radical - changes in the law which are effected by the Children Act and indeed much more difficult to prophesy what impact the changes will have.

It is true that the Act seeks to remove the potential for injustice which existed in the 'place of safety' and other emergency provisions of the legal structure.[41] It can also be said that by restricting the availability of wardship the Act again emphasises that

37   *Report of the Matrimonial Causes Procedure Committee* (1985).
38   Ibid., para. 3.2.
39   Ibid., para. 2.24.
40   This point of view is put by Stuart Bell MP, *When Salem came to the Boro* (London: Pan Books, in assoc. with Sidgwick & Johnson, 1988).
41   The routine use of place of safety orders as the first stage of authoritative intervention in a family's affairs was criticized in the *Report of the Inquiry into Child Abuse in Cleveland* 1987, Cm. 412, para. 16.14. The Children Act 1989 will replace 'place of safety' orders by 'emergency protection' orders available in a procedure which will contain many more safeguards for the family.

the function of the courts is to decide issues, and that it is no part of a court's business to 'take a child into its care and to decide how . . . it is to be brought up.[42] And it can be said that the restriction on the availability of wardship is intended to protect families against unwarranted interference based on the philosophy that because the child's welfare is paramount children may properly be removed from parental care simply on the basis that a court considers that the state could do better for the child than his family.[43] Indeed the Lord Chancellor has specifically said that whereas a broad welfare discretion 'may be appropriate and defensible where a court is deciding a dispute between warring members of a family', to allow a broad discretion without defined minimum criteria to justify state intervention in the integrity and independence of the family would constitute a threat to the 'poor and to minority groups, whose view of what is good for a child may not coincide closely with that of the majority . . .'.[44]

What then are the circumstances in which such intervention is to be permitted? Before a court can make a care order (which has the effect that the local authority will be responsible for the child and the child's welfare free from mandatory directions from outside, three conditions must be satisfied:

(i) The 'threshold' conditions - including the requirement that the child be shown to be suffering or likely to suffer significant harm - set out in the Act must be proved to exist.[45]

(ii) The making of an order will be better for the child than not making any order at all;[46] and

(iii) The child's welfare has been treated as paramount. The court must specifically direct itself to this issue, and have regard in particular

---

42   Cross (1967) 83 LQR 200, 202.

43   Lord Mackay of Clashfern, *Joseph Jackson Memorial Lecture* (1989) 139 NLJ 505; Review of Child Care Law (1985) para. 15.10. The view that a parent has a 'natural' right to the care of a child has recently been articulated in case law: see n. 20 above.

44   Lord Mackay of Clashfern, ibid., p. 508.

45   s. 31(2).

46   s.1(5)

to a number of factors enumerated in the Act.[47] In carrying out this aspect of the decision-taking procedure the court must have regard to the range of powers available to the court; and in a proper case the court will be able to make a residence order in favour of a friend or relative rather than a care order.[48]

This is certainly a much more complex process than is involved in care proceedings under the Children and Young Persons Act 1969; and the threshold condition referred to above seems almost calculated to give rise to a great deal of litigation and uncertainty in marginal cases.

It is provided[49] that the court shall not make a care or supervision order unless it is satisfied:

(a)   that the child concerned is suffering, or is likely to suffer, significant harm; and

(b)   that the harm, or likelihood of harm, is attributable to -

  (i)   the care given to the child, or likely to be given to him if the order were not made, not being what it would be reasonable to expect a parent to give to him; or

  (ii)   the child's being beyond parental control.

The Act[50] gives further guidance about the meaning of many of the terms ('harm', 'development', 'health' and 'ill-treatment').

This is not the place for a detailed examination of these

---

47   s. 1(4) (a); s. 1(3).
48   s. 1(3)(g) and s. 8(1). It would appear that such orders can be made even if the 'threshold' condition is not satisfied.
49   s. 31(2).
50   s. 31(9).

provisions;[51] but two points must be made. First, the scope for the introduction of expert evidence is obviously made potentially enormous. What, for example, is likely to constitute harm to a child's emotional development? What evidence is there that the course proposed by the Local Authority - and it is envisaged that Local Authorities will be required to indicate what they intend to do for the child if an order is made[52] - will better promote the child's welfare than making no order at all? It is not surprising that one experienced High Court judge has expressed concern that the 'unwieldy and intractable jurisdiction' will 'swamp the courts'.[53]

The second point which should be made is that it is far from clear that the threshold condition will be satisfied in at least some cases in which a child's welfare may be seriously at risk. The most disturbing of these situations is where an 'unimpeachable' parent - who is able to provide good material facilities for a child - proposes to remove a child from foster parents who have cared for the child and with whom the child has established strong links. There would be no difficulty in establishing that such a child would be likely to 'suffer significant harm'; but can it be said that such harm is attributable to the care likely to be given to the child not being what it would be reasonable for a parent to give to him?

A revolution in the courts' role?

In this area, therefore, there must be concern that the courts have been given a task which will prove extremely difficult for them to carry out. But perhaps the most striking, and in some ways disturbing, feature of the legislation is the revolution which it envisages in judicial practice. The Official Introduction to the Children Act 1989, gives the flavour of what is intended by the use of headings such as 'Mobilising the Courts' and 'A More Active Court'.[54] Much of the

51   See for full discussions, A. Bainham, *Children: The New Law* (Bristol: Jordans, 1990) paras 5.6 - 5.22; R. White, P. Carr and N. Lowe, *A Guide to the Children Act 1989* (London: Butterworths, 1990) 6.9-19 and J. Masson, *The Children Act 1989* (London: Sweet and Maxwell, 1990).

52   Lord Mackay of Clashfern, p. 506

53   Per Anthony Lincoln J, *Re L, The Times*, 12 Oct., 1989.

54   paras 1.47-50. It may also be said that the courts' powers to make detailed access arrangements in respect of a child committed to care are difficult to reconcile with the general approach that courts are to be concerned with adjudication and not with administration.

detail is left to rules; but some provisions of the Act give an indication of the new managerial role which the courts are to be expected to play: they are, for example, to draw up timetables with a view to disposing of the issue without delay; and they are empowered to give such directions as are considered appropriate to ensure so far as practicable that the timetable is adhered to.[55] Clearly a great deal of thought will have to be given to formulating procedures which will enable these well-intentioned measures to be effective.

The same is true of the rules which are to be made to ensure that in magistrates' courts there will be

> much more disclosure of the parties' evidence and cases ahead of the hearing, greater reliance on written material and magistrates reading the papers before the hearing and giving reasons for their decision at the end.[56]

The requirement that lay magistrates should formulate reasons in a way which will sufficiently explain the decision and the reasons which have led to it to the parties before them, and yet be sufficiently precise to minimise the risk of successful appeals arising from defects in the way in which the reasons for the decision are expressed, is likely to be particularly demanding; and the task of training magistrates for this new role will be a formidable one. It is encouraging that the Government is establishing a Central Advisory and Monitoring Committee Structure, and that an experienced Circuit Judge (Her Honour Judge Bracewell) has been appointed to provide advice and assistance to the Judicial Studies Board on the training of judicial officers, and to be responsible to the President of the Family Division for advising on the judicial administration which will be involved in the new structure, and on the procedures for allocating cases between the three levels of court (High Court, County Court, and Magistrates' Family Proceedings Court) which will have jurisdiction.[57]

55   s. 11 ['private law' orders] and s. 32 [care proceedings].
56   HMSO, *Introduction to the Children Act 1989*, para. 1.49.
57   Lord Mackay of Clashfern, above n. 43, p. 507.

This raises the whole question of the procedures which the courts are going to use in order to resolve cases. It is clear that the essential first step will still be to establish the relevant facts;[58] but how is that to be done? The answer in the English Common Law system has traditionally been by adopting the adversarial model of adjudication. The word 'adversarial' has unfortunate overtones of hostility and antagonism; but in reality it simply describes a system under which the court sits to hear and determine the issues raised by the parties, 'not to conduct an investigation or examination on behalf of society at large'.[59] In consequence the court itself has no power to investigate matters if the parties do not choose to do so. It is for the party on whom the law places the onus of proof to produce evidence which establishes the case; the other party need make no reply. The parties may test such evidence as is put forward by cross-examination; but it is not for the judge to ask why witnesses have or have not been called.[60] The adversarial system is thus in part based on the traditional dialectical approach that the truth may best emerge if each interested party is allowed to state the case from that party's own perspective. The truth (or synthesis) will then emerge from the opposition of thesis and antithesis.

Partly for historical reasons,[61] and partly because of concern that the parties to divorce proceedings might collude to deceive the court,[62] this traditional common law approach has never been universally applied in the courts dealing with family law. In particular, it never applied to the exercise of the Crown's prerogative jurisdiction over wards of court which was parental and

58   *M* v *M (Custody Application)* [1988] 1 FLR 225.
59   *Jones* v *National Coal Board* [1957] 2 All ER 155, 159, *per* Lord Denning MR.
60   Cf. *R* v *Blundeston Prison Board of Visitors, ex parte Fox-Taylor* [1982] 1 All ER 646, 648, *per* Phillips J.
61   The fact that until 1857 the Ecclesiastical Courts (which adopted an inquisitorial procedure) administered the law governing marriage was particularly significant.
62   The fact that in divorce proceedings the court is still required to inquire into the facts alleged by the petitioner and into any facts alleged by the respondent [Matrimonial Causes Act 1973, s. 1(3)] indicates the force of historical precedent in this respect.

administrative by nature.[63] More recently, it has become the fashion for judges to assert that care proceedings in magistrates' courts are not adversarial[64] (although such statements are difficult to reconcile with the structure of the existing legislation and rules.[65])

But all this may now change. Are the courts not only to manage the timetable of cases, but also to intervene in the process of getting at the truth - perhaps in care cases even before the threshold condition has been made out - whether or not the parties choose to lead evidence? Welfare and Guardian *ad Litem* reports are, of course, one well recognised method whereby an inquisitorial element is brought into the disposal of cases; but it seems to be suggested that much more significant changes of procedure - or perhaps style - are in contemplation. If so, the effect in the Family Proceedings Court will be far more revolutionary than any of the changes made by the Children Act in the substantive law. Participatory justice is an appealing phrase; but the danger of adjudicators who have the responsibility of deploying the coercive power of the state appearing to 'descend into the arena' is a real one. To arrive at the appropriate balance whereby magistrates and others will go beyond merely acting as umpires whilst not appearing to become partisans will require a revolution in training and approach.

63   The 'disposal of controverted questions is an incident only in the jurisdiction' [*Scott* v *Scott* [1913] AC 417, 437, *per* Lord Haldane LC]; and in pursuing the ward's best interests the court will if need be look beyond the submissions of the parties: *Re E(SA) (a minor)(wardship)* [1984] 1 All ER 289, 290, *per* Lord Scarman. It has been said that the role of the parties is simply to put before the judge for his consideration their suggestions for the ward's upbringing: Cross (1967) 83 LQR 200, 207.

64   See e.g. *Humberside CC* v *DPR* [1977] 1 WLR 1251; *R* v *Birmingham Juvenile Court, ex parte G and others (minors)* [1989] 2 FLR 454.

65   See e.g. *R* v *Hampshire CC, ex parte K and K* [1990] 2 WLR 649 (where the Local Authority took 'every tactical advantage' in not revealing evidence favourable to the parents' case) and *R* v *Birmingham Juvenile Court, ex parte G and others (minors)* [1989] 2 FLR 454.

4

The European Convention on Human Rights and the 'Illegitimate' Child

J. S. Davidson

In the latter half of the twentieth century the dominant feature of international human rights law has been the emergence of instruments which seek to ensure equality of treatment for all people regardless of race, religion, sex or status of birth. It is perhaps surprising therefore that discrimination against those born out of wedlock has endured for so long, and perhaps even more surprising that the Member States of the Council of Europe, which have been bound by the European Convention on Human Rights since 1950 and the European Social Charter since 1961, have, in a significant number of instances, perpetuated both the stigma and the inequalities attached to illegitimate[1] children. On three occasions in the last decade the European Court of Human Rights (the Court) has had cause to rule on

1   The term 'illegitimate' is enclosed in inverted commas in the title in order to concur with the usage of the European Court of Human Rights. Schermers suggests that the usage itself may signify that the terminology is discriminatory or unclear and that the expression 'extra-matrimonial' child may be more acceptable. H.G. Schermers, *European Law on Illegitimate Children*, The Dominik Lasok Lecture on European Community Law, Centre for European Legal Studies, University of Exeter Faculty of Law 24 Feb. 1989, p. 2 and footnote 2. For the sake of brevity and consistency, the terms legitimate and illegitimate will be used to describe those born within and without wedlock.

issues affecting the status and rights of children born out of wedlock. First, in the important *Marckx* [2] case, then in *Johnston* [3] and finally in *Inze*.[4]   While each of these decisions is significant in terms of the elaboration of the rights of illegitimate children in the cases under consideration, they are also important in a much wider sense, for they contribute to the development of European human rights law on children born out of wedlock, and to the development of the law of the European Convention in general.   Such developments have not been uncontroversial and the expansive approach to interpretation of the Convention employed by the Court has been criticised by one eminent jurist as a misguided attempt to read a code of family law into a document concerned only with the prevention of state interference in domiciliary rights.[5]   Despite such criticisms, it is nonetheless clear that the Court's interpretation of the Convention has developed international standards against which the behaviour of the Contracting Parties towards illegitimate children within their jurisdiction will be measured.

The purpose of this essay is to examine the *Marckx* case in detail in order to illuminate the development of the European Convention's law on the illegitimate child and to point up areas of controversy in the Court's techniques of interpretation and application of the law. It will also analyse the wider implications of the judgment for European human rights law in general, and examine the subsequent cases on illegitimacy where the principles enunciated in *Marckx* have been reaffirmed, developed or refined. Finally, an attempt will be made to draw some conclusions about the role of the European Court of Human Rights in contributing to European social development in this field.

International standards and the illegitimate child

Among the various human rights instruments only the Universal

---

2   *Marckx* v *Belgium,* Eur Court HR, Series A, No 31.
3   *Johnston and others* v *Republic of Ireland*, Eur Court HR, Series A, No 112.
4   *Inze* v *Austria*, Eur Court HR, Series A, No 126.
5   See below, pp. 82 ff.

Declaration of Human Rights,[6] the American Convention on Human Rights[7] and the Convention on the Rights of the Child[8] specifically refer to the equal treatment of children born out of wedlock. Article 25(2) of the Universal Declaration calls for the equal treatment of all children 'whether born in or out of wedlock', and Principle 1 of the Declaration of the Rights of the Child requires children to be granted the rights contained therein without discrimination on account of 'social origin, property, birth or other status'. The American Convention also states that 'the law shall recognize equal rights for children born out of wedlock and those born in wedlock'. The equal treatment of illegitimate children is, however, implicit in the texts of other international instruments. The United Nations Covenant on Civil and Political Rights[9] requires states not to discriminate against children on grounds of their birth and the Covenant on Economic and Social Rights obliges states not to discriminate against children 'for reasons of parentage'.[10] Similarly, the rights contained in the European Social Charter are to be granted 'irrespective of marital status and family relations'.[11] The Organisation of African Unity's Charter on Human and Peoples Rights also incorporates non-discrimination against

6   GA Resolution 217A(III), GAOR, 3rd Session, Part I, Resolutions, p. 71. While the Universal Declaration is not of itself legally binding, it has had a profound influence on the development of customary international law, and may, in its own right, be regarded as both a statement of general principles of law and an authoritative interpretation of the UN Charter. See further, I. Brownlie, *Principles of Public International Law* (Oxford: University Press, 3rd edn, 1980) pp. 570-1.
7   (1970) 9 ILM 673.
8   The UN Convention on the Rights of the Child (the text of which is reproduced below at pp. 294 ff.) was adopted without a vote by the UN General Assembly on 20 November 1989, thirty years to the day after the adoption of the Declaration on the Rights of the Child. See further J. S. Davidson (1990) *NZ Family Law Bulletin*.
9   UKTS 6 (1977); (1967) ILM 368.
10   UKTS 6 (1977); (1967) ILM 360.
11   The mechanism for the enforcement of the European Social Charter is a system of reporting by Contracting Parties on measures of implementation which they have taken. These reports are then assessed by an Independent Committee of Experts. While the Social Charter therefore plays an important role in developing standards of treatment for illegitimate children, it contains no right of individual petition as does the European Convention on Human Rights. In terms of individual remedies therefore, the Social Charter is clearly lacking. See D. J. Harris, *The European Social Charter*: (Virginia: University Press, 1987).

discrimination against illegitimate children by providing that the 'State shall . . . ensure the protection of the rights of . . . the child as stipulated in international declarations and conventions'.[12] Of all the regional instruments only the European Convention on Human Rights does not refer either expressly or by implication to the requirement of equality of treatment of the child born out of wedlock in any of its substantive provision.[13] It has therefore been left to the Court to determine whether or not non-discriminatory treatment of illegitimate children is implicit in the rules established by the Convention.

The *Marckx* case

The case of Paula and Alexandra Marckx was the first in which the Court had to decide whether the Convention protected the rights of the illegitimate child. The Court sat *in plenum* making this judgment of the utmost importance in the development of the law of the Convention or, as Schermers calls it, European constitutional law.[14] The case concerned certain provisions of the Belgian Civil Code which the applicants contended discriminated against illegitimate children and their mothers and which therefore violated their right to family life contrary to Article 8 of the Convention. Under the Belgian Law complained of, no legal bond arose between an unmarried mother and her child from the mere fact of birth, whereas the converse was true in the case of legitimate children. Maternal affiliation of illegitimate children could only be achieved either by voluntary recognition or by the child taking legal proceedings within five years of his attaining majority. Even if affiliation was established, it gave rise only to limited rights for the illegitimate child. First, the child did not become a member of the mother's family, thus excluding the possibility of the child inheriting on intestacy and precluding his grandparents from acting *in loco parentis* in the event of the death of the child's mother. Second, and perhaps more important, the illegitimate child's patrimonial rights *vis-à-vis* its

12   (1982) ILM 59.
13   Article 14 does, however, refer to non-discrimination on grounds of birth, but this provision is incapable of standing alone and may only be used in conjunction with the other substantive articles in Part 1 of the Convention. For the text of article 14 see below n. 16. For a consideration of the operation of Article 14 see below, pp. 89-92.
14   *European Law*, above, n. 1.

mother were severely curtailed. An illegitimate child which was the sole heir was entitled only to three-quarters of the share in its mother's estate of which it would have been entitled had it been legitimate. Dispositions *inter vivos* were also limited to this amount. Paradoxically, if affiliation between mother and illegitimate child was not established, the mother could give or bequeath all her property to the child who remained to her a stranger in law. The mother was therefore faced with two alternatives: either she could recognise the child and prejudice his patrimonial rights on intestacy or she could desist from affiliation and thus renounce establishing a family connection with the child in the eyes of the law. She could avoid these consequences either by adopting the child or by marrying and retrospectively legitimating the child. In the former case, the child still remained a stranger to his mother's family, and in the case of latter the mother was obliged to marry.

Paula Marckx contended that these provisions of the Belgian code violated the fundamental rights guaranteed by the Convention both of her and of her daughter and she lodged an application with the European Commission on Human Rights claiming that they were both 'victims' of such a violation within the meaning of Article 25(1).[15] In particular, she claimed that there had been violations by Belgium of Article 8 taken by itself and in conjunction with Article 14, Article 3, Article 12, and Article 1 of the First Protocol to the Convention

15   Article 25(1) provides:
      The Commission may receive petitions addressed to the Secretary-General of the Council of Europe from any person, non-governmental organisation or group of individuals claiming to be the victim of a violation by one of the High Contracting Parties of the rights set forth in this Convention, provided that the High Contracting party against which the complaint has been lodged has declared that it recognizes the competence of the Commission to receive such petitions . . .

16   The relevant provisions state:
      Article 3:
      No one shall be subjected to torture or to inhuman or degrading treatment.

taken by itself and in conjunction with Article 14.[16] The Commission rejected the claims based on Article 3 since it considered that although the treatment of the applicants may have been humiliating, it was not degrading in the sense of the Convention. Furthermore, it rejected the claim based on Article 12, maintaining that the guarantee

Article 8:

(1)   Everyone has the right to respect for his private and family life, his home and his correspondence.

(2)   There shall be no interference by a public authority with the exercise of this right except such as is in accordance with the law and is necessary in a democratic society in the interests of national security, public safety or the economic well-being of the country, for the prevention of disorder or crime, for the protection of health or morals, or for the protection of the rights and freedoms of others.

Article 12:

Men and women of marriageable age have the right to marry and to found a family, according to the national laws governing the exercise of this right.

Article 14:

The enjoyment of the rights and freedoms set forth in this Convention shall be secured without discrimination on any ground such as sex, race, colour, language, religion, political or other opinion, national or social origin, association with a national minority, property, birth or other status.

Article 1, Protocol 1:

Every natural or legal person is entitled to the peaceful enjoyment of his possessions. No one shall be deprived of his possessions except in the public interest and subject to the conditions provided for by law and by the general principles of international law.

The preceding provisions shall not, however, in any way impair the right of a State to enforce such laws as it deems necessary to control the use of property in accordance with the general interest or to secure the payment of taxes or other contributions or penalties.

of a right to marry did not imply a right not to marry. Both these findings were upheld by the Court. Nevertheless, the Commission found that the applicants had been the victims of breaches of Article 8 and of Article 1 of the First Protocol both taken independently and in conjunction with Article 14.

Preliminary issues of the Convention's applicability

The Court considered that the applicants' complaints concerning the manner of establishing affiliation, the extent of Alexandra's family relationships and the patrimonial rights of the child and the mother turned principally upon an interpretation of Article 8 of the Convention taken alone and in conjunction with Article 14.[17] However, neither Judge Sir Gerald Fitzmaurice in a vigorous and acerbic dissenting judgment, nor Belgium in its submissions to the Court, took the view that the applicants had suffered a violation of any rights protected by the Convention. The reasons upon which they based their objections were essentially different in nature, although there was a degree of convergence in their reasoning when it came to a consideration of whether or not the applicants were seeking to challenge Belgian law *in abstracto*.

Judge Fitzmaurice was of the opinion that the complaints did not lie within the scope of the Convention *ratione materiae*, asserting that there was a distinction between the applicability of a provision and its breach. He argued that there could only be a breach of a provision if that provision applied *ab initio* to the facts under consideration. He took the view in the instant case that Article 8 was not applicable because the Convention was simply not designed to deal with such circumstances.[18] Here Judge Fitzmaurice joined battle with the legal methodology applied by the majority in the Court. Following his brief exposition on questions of applicability and breach of legal norms, he observed somewhat trenchantly:

---

17   Series A, No 31, paragraph 28, p. 14.
18   Ibid., paras 3 and 4, pp. 39-40.

The foregoing are elementary, standard propositions
which should not need stating because they are such as
everyone would assent to in principle, - but principle
is easily lost sight of when eagerness for specific
results - however meritorious they may be in
themselves - overreaches the still, small voice of the
juridical conscience.[19]

The necessary consequence of the non-applicability of the relevant
provisions meant, in essence, he considered that neither Paula nor
Alexandra Marckx had fulfilled the requirements of Article 27
governing the admissibility of petitions, since the facts did not
disclose a violation of any rights protected by the Convention.[20]

Judicial activism or restraint?

Judge Fitzmaurice pursued the rigorous logic of his argument
throughout a critique of the way in which the Court had interpreted
Article 8 in the instant case. His view was that Article 8(2), dealing
with limitations which could be imposed on family life by the state on
broad grounds of public policy, demonstrated clearly the background
against, and the purpose for, which the Convention had been drafted.
In short, the Convention was designed not to create a detailed code of
European family law, but to protect individuals against the dangers of
state interference in their lives. Here it is appropriate to set out
Fitzmaurice's reasoning at length since it gives the key to his judicial
philosophy:

It is abundantly clear (at least it is to me) - and the
nature of the whole background against which the idea
of the European Convention on Human Rights was
conceived bears out this view - that the main, if not
indeed the sole object and intended sphere of

19   Ibid., para. 5, p. 40.
20   The material part of Article 27 reads:
              (2)   The Commission shall consider inadmissible any
              petition which submitted under Article 25 which it considers
              ... manifestly ill-founded ...

application of Article 8, was that of what I will call
the 'domiciliary protection' of the individual. He and
his family were no longer to be subjected to the four
o'clock in the morning rat-a-tat on the door; to
domestic intrusions, searches and questionings; to the
examinations, delaying and confiscation of
correspondence; to the planting of listening devices
(bugging); to restrictions on the use of radio and
television; to telephone tapping or disconnection; to
measures of coercion such as cutting off the electricity
or water supply; to such abominations as children
being required to report upon the activities of their
parents and even sometimes the same for one spouse
against another, - in short the whole gamut of fascist
and communist inquisitorial practices such as had
scarcely been known, at least in Western Europe,
since the eras of religious intolerance and oppression,
until (ideology replacing religion) they became
prevalent again in many countries between the two
world wars and subsequently. Such, and not the
internal, domestic regulation of family relationships,
was the object of Article 8, and it was for the
avoidance of these horrors, tyrannies and vexations
that 'private and family life . . . home and . . .
correspondence' were to be respected, and the
individual endowed with a right to enjoy that respect -
not for the regulation of the civil status of babies.[21]

Judge Fitzmaurice further observed that matters of civil status and the
protection of family life related to two different orders of juridical
concept. Thus his colleagues had deviated from the juridical
orthodoxies of interpretation and had instead engaged in that most
heinous of activities - judicial legislation. Fitzmaurice argued that
even the paragraph headings of the judgment constituted:

> [A] misguided endeavour to read - or rather introduce
> - a whole code of family law into Article 8 of the

21　　Ibid., para. 7, pp. 41-2.

Convention, thus inflating it in a manner and to an extent, wholly incommensurable with its true and intended proportions. Family *law* is not family *life* and this Article constitutes too slender and uncertain a foundation for any process of grafting the complexities and details of the one onto the relative simplicities of the other. The pretension to do so, in order to force the case within the (actually) quite narrow limits of Article 8 is, as the French saying aptly puts it, '*cousu de fil blanc*' ('sticking out a mile').[22]

These objections, which were aimed at the Court's techniques of interpretation, are clearly those of a common lawyer whose primary approach to statutory or treaty interpretation is textual or literal: the function of the judge here is not to make the law but simply to interpret it as he finds it.[23] Of course, Judge Fitzmaurice, in order to buttress his argument that the Court was exceeding its proper function of interpretation, resorted to an examination of the context within which the Convention had been concluded. Here he examined the mischief which the Convention had been designed to guard against and interpreted it within that context. In his view the principle reason for the drafting of the Convention was to protect individual liberty

22   Ibid., para. 15, p. 45.
23   This is not, however, simply a common law foible since some support for the textual approach to treaty interpretation can be found in Article 31 of the Vienna Convention on the Law of Treaties which provides:
> A treaty shall be interpreted in good faith in accordance with the ordinary meaning to be given to the terms of the treaty in their context and in the light of its object and purpose.

However, as the International Law Commission made clear in its Commentary, the principle of effectiveness is inherent in Article 31. 'When a treaty is open to two interpretations one of which does and the other does not enable the treaty to have appropriate effects, good faith and the objects and purposes of the treaty demand that the former interpretation should be adopted.' YBILC, 1966, II, p. 219. It is clear that the Court has, wherever it has been able, adopted the principle of effectiveness in interpreting the Convention. See J. Merrills, *The Development of International Law by the European Court of Human Rights* (Manchester: University Press, 1988), chapter 4.

against totalitarianism of both the left and the right.[24]

This was not the first or the last time Judge Fitzmaurice had taken a stand against the dynamic approach to interpretation of the Convention by his colleagues.[25] In *Tyrer* [26] for example, he resisted a broad interpretation of Article 3 arguing that such an interpretation would transform it into 'a vehicle of indirect penal, reform for which it was not intended'.[27] Furthermore, in *Ireland* v *United Kingdom*,[28] Judge Fitzmaurice, in a statement of his understanding of the judicial function, drew a subtle distinction between what he saw as legitimate and 'natural' incremental developments through interpretation of the Convention and 'development as a conscious aim . . . a quasi - legislative operation exceeding the normal judicial function'.[29]

Whether or not one has sympathy with Judge Fitzmaurice's call for judicial restraint, it is clear that the majority of the Court has been involved in the process of development of the effectiveness of the Convention through judicial activism, and it is perhaps natural that this has been so. The Court, in effect, functions as a European constitutional court and its techniques are consonant with those of national constitutional courts.[30] As will be seen subsequently, the Court has interpreted the Convention as a living instrument designed to cope with the problems created not by European society as it was in the 1950s, but by European society as it is at the time of interpretation.[31] While Fitzmaurice was probably correct in asserting that the Convention was originally drafted to provide a bulwark against fascism and communism,[32] its function has, in the Court's

24   Above pp. 82-3.
25   For a full consideration of Judge Sir Gerald Fitzmaurice's dissent against the style of interpretation adopted by the Court see C. C. Morrisson, *The Dynamics of Development in the European Human Rights Convention System*, (The Hague: Nijhoff, 1981), chapter 1 and Merrills, *Development*, pp. 211-29.
26   Eur Court HR, Series A, No. 26.
27   Ibid. Separate Opinion of Judge Sir Gerald Fitzmaurice, para. 14.
28   Eur Court HR, Series A, No. 25.
29   Ibid. Separate Opinion of Judge Sir Gerald Fitzmaurice, para. 6.
30   See Morrisson, *Dynamics*, pp. 3-8 and D. J. Harris, 'Human Rights Developments in 1979' (1979) *BYIL* 260-4.
31   Below pp. 94-7.
32   See R. Beddard, *Human Rights and Europe* (London: Sweet and Maxwell, 2nd edn 1980) pp. 17-30.

view, been transformed by European socio-political developments.

An *actio popularis* under the Convention?

Belgium's main objection before the Court was that the applicants were effectively seeking a ruling on the Belgian Civil Code *in abstracto*, because they had never suffered any actual damage from an application of the relevant domestic law. Since no actual damage had been suffered, the Belgian government contended that the applicants could not be victims within the meaning of Article 25.[33] This position was also taken by Sir Gerald Fitzmaurice when he inquired whether someone could be a victim if he was affected by the law in question 'in a purely or largely formal, nominal, remote, or trivial way'.[34] Here the Court reaffirmed its decision in *Klass*[35] in which it had rejected the concept of rulings on the validity of laws *in abstracto*, thus denying the possible existence in the law of the Convention of an *actio popularis*. As the Court remarked:

> In principle it does not suffice for an individual applicant to claim that the mere existence of a law violates his rights under the Convention, it is necessary that the law should have been applied to his detriment.[36]

However, in *Klass* the Court seemed to suggest that the existence of legislation permitting the state to intercept private individuals' telephone communications could of itself constitute a breach of the Convention since the law might be used against an individual without his knowledge. This view was confirmed by the Court in *Marckx* where it said:

> Article 25 of the Convention entitles individuals to contend that a law violates their rights by itself and in

---

33   *Marckx*, above n. 2 at para. 26.
34   Ibid., Dissenting Opinion of Judge Sir Gerald Fitzmaurice, Postscript, para. 3.
35   Eur Court HR, No. 28.
36   Ibid., para. 33.

the absence of an individual measure of implementation, if they run the risk of being directly affected by it.[37]

This confirmation of a broad interpretation of Article 25 in *Marckx*, which was subsequently reaffirmed in *Johnston*,[38] brings the Court extremely close to an acknowledgment of an *acto popularis* without it actually affirming the existence of such a doctrine. Merrills, however, prefers to see the Court's approach as part of its desire to increase the effectiveness of the Convention. He argues:

> While the Convention clearly precludes an *actio popularis* the Court sees itself as much more than a provider of remedies for isolated complaints. In the interest of the effectiveness of the Convention as a whole it is prepared to use individual applications as an opportunity to make points which it considers need to be made and interprets the concept of 'victim' accordingly.[39]

The interpretation of Article 8[40]

Having disposed of the question of admissibility, the first issue considered by the Court was, what was meant by the words 'respect for . . . private and family life' in Article 8? The Court observed that respect for family life presupposed the existence of a family, but did not distinguish between the legitimate or illegitimate family: to do so would be inconsistent with the enjoyment of the right by 'everyone'.[41] The Court found that this position was confirmed by Article 14 which guaranteed, *inter alia*, that the rights guaranteed in the Convention should be secured without discrimination on the

---

37   *Marckx* above, note 2 at para. 27.
38   Eur Court HR, Series A, No. 112.
39   *Development*, p. 50. See also P. van Dijk, and G. J. H. van Hoof, *Theory and Practice of the European Convention on Human Rights*, (Deventer: Kluwer, 1984) pp. 36-41.
40   For the text of Article 8, see above n. 16.
41   *Marckx*, at para. 31.

grounds of a person's birth or other status. It also noted by way of extraneous evidence that the Committee of Ministers of the Council of Europe in a 1970 resolution had indicated that it regarded one-parent families as a form of family requiring the same degree of social protection as other families.[42] Thus the applicants fell within Article 8 *ratione personae.*

Positive obligations from a negative formulation

In a further preliminary consideration the Court also dealt with the rather more controversial matter of whether Article 8 only placed negative obligations on the state not to interfere with family life or whether it also implied positive obligations on the state to promote the development of family life. Here it found that while Article 8 was 'essentially' concerned with protecting the family from arbitrary interference by public authorities, the state was also under an obligation to 'act in a manner calculated to allow those concerned to lead a normal family life'.[43] The Court further observed:

> As envisaged by Article 8, respect for family life implies in particular, in the Court's view, the existence in domestic law of legal safeguards that render possible as from the moment of birth the child's integration in his family. In the connection, the State has a choice of various means, but a law that fails to satisfy this requirement violates paragraph 1 of Article 8 without there being any call to examine it under paragraph 2.[44]

The notion of imposing positive obligations upon the Contracting Parties by an application of Article 8, which of itself seemed merely to require state abstention from interference, is controversial and elicited dissent from a number of judges. Some based their dissent on the view that Article 8 was not relevant to the

42   Ibid.
43   Ibid.
44   Ibid.

issues confronted in the instant case,[45] while Judge Matscher argued that although Article 8 was applicable, matters of such complexity should be left within the state's margin of appreciation. Although it now appears to be accepted that states may be under positive obligations, even from provisions of the Convention which simply impose negative obligations, it is a matter of criticism that the precise extent of such obligations may not be apparent and are likely to develop from time to time in response to social changes. Although Judge Matscher stated in his partly dissenting opinion that it was correct to say that Article 8(1) imposed both positive and negative obligations on Contracting Parties, he urged that the Contracting Parties should be given a wide measure of discretion in the application of this doctrine:

> [I]t must be stressed that this positive obligation flowing from Article 8 of the Convention, is limited to what is necessary for the creation and development of family life according to the ideas which contemporary European societies have of this concept. Furthermore, States enjoy a certain power of appreciation as regards the means by which they propose to fulfil this obligation. In no case does Article 8 impose on the Contracting States a duty to adopt a family code comprising rules which go beyond this requirement.[46]

Applying Articles 8 and 14

Before turning to each of the applicant's cases individually, the Court examined the role of Article 14 in the proceedings. Here the Court recalled its earlier jurisprudence which had determined that Article 14 has no independent existence, but nonetheless plays a vital role in complementing the Convention and its Protocols.[47] In this field the

---

45 Judges Vihjalmson, Fitzmaurice, Bindschedler Robert and Pinheiro Farinha.

46 *Marckx*, Partly Dissenting Opinion of Judge Matscher, Part I.

47 Ibid., para. 32. See also *Belgian Linguistics Case*, Eur Court HR, No. 19, para. 44; van Dijk and van Hoof, *Theory*, pp. 386-98; Merrills, *Development*, pp. 152-7; F. G. Jacobs, *The European Convention on Human Rights*, (Oxford: University Press, 1975) pp. 188-93.

Court has also adopted an expansive approach to the interpretation of the Convention finding that although there may be no infringement of a substantive right in itself, nonetheless a rule may, if it is discriminatory, violate both the substantive right and Article 14 taken in conjunction. In this sense, the Court has always considered a rule to be discriminatory 'if it has no "objective and reasonable justification", that is if it does not pursue a "legitimate aim" or if there is not a "reasonable relationship of proportionality between the means employed and the aim sought to be realised"'.[48] Thus, as a preliminary observation, the Court held that as part of its positive obligations under the Convention, Belgium was obliged to allow the family life of the unmarried child and its mother to develop normally and with the absence of any discrimination against the illegitimate child based on the status of its birth: such was dictated by Articles 8 and 14 taken together.[49]

The Court then proceeded to deal with Paula Marckx's claim that the affiliation rules contained in the Belgian legal code violated Article 8 alone. Here the Court noted that the procedure for affiliation did not involve difficulties, but that it placed the mother in an invidious position: if she recognised the child, it restricted her capacity to grant or bequeath property to it, but if she refused to recognise the child in order to preserve her patrimonial rights, then she was obliged to renounce any family relationship with it.[50] The Court found that this dilemma was not consonant with 'respect' for family life since it 'thwarte[ed] and impede[d] the development of such life'.[51]

As regards Alexandra, the Court noted that the failure of a mother to recognise her illegitimate child meant that no family relationship with the child could be established until either the mother undertook such recognition or until the child was of full age and therefore able to seek a judicial declaration in its own right. In this case Paula had recognised Alexandra very quickly, but Alexandra, because of the operation of Belgian law, had been legally motherless from 16-29 October 1983. The Court therefore ruled that, despite the

---

48   *Marckx*, at para. 33.
49   Ibid., para. 34.
50   Ibid., para. 36.
51   Ibid.

brevity of the period, there had been a lack of respect for Alexandra's family life.[52]

The Court then turned its attention to the question of whether there had been a violation of the applicants' rights under Articles 8 and 14 taken in conjunction. Again, the Court applied a dynamic mode of interpretation to the Convention provisions in this area. It began by applying the presumption that the illegitimate child had as much interest in establishing the bond of affiliation as the legitimate child, but under Belgian law, the illegitimate child was likely to remain motherless if recognition was not undertaken by the mother. The Court therefore felt that this requirement lacked objective and reasonable justification and held that the distinction between the automatic maternal affiliation of the legitimate child and the non-automatic affiliation of the illegitimate child violated both the applicants rights in Article 14 taken together with Article 8.[53]

During the Court's consideration of these issues Belgium had argued that its law was designed to encourage and favour the traditional family unit and that this was therefore in line with the objectives of the Convention; the law was founded on objective and reasonable grounds relating to morals and public order. While the Court rejected this argument, it nevertheless made the following observation:

> [T]he Court recognises that support and encouragement of the traditional family is in itself legitimate or even praiseworthy. However, in the achievement of this end recourse must not be had to measures whose object or result is, as in the present case, to prejudice the 'illegitimate' family; the members of the 'illegitimate' family enjoy the guarantees of Article 8 on an equal footing with the members of the traditional family.[54]

Judge Fitzmaurice preferred to go further, arguing that the Belgian government should not be condemned for the operation of a

---

52   Ibid., para. 37.
53   Ibid., para. 39.
54   Ibid., para. 40.

law which had much in its favour (although he did not say what this was) and should be allowed a margin of appreciation in dealing with changes in social mores.[55] He was, in any event, of the view that the evidence cited by the Court did not seem to suggest that there was in fact a general trend towards the 'obliteration' of the distinction between legitimate and illegitimate children.[56] This point was raised again in *Johnston* [57] where it revealed stark differences of opinion between certain of the dissenting judges.

Support for the traditional family?

The *Johnston* case concerned the absence of any provision in Irish law for the divorce of spouses whose marriages had irretrievably broken down. Here, the first and second applicants, who lived together as man and wife, were both married in the eyes of Irish law to persons with whom they no longer had a matrimonial relationship. Indeed, the second applicant, Janice Williams-Johnston, had taken the name of her male cohabitee and had borne his child, Nessa, the third applicant. Because her parents could not divorce and remarry, Nessa was regarded in Irish law as an illegitimate child and therefore suffered all the disabilities of such a child under the law. Although Irish law, unlike Belgian law in the *Marckx* case, recognised the principle of *mater semper certa est*, nonetheless, Nessa Williams-Johnston suffered a similar *capitis diminutio* as had Paula Marckx in relation to her patrimonial rights. Furthermore, Nessa was prejudiced by the fact that she could never be legitimated nor jointly adopted by her natural parents. Here the Court reaffirmed its judgment in *Marckx* indicating that under Article 8 there was a positive obligation upon the state to act in a manner calculated to allow those concerned

---

55   Ibid., Dissenting Opinion of Judge Sir Gerald Fitzmaurice, para. 29. The margin of appreciation doctrine constitutes a recognition by the Commission and the Court that the Contracting Parties have a certain area of discretion in applying the derogations under Articles 8-11 and Article 15. Nevertheless, the Commission and the Court will test the reasonableness of the exercise of each Contracting Party's exercise of its discretion. See Jacobs, *European Convention*, pp. 201-2; van Dijk and van Hoof, *Theory*, pp. 194-6.

56   *Marckx*, Dissenting Opinion of Judge Sir Gerald Fitzmaurice, para. 29.

57   Above, n. 3.

to lead a normal family life.[58] However, two Judges took different views on whether the Court should have pronounced, as it did in the *Marckx* case, whether or not it supported the concept of the traditional family. Judge Pinheiro Farinha in a Declaration appended to the judgment opined that the Court should have included the statement supporting the traditional family from the *Marckx* judgment.[59] In his separate opinion, however, Judge De Meyer adopted a much more liberal stance arguing:

> [I]t seems to me that it is not sufficient to say that the third applicant should be 'placed . . . in a position akin to that of a legitimate child': in my view we ought to have stated more simply that the legal situation of a child born out of wedlock must be identical to that of a child of a married couple and that, by the same token, there cannot be, as regards relations with or concerning a child, any difference between the legal situation of his parents and of their families that he was a child of a married couple or a child born out of wedlock.[60]

This difference of opinion between Judge Pinheiro Farinha and Judge De Meyer is a clear example of what Merrills describes as a divergence in judicial ideology between hard conservatism and benevolent liberalism.[61] It must be said, however, that the Court, by adopting the formulation that the illegitimate child should be placed in a position akin to that of the legitimate child, left open the possibility that absolute equal treatment may not be possible in relation to the illegitimate child. This indicates that a certain level of discrimination may still be tolerated by the Court in cases of illegitimacy. It may even signify an acknowledgment by the Court that, strive as they might to eliminate inequalities of treatment between those born in and out of wedlock, the reality of the situation

---

58   Ibid., para. 72
59   Declaration by Judge Pinheiro Farinha. (Translation).
60   Separate Opinion, Partly Dissenting and Partly Concurring of Judge de Meyer, Section III, para. 1.
61   Merrills, *Development*, chapter 10.

is that an absolute elimination of inequality might never be possible. Indeed, some support for this view may be found in the *Inze* case which dealt once again with discrimination against illegitimate children in the area of patrimonial rights on succession. Here, a chamber of the Court held that:

> Very weighty reasons would . . . have to be advanced
> before a difference of treatment on the ground of birth
> out of wedlock could be regarded as compatible with
> the Convention.[62]

This clearly suggests that some discrimination against illegitimate children may be tolerated, but that it would have to be underpinned by reasonable and objective justifications for the difference in treatment.

The Convention as a living instrument

In *Marckx* the Court observed that although it was true that at the time the Convention was drafted it was regarded as permissible in many of the contracting states to distinguish between legitimate and illegitimate families, nonetheless, recalling its judgment in the *Tyrer* case,[63] the Convention must be interpreted in the light of present-day conditions and thus:

> In the instant case the Court cannot but be struck by
> the fact that the domestic law of the great majority of
> the member States of the Council of Europe has
> evolved, and is continuing to evolve, in company with
> the relevant international instruments towards full
> recognition of the maxim '*mater semper certa est.*'[64]

The Court referred in particular here to the Brussels Convention on the Establishment of Maternal Affiliation of Natural Children 1962[65]

---

62   *Inze*, n. 4, para. 41.
63   Eur Court HR, Series A, No. 26, para. 31.
64   *Marckx*, para. 41.
65   932 UNTS 73.

and the Council of Europe Convention on the Legal Status of Children Born out of Wedlock 1975.[66] Although these conventions had at the time of the *Marckx* decision only a small number of contracting states, they were nevertheless in force, and the Court observed that when taken in conjunction with the Convention itself they denoted 'a clear measure of common ground in this area amongst modern societies'.[67] Indeed, at the time of proceedings in the instant case the Belgian government had introduced a bill to reform its laws relating to the illegitimate child, and in the statement of reasons accompanying the bill the government noted that the discriminatory treatment between legitimate and illegitimate citizens amounted to a 'flagrant exception to equality before the law as established in Article 6 of the Belgian Constitution'.[68]

It may, in fact, be questionable whether the proposed trend evidenced in the Conventions referred to by the Court had indeed become crystallized in such a conclusive way. While it is accepted that human rights law is not static and must respond to clearly evidenced social changes, it is perhaps doubtful whether the social trend towards equal treatment of legitimate and illegitimate children which was identified in *Marckx* had been fully consummated. The international instruments to which the Court referred, while admittedly in force, had been signed by less than half the Member States of the Council of Europe and ratified by only four. At first sight this would not seem to suggest that the Court's position was tenable. Nevertheless, the Court was not to be diverted by such a possibility. After considering the small number of ratifications it ruled:

> [T]his state of affairs cannot be relied on in opposition to the evolution noted above. Both the relevant Conventions are in force and there is no reason to attribute the currently small number of Contracting States to a refusal to admit equality between 'illegitimate' and 'legitimate' children on the point under consideration. In fact the existence of these two

66   UKTS 43 (1981); ETS 85.
67   *Marckx*, para. 41.
68   Ibid.

treaties denotes that there is a clear measure of
common ground in this area amongst modern
societies.[69]

In *Johnston* the Court further prayed in aid the Preamble to
the 1975 Convention on Children Born out of Wedlock as justification
for its conclusion that a more liberal position had evolved in Europe
in recent years. Here, the Preamble to the Convention referred to the
fact that 'in a great number of member States [of the Council of
Europe] efforts have been, or are being, made to improve the legal
status of children born out of wedlock by reducing the differences
between their legal status and that of children born in wedlock which
are to the legal or social disadvantage of the former.'[70] Again, in
Inze, after stating the proposition that the Convention was a living
instrument, the Court reaffirmed the judgment in *Johnston* observing
that now nine member States were parties to the Convention on
Children Born out of Wedlock![71]

While it will always be a matter of some delicacy to
determine whether or not certain social trends have been completed or
whether they are simply in the process of development, it may well be
thought that the Court exaggerated the velocity of progress towards
equal treatment of legitimate and illegitimate children in all 21
member States of the Council of Europe on the somewhat slender
evidence available to it in the *Marckx* case. While the Court is
probably here in the juridical equivalent of Morton's fork - it will be
criticised if it identifies a social development prematurely or if it fails
to identify developments which have already crystallized[72] - it is

---

69   Ibid.
70   *Johnston,* above n. 3, para. 74. The Court also referred to the Irish Legal
      Status of Children Bill which had been laid before the Dail during the
      currency of the case, which, it noted, gave effect to the principles it was
      enunciating in *Johnston.*
71   *Inze,* above n. 4, para. 41.
72   Which was arguably the situation in *Ozturk* which dealt with
      decriminalization of traffic offences in Germany. Here, the majority held
      that despite decriminalization, Article 6 of the Convention applied and thus
      a person subject to such proceedings was entitled to be assisted by an
      interpreter. Five judges dissented, indicating that the notion of
      decriminalization was for the benefit of the individual, and consequently
      disengaged the application of Article 6.

nonetheless crucial that it aspires to as accurate a representation of the current state of affairs as possible in order to do justice to the Contracting Parties. The reason for this is that while each judgment of the Court is technically declaratory of the law only in the case at hand, it is clear that judgments of the Court have a much wider significance since they are an authoritative interpretation of the rights in question and are therefore probably binding in fact upon all Contracting Parties.[73] Each of those parties is consequently under an obligation under Article 1 of the Convention to 'secure to everyone within their jurisdiction the rights and freedoms defined in . . . this Convention'. If therefore a particular social development is identified and given sanction by the Court prematurely, certain Contracting Parties may well consider that they are being obliged to undertake actions to implement rights which may not necessarily have the approval of their populace. At its extreme, this would result in the Court effectively undermining, rather than contributing toward, the principles of democracy and the rule of law.

Protecting family relationships under the Convention

In *Marckx* the Court observed that under the Belgian Civil Code a legitimate child was integrated from the moment of birth into the families of each of its parents, but a recognised illegitimate child or an adopted illegitimate child remained in principle a stranger to its parents' families. This operated to deny illegitimate children rights in intestacy over the estates of its mother's or father's relatives, and also prevented the creation of any obligations between the illegitimate child and its parents' families. Thus in the instant case Alexandra was denied any relationship in law with either her maternal grandmother or aunt. The court held that this denial of any familial ties between Alexandra and her mother's family was a violation of the right to family life in Article 8:

> In the Court's opinion, 'family life', within the meaning of Article 8, includes at least the ties between near relatives, for instance those between grandparents

---

73   See Schermers, *European Law*, pp. 4-6.

and grandchildren, since such relatives may play a considerable part in family life.[74]

The Court further held, consistently with the earlier part of its judgment, that 'respect' for family life created an obligation on the part of the state to act in a manner calculated to allow these ties to develop normally. It therefore followed, in the Court's view, that the prevention of a child becoming part of its mother's family represented a hindrance to this normal development and thus amounted to a breach of Article 8.[75] The discriminatory treatment between legitimate and illegitimate children as regards their family relations also in the court's view could not find any objective and reasonable justification:

> Admittedly, the 'tranquillity' of 'legitimate' families may be disturbed if an 'illegitimate' child is included, in the eyes of the law, in his mother's family on the same footing as a child born in wedlock, but this is not a motive that justifies depriving the former child of fundamental rights.[76]

Patrimonial rights

The question of the applicants' patrimonial rights was then considered by the Court. It found that, until she was recognised, Alexandra had no inheritance rights in her mother's estate on intestacy. Only her adoption conferred upon her the rights of a legitimate child, but between inheritance and adoption she could receive no more by disposition *inter vivos* or by will than her entitlement under the Belgian Civil Code's title on intestacy. Furthermore, Alexandra had no inheritance rights on intestacy in the estates of the members of her mother's family. These conditions, the applicants alleged, violated Article 8 alone and in conjunction with Article 14 in Alexandra's case, and Article 1 of Protocol 1 taken alone and in conjunction with Article 14 in Paula's case.

74   *Marckx,* above n. 2, para. 45.
75   Ibid., para. 46.
76   Ibid., para. 48.

As regards Alexandra, the Court decided that the issue could be decided on the basis of Article 8 and Article 14 alone and without reference to Article 1 of the Protocol. It concurred with the Commission's view that the latter provision applied only to peaceful enjoyment of existing possessions and did not guarantee the right to acquire possessions through intestacy or voluntary dispositions.[77] The Court did agree with the Commission, however, that matters of property disposal between near relatives was intimately connected with family life. It held:

> Family life does not include only social, moral or cultural relations . . . it also comprises interests of a material kind, as is shown by, amongst other things, the obligations in respect of maintenance and the position occupied in the domestic legal systems of the majority of the Contracting States by the institution of a reserved portion of an estate.[78]

However, the Court noted that although it was implicit in Article 8 that a child was entitled to some portion of its parent's estate, it left open the choice and means to each Contracting Party to determine the extent of a child's entitlement *vis-à-vis* other relatives so as to comply with the requirements of allowing the normal development of family life. Thus the restrictions in the Belgian Civil Code did not of themselves violate Article 8, but when taken with Article 14, there was no objective or reasonable justification for the differential treatment of the illegitimate family from the legitimate family.[79]

In analysing Paula's patrimonial rights the Court observed that her circumstances were the same as those of Alexandra: there was no violation of Article 8 alone, but there was a violation of Article 8 in conjunction with Article 14.[80] As regards Article 1 of Protocol 1, the Court ruled that the right to dispose of one's property was a traditional and fundamental aspect of the right of property.

77   Ibid., para. 50.
78   Ibid., para. 52.
79   Ibid., para. 59.
80   Ibid., para. 62.

However, it noted that Article 1(2) of the Protocol gave the Contracting Parties the right to control the use of property in accordance with the general interest, and that it might therefore be in the 'general interest' to control dispositions *inter vivos* or by will.[81] The relevant paragraphs of the Belgian Civil Code governing such dispositions in the cases of illegitimate children were therefore not of themselves a violation of Article 1 of Protocol 1. Nonetheless, the Court referred to the discrimination inherent in Belgian law, in that unmarried mothers were treated differently from married mothers without any objective or reasonable justification.[82]

Not unnaturally, Judge Fitzmaurice took issue with this finding by the majority. Again, he applied the devices of literal construction and the mischief rule taken in conjunction. He took the view that 'peaceful enjoyment of . . . possessions' in Article 1 of Protocol 1, in no way implied any concern by the drafters of the Convention with inheritance or disposal rights; it was intended to deal only with unlawful or arbitrary interference with enjoyment of property by the state.[83] Indeed, Judge Fitzmaurice accused the Court of the 'language of hyperbole' by reading into Article 1 of the Protocol a guarantee to the *right* of property rather than simple enjoyment.[84] As noted above in the context of Articles 8 and 14,[85] the divergence between Judge Fitzmaurice and the dominant remainder of the Court indicates particular preferences both as to the techniques of interpretation applied and the result to be achieved therefrom.

Retroactivity and legal certainty

The Court's ruling on the extent of illegitimate children's property rights under the Convention caused some consternation to the Belgian government, since the declaratory nature of the Court's judgment meant that all dispositions which had taken place under the Belgian Civil Code to illegitimate children since the entry into force of the

---

81   Ibid., para. 64.
82   Ibid., para. 65.
83   Dissenting Opinion of Judge Sir Gerald Fitzmaurice, para. 17.
84   Ibid., para. 18.
85   Above, pp. 89-92.

Convention would have to be revoked. Belgium therefore requested, in the interests of legal certainty, that the ruling be pronounced *ex nunc* rather than *ex tunc*.[86]   The Court agreed that, although its rulings had declaratory effect only in the case which was the subject of proceedings, it nonetheless recognized that the judgment would have effects beyond those of the instant case. Referring to the judgment of the European Court of Justice in *Defrenne*[87] the Court held:

> Having regard to all the circumstances, the principle of legal certainty, which is necessarily inherent in the law of the Convention, as in Community law, dispenses the Belgian Government from reopening legal acts or situations that antedate the delivery of the present judgment.[88]

In so holding, the Court noted that *ex nunc* rulings were a feature of the constitutional courts of European states which possessed such institutions.

This part of the *Marckx* judgment is interesting from a number of perspectives. First, it demonstrates clearly that the Court is prepared to acknowledge that general principles of law are an integral part of the Convention, and second, that rulings of the European Court of Justice of the European Community (ECJ) are of persuasive authority.

The notion of general principles of law is readily accepted as a feature in the judicial functions of both the International Court of Justice (ICJ) and the ECJ. While the ICJ is specifically enjoined by Article 38(1)(c) of its Statute to apply 'general principles of law

---

86   Ibid., para. 58.
87   Case 43/75, *Gabrielle Defrenne v SABENA* [1976] ECR 455; [1976] 2 CMLR 98. For a common lawyer's critique of this case see K. Hampson, *Reports of the Judicial and Academic Conference* (Luxembourg: European Court of Justice, 1976) p. II-3. Discussed in D. A. C. Freestone, and J. S. Davidson, *The Institutional Framework of the European Communities* (London: Croom Helm, 1988) pp. 28-44.
88   *Marckx*, para. 58.

recognised by civilised nations',[89] the ECJ has developed a distinctively European system of general legal principles. These principles have been culled from the administrative legal systems of each of the EC's member States and are utilised by the ECJ to measure the legality of Community acts challenged under Articles 173 and 184 of the EEC Treaty.[90] In both the ICJ and the ECJ, general principles of law are used to complement and complete the legal systems of which they are part. In the case of the Convention, it is clear that the Court, like the ECJ, has implied the existence of general principles in order to complete and enhance the effectiveness of the Convention system.[91]

The reference by the Court to the ECJ's judgment in *Defrenne* is also particularly noteworthy since it is indicative of cross-fertilization between the work of the ECJ and the Court of Human Rights. While the ECJ has been more vigorous in asserting that the Convention is part of the European Community's common legal heritage and that its rules are binding on the Community, *Marckx* demonstrates that both courts are now taking judicial notice of each other's decisions.[92] This would seem to represent a confluence of European legal principles which may in time come to be seen as the basis of a truly European constitutional law.[93]

89   On 'general principles' in the ICJ see e.g. B. Cheng, *General Principles of Law Applied by International Courts and Tribunals* (London: Stevens, 1953); Sir G. Fitzmaurice, 'The General Principles of International Law Considered from the Standpoint of the Rule of Law' 92 *Hague Recueil* 7.

90   For a full discussion of these general principles under the EC system see H. G. Schermers, *Judicial Protection in the European Communities* (Deventer: Kluwer, 1983); T. C. Hartley, *Foundations of European Community Law* (Oxford: University Press, 2nd ed 1988) and Freestone and Davidson, *Institutional Framework*.

91   It should be noted that the Convention also makes express reference to general principles in Article 7(2) and in Article 1, Protocol 1. See Merrills, *Development*, chapter 8 and van Dijk and van Hoof, *Theory*, pp. 279-81.

92   On the EC and the Convention see P. Pescatore, 'The Context and Significance of Fundamental Rights in the Law of the European Communities' (1981) HRLJ 295; H. G. Schermers, 'The Communities under the European Convention on Human Rights' [1978/1] LIEI 1; Beddard, *Human Rights*, pp. 30-5; van Dijk and van Hoot, *Theory*, pp. 479-86; A. Drzemczewski, 'The Domestic Application of the European Convention on Human Rights as European Community Law' (1981) 30 ICLQ 1-50.

93   For an elaboration of this argument see Schermers, *European Law, passim*.

Compensation

The applicants requested the court to award nominal compensation of one Belgian franc under Article 50 of the Convention for the moral damage which they had suffered. The majority of the court rejected this, arguing that the finding of the several breaches of the Convention was of itself a sufficient remedy. A sizeable minority of six judges disagreed with the majority position on Article 50. They argued that Paula had suffered affront to her feelings, her sense of family and her dignity as a mother. She was also faced with 'painful and distressing' alternative of either recognising her daughter and thereby prejudicing her rights of inheritance and gift, or of keeping these intact by refusing to recognise Alexandra and thus renounce any legal family ties. Although Alexandra by 'reason of her young and tender age' been spared the 'anxiety, pangs and anguish' involved in the determination of her legal status, she had, from the moment of her birth, been the object of public discrimination, elements of which persisted even after her adoption. Because of these factors, the minority considered that the applicants were entitled to the compensation which they sought. They further took the view that the restraint exercised by the applicants in their claim contributed to the merit of their case under Article 50.

In *Johnston*, however, it appears that although the factors influencing the minority position in *Marckx* were in evidence, the Court spoke with one voice in holding that the finding of a breach of the third applicant's right to family life was in itself just satisfaction for the injury suffered. Only Judge de Meyer gave a different reason from the majority for holding that compensation ought not to be awarded. He argued:

> [S]uch compensation would be warranted if there were measures or decisions which, in the guise of provisions of general or impersonal application, had the object or the result of affecting the applicants directly and individually. But that is not the situation here.

Judge de Meyer's formulation here is reminiscent of the terminology applied by the ECJ when considering direct actions for

judicial review of Community acts under Article 173 of the EEC
Treaty. The ECJ's formulation has been criticised as being too
rigorous and potentially a denial of rights. It would also seem that
Judge de Meyer's statement is also too strict, for it is unlikely that
very many, if any, complainants under the Convention could meet the
stringency of the test advanced. As in Community law, a victim of a
violation of the Convention would have to demonstrate that they were
a member, perhaps the only member, of a small, closed class of
persons affected by the national measure or decision in question. The
correct view of Article 50 is probably that adopted by the minority in
Marckx; Judge de Meyer's reading of the provision is not consonant
with its wording or tenor and would lead to a denial of justice in the
Convention system itself.

Conclusions

The decisions of the European Court of Human Rights in *Marckx*,
Johnston, and *Inze* taken at their simplest levels clearly indicate that
the law of the Convention will no longer tolerate the discriminatory
treatment of illegitimate children within the legal systems of the
contracting Parties, in spite of the absence of a clear substantive
provision to that effect within the Convention itself. However, to read
the decision in *Marckx*, the most important of the three cases, simply
as finding within Article 8 of the Convention an implied right of equal
treatment for illegitimate children would be to underestimate the
significance of the decision, for not only did the Court create a new
standard of obligatory behaviour for the Contracting Parties, but it
also established, confirmed and developed a number of important
principles of European human rights law.

Perhaps the first and most important observation is that the
finding of a positive obligation from a negatively phrased provision
relating to family life has implications for the whole gamut of family
relations. As the Court made clear, the obligations of States are not
simply to refrain from interference with the enjoyment of family life
but to act in a manner calculated to create the conditions in which
family life might develop normally. This is certainly an important
interpretation of the Convention, although clearly not one that Judge
Sir Gerald Fitzmaurice was prepared to endorse, since it places upon
the Contracting Parties an open-ended obligation actively to facilitate

individuals' enjoyment of family life in the round. The problem which arises from such an interpretation of the Convention is that it will not be clear, either to individuals or the Contracting Parties, what their respective rights and obligations are likely to be at any given point, since these are likely to change with the passage of time and with social developments. This of course is a problem which also stems from the fact that the Convention itself is regarded and interpreted by the Court as a living, dynamic instrument. In adopting such a view of the Convention the Court must take account of the evolution of social and legal developments within and between its Contracting Parties. This position, and the problems associated with it, were referred to above. Briefly restated, these problems are that the adoption of an evolutive approach to interpretation of the substantive rights within the Convention may give rise to the possibility either that the Court will fail to identify a newly crystallized position or that it will identify a social development prematurely. It is arguable that this latter occurred in *Marckx*, for it was by no means well-established that equality of treatment either existed or was accepted as a whole by the Contracting Parties or their people. Nonetheless, the judgment of the Court undoubtedly played a catalytic role in the development of a more liberal and enlightened approach to those born out of wedlock. Whether the Court should be a catalyst in the development of such moral issues must probably remain a matter of personal and, ultimately, judicial preference.

The *Marckx* case is also significant in that it confirmed a very broad interpretation of the concept of a victim within the meaning of Article 25. While the Court did not accept that an *actio poularis* existed within the Convention system, it nevertheless made it quite clear that it would allow petitions where individuals were potential victims of a violation of rights protected by the Convention. This confirmation of a broad view suggests that the Court is concerned to maximise the effectiveness of the Convention system.

While one may commend the breadth of the Court's view of Article 25, it seems that its approach to Article 50 was rather too restrictive. A finding of a violation of a protected right may have given Alexandra Marckx and Nessa Johnston a feeling of moral vindication, but the absence of financial rectification of injured feeling appears to render the victory less complete. Certainly, if the Court decided to follow the lead taken by Judge de Meyer in

Johnston it is doubtful whether compensation would ever be available to a victim of a breach of the Convention since it is unlikely that anyone would be individually affected by a general provision in the way suggested.

In the cases of illegitimate children therefore, the Convention has acted as more than a safety net to catch those who have fallen victim to maltreatment by the state; rather it has set a new, higher standard of treatment not only for illegitimate children, but for the family in general. One may cavil at the Court reading a code of family law into a provision which appears to be concerned solely with preventing state interference in family life, but the effect has been to speed progress to more civilised standards of behaviour towards those who are, or were, the victims of discriminatory treatment through no fault of their own. Such a result, achieved through perceptive and well-measured judicial intervention, can only be commendable.

5

Juvenile Suspects and the Police and Criminal Evidence Act

David Dixon

This chapter will assess some effects of the Police and Criminal Evidence Act 1984 (PACE) on the way in which juvenile suspects[1] are dealt with by the police. It draws principally on some findings of two research projects which focussed on the package of powers for the police and safeguards for suspects' rights which make up parts I-VI of PACE. The smaller project[2] was a series of extended semi-formal interviews with legal advisers who operate in the police stations covered by the main project. The latter studied the effects of PACE on policing in a medium-sized force in the North of England.[3]

1   Those aged 10-16 inclusive, and younger suspects in homicide cases.
2   Funded by Hull Law School and carried out by David Dixon and David Wall.
3   Funded by the ESRC (grant E1125 0001) and carried out by Keith Bottomley, Clive Coleman, David Dixon, Martin Gill and David Wall. For their help in preparing this chapter, I am very grateful to Clive and Keith, and also to John Wright, Michael Hogan, Mike Pinnock and Elaine Fishwick. I also thank the officers of our research force and the interviewed legal advisers for their co-operation.

The research was carried out in three sub-divisions covering contrasting geographical areas (city centre, outer estate, and a rural/small town mix). Methods included: documentary analysis (of, *inter alia*, 2844 custody records from four years, chosen from before and after PACE's implementation in January 1986); formal interviews (with 160 officers); some 870 hours of observation; analysis of internal rules and policy documents; and a great deal of informal conversation and discussion.

My concern here is principally with the detention and questioning of young people before charge. It is in this area that PACE includes specific provisions for such suspects. The Royal Commission on Criminal Procedure, on whose Report PACE was to a considerable extent based, was 'very aware of the need to keep in mind the special position of juveniles' and consequently recommended the introduction of increased and more powerful safeguards for them.[4] The effectiveness of a range of earlier special provisions for juveniles was limited by the discretion allowed to the police by the criterion of 'practicability'.[5] The result was that, as the Policy Studies Institute (PSI) reported, rules about the questioning of juveniles were 'frequently ignored'.[6]

A considerable proportion of people dealt with by the criminal justice system are juveniles: 'between 25 and 30 per cent of known offenders are juveniles, covering those persons either sentenced by the courts or cautioned for indictable offences by the police'.[7] In our custody record samples from 1986 and 1987, 14% of detained suspects were juveniles (compared to 11% in 1984). There were considerable sub-divisional differences: in 1987, rates varied from 6% in the rural subdivision to 19% in the outer estate subdivision. A Home Office survey of custody record data from 32

---

4   *Report of Royal Commission on Criminal Procedure* (1981) Cmnd 8092, para. 10.2.

5   *The Investigation and Prosecution of Criminal Offences in England and Wales (Report of Royal Commission on Criminal Procedure)* (1981) Cmnd 8092-1, pp. 33-4.

6   D. Smith and J. Gray, *Police and People in London: the PSI Report* (Aldershot: Gower, 1985) p. 475.

7   *Report of Her Majesty's Chief Inspector of Constabulary for 1987* (1988) HC 521, p. 29.

stations in March 1987 reported that 18% of detained suspects were juveniles, with rates varying from 5% to 38%.[8] While such variations are partly accounted for by social and geographical contrasts, differing police practices in informally cautioning, summonsing, and arresting young suspects are also influential.

PACE, juveniles and street policing

Our research also examined major PACE powers used in policing outside the station - stop and search, search of premises, and arrest. By contrast with the regime for detention and questioning, none of these makes separate, specific provision for young people. This is not, of course, to imply that there are no significant differences between the way such powers are *used* in the cases of adults and young people. In our research force in 1987, 27% of recorded stops and searches were of people under 17 years, while a further 32% were of those aged between 17 and 20. It is important to note the limitations of such data. As we explain elsewhere, by no means all stops and searches are recorded: non-statutory, 'consensual' searches are particularly likely to be of people, like juveniles, who are dealt with regularly and/or who are not thought likely to protest or complain.[9]

Since the late nineteenth century, the attention of the police in the policing of social space and public order has predominantly been focussed on young people; this has been central to the police mandate in street policing.[10] In particular, young black people are subject to more intensive policing than their white peers. An important part is

8   D. Brown, *Detention at the Police Station under the Police and Criminal Evidence Act.* Home Office Research Study 104. (London: Home Office, 1989) p. 38. See also A. Sanders, *et al., Advice and Assistance at Police Stations and the 24 Hour Duty Solicitor Scheme* (London: Lord Chancellor's Department, 1989) p. 34.

9   D. Dixon, *et al.,* 'Reality and rules in the construction and regulation of police suspicion' (1989) 17 *International Journal of the Sociology of Law* 185 and D. Dixon, *et al.,* 'Consent and the legal regulation of policing' (1990) 17 *Journal of Law and Society* 1 (1990a).

10   M. Brogden, *et al., Introducing Police Work* (London: Unwin Hyman, 1989) pp. 102-11.

played by wide discretionary powers (provided either by law or custom) to move on; to stop, question, and search; to arrest. These are complemented by vague, flexible offences (such as drunk and disorderly, abusive language, obstruction).

As a result of these factors, the attempt in PACE to apply techniques of legal regulation to policing has been much less successful outside the police station than inside it. Notably, there is a marked contrast between, on one hand, the very limited effect of the PACE provisions for regulating stop and search, and on the other, that of the detention procedures, supervised by the custody officers created by PACE.[11] In the discretionary world of street policing, restrictive legal procedures defining police powers and suspects' rights are seen as incongruous and inappropriate: 'invocations of "rights" are . . . interpreted as challenges to police authority, as disrespect, as lack of deference, as being a "smart-arse"'.[12] The outcomes will usually range from increased suspicion on the part of the police (knowledge of rights as implying previous contact with the law), to provocation and, ultimately, creation of offences.

PACE and the detention of juvenile suspects

While these factors mean that the policing of young people is, in many respects, a distinct social practice, the legal powers and safeguards utilised therein are not specific. It is only when detention and, most importantly, questioning occurs that additional safeguards are provided for the protection of juvenile suspects. The reasons for this are made clear in the *Code of Practice for the Detention, Treatment and Questioning of Persons by Police Officers* (issued under PACE s. 66):

> It is important to bear in mind that, although juveniles or persons who are mentally ill or handicapped are often capable of providing reliable evidence, they

11   K. Bottomley, *et al.*, *The Impact of Aspects of the Police and Criminal Evidence Act 1984 on Policing in a Force in the North of England* (Hull: Centre for Criminology and Criminal Justice, 1989), D. Dixon, *et al.* (1989) and D. Dixon, *et al.*, 'Safeguarding the rights of suspects in police custody' *Policing and Society,* forthcoming 1990.

12   D. B. Brown, Book Review, *Legal Service Bulletin,* August 1984, p. 187.

may, without knowing or wishing to do so, be particularly prone in certain circumstances to provide information which is unreliable, misleading or self-incriminating. Special care should therefore always be exercised in questioning such a person . . . Because of the risk of unreliable evidence it is also important to obtain corroboration of any facts admitted whenever possible.

(Code C, Note for Guidance 13B)

Juveniles are treated in broadly the same way as others classified as 'persons at risk' - the mentally ill or mentally handicapped. Serious, intractable problems are caused (to suspects and police) by the difficulty often experienced in identifying mental illness and, particularly, mental handicap. Statistics of suspects recorded as mentally ill or mentally handicapped suggest that a substantial number of people are detained and questioned without being identified as such.[13] However, it is easier to point this out than it is to suggest remedies, given the very real problems of diagnosis and of inadequate expert advisory and support services.[14] While it is not possible to discuss in detail the mentally ill and mentally handicapped, it is important to remember that categories of suspects may overlap: a juvenile who is also mentally ill or mentally handicapped may encounter and cause particular problems in the process of detention and questioning.[15] The Code of Practice provides that, if there is any doubt, the suspect is to be treated as 'at risk'. In the case of juveniles, if the suspect 'appears to be under the age of 17 then he shall be treated as a juvenile for the purposes of this code in the absence of clear evidence to show that he is older' (Code C, 1.5).

---

13   Dixon, *et al.* (1990).

14   B. Irving and I. McKenzie, *Police Interrogation* (London: Police Foundation, 1989) pp. 202-4, 225-6.

15   PACE s. 77 requires courts to exercise special caution in considering confessions made by the mentally handicapped. As Mirfield argues, there is no good reason why this protection should not be extended to all vulnerable suspects (P. Mirfield, *Confessions* (London: Sweet and Maxwell, 1985) pp. 165-6).

The central purpose of PACE in the area of detention and questioning was to provide the police, for the first time, with a general statutory power to detain suspects for questioning. The length of such detention is controlled by the requirement that a suspect should be charged as soon as sufficient evidence is available, and by a series of reviews carried out by progressively more senior officers (and eventually by a court) beginning no more than six hours after the suspect is brought to the station. This power to detain for questioning is balanced by a series of suspects' rights, notably the involvement in the detention and questioning process of 'appropriate adults' and legal representatives.

The procedures for admitting a suspect to custody and for arranging the attendance of legal advisers and appropriate adults at the station are inevitably time consuming. As a result, the effect of PACE has been that in cases at the lower end of the distribution, suspects are detained for rather longer than before 1986. However, at the higher end, the effect of time-limited review periods is that suspects are detained for rather shorter periods than before.[16]

Juveniles tend to be detained for less serious offences: for example, shoplifting accounted for 35% of juveniles and 9% of ordinary adult suspects in the Home Office sample.[17] Consequently, our custody record survey found juveniles being detained before charge or release for shorter periods than adults, with the difference ranging from 2.7 hours in 1984 to just over one hour in 1987. Given the special arrangements for dealing with juveniles (discussed below), it is perhaps not surprising to find that PACE resulted in slightly greater increases in the length of detention for juveniles than for adults, particularly in the outer city and rural subdivisions in which legal advice and appropriate adults were less readily available. The Home Office survey of 32 areas found that the median time for making contact with an appropriate adult was 25 minutes after arrival at the station; the time then taken for the adult to reach the station was an additional 70 minutes.[18] Comparative details in our subdivisions are shown below:

---

16   Bottomley, *et al.* (1989) chapter 6 and Irving and McKenzie (1989)
17   Brown (1989) p. 39.
18   Ibid., pp. 40-1.

Mean detention lengths, before charge or release, of adults and juveniles (hours)

	TOTAL		CITY CENTRE		OUTER CITY		RURAL	
	ad.	juv.	ad.	juv.	ad.	juv.	ad.	juv.
1981	4.5	3.2	4.5	3.3	4.7	3.3	3.5	1.7
1984	4.7	2.0	5.4	2.7	4.6	1.9	3.6	1.0
1986	4.7	3.1	5.2	2.9	4.4	3.3	4.2	3.2
1987	5.6	4.4	5.6	3.8	6.1	5.5	5.0	3.7

As these figures indicate, the process of change in police practice in the 1980s was not straightforward. Between 1981 and 1984, there was a substantial decrease in detention lengths for juveniles, while at the same time there was a marginal increase in those for adults. While developments in other areas such as cautioning during this period may have been influential, one reason for this was that our research force had pre-empted PACE by introducing a system for dealing with suspects in custody based on some of the recommendations of the Royal Commission on Criminal Procedure. The occasion for this was concern over the way in which some juvenile suspects had been dealt with. As these procedures were introduced by internal force standing order rather than by legislation, they did not include the mandatory involvement of third parties which was responsible for the subsequent increase in detention lengths. While juvenile detention times increased progressively from 1984 to 1987, in the case of adults, the significant increase occurred not in 1986 (as might have been expected with the introduction of PACE), but in 1987. A major reason for this would appear to have been a substantial general increase in requests for legal advice in the outer city subdivision (from 26% in 1986 to 34% in 1987). As will be noted below, this included a considerable increase in requests for access to legal advice by juveniles.

One additional, specific provision relating to the detention of juveniles can be noted here. The Code of Practice forbids the placing of a juvenile in a cell 'unless no other secure accommodation is available and the custody officer considers that it is not practicable to supervise him if he is not placed in a cell' (Code C, 8.8). This is a good example of what the PSI classified as 'presentational rules' which 'exist to give an acceptable appearance to the way that police work is carried out'.[19] Our research force, like others, met this requirement by simply designating a couple of otherwise standard cells as 'Juvenile Detention Rooms'.

Juveniles and appropriate adults

The principal device used in PACE to safeguard juvenile suspects' rights is to require the presence of an 'appropriate adult' at several significant stages of a young person's detention. In the case of a juvenile, the 'appropriate adult' means either (i) a parent or guardian (or the body responsible for a juvenile who is in care), or (ii) a social worker. Failing these, the appropriate adult can be 'another responsible adult who is not a police officer or employed by the police' (Code C, 1.7).

The Home Office survey found that parents or relatives were called to act as appropriate adults in 77% of cases, social workers in 17% and others, such as friends or legal advisers (whose dual role is discussed in the following section) in 5%.[20] In draft revisions to the Codes of Practice laid before Parliament in July 1990, it is suggested that parents are preferable to social workers:

> The parent or guardian of a juvenile should be the appropriate adult unless he is suspected of involvement in the offence, is the victim, is a witness, is involved in the investigations or has received admissions . . . (or) is estranged from the juvenile. (Note 1C).

This belatedly acknowledges the Royal Commission's view that 'a parent has a right to know where his child is and to be with his child during an interview . . . parents should have the opportunity to be present when their child is in trouble'.[21] However, the issue which the Royal Commission did not address is whether priority should be given to the rights of parents or to the provision of effective support

---

19   Smith and Gray (1985) p. 442.
20   Brown (1989) p. 39.
21   *Report of Royal Commission on Criminal Procedure* (1981) Cmnd 8092, para. 4. 104.

and advice to juvenile suspects. If, as I would suggest, the latter is more important, it may be that properly trained, specialist social workers are needed as well as parents. It would be unfortunate if the revised Code were to discourage the development of specialist units within social work departments.

When any suspect is brought to a police station under arrest, he/she must be told *inter alia* of the right to have someone informed of the arrest (PACE s. 56; Code C, 3.1). If a suspect is a juvenile, PACE s. 57 requires the police to inform 'a person responsible for the welfare of the child or young person' that he/she has been arrested, what the arrest was for, and where he/she is in custody. In addition, the Code of Practice requires that 'the custody officer must as soon as practicable inform the appropriate adult of the grounds for his detention and his whereabouts, and ask the adult to come to the police station to see the person'. In practice, these procedures are combined: the custody officer will simply ask for the parents' address and telephone number when completing the section of the custody record dealing with the right of intimation. Normally, only if there are problems with the attendance of a parent will the custody officer turn to social services.

The suspect must be informed of his/her rights in the presence of the appropriate adult; this means that the custody officer should repeat the offers of legal advice, intimation, and a copy of the Codes of Practice if the appropriate adult was not present at the original reception into custody (Code C, 3.6). The appropriate adult can request legal advice on the juvenile's behalf (Code C, 13.2). Some PACE procedures for the identification of suspects (such as taking a physical sample) require the suspect's consent: 'in the case of a juvenile the consent of his parent or guardian is required as well as his own, (unless he is under 14, in which the consent of his parent or guardian is sufficient)' (Code D, 1.10. Note that other appropriate adults, e.g. social workers, cannot give such consent). The appropriate adult must be present while any identification procedures are carried out (Code D, 1.11-12).

Most important is the requirement that an appropriate adult should be present whenever a juvenile is 'interviewed or asked to provide or sign a written statement' (Code C, 13.1). It should be noted that this requirement is not limited to questioning in police stations: the case of *Delroy Fogah* made clear that evidence of an 'interview' in the street or in a police car after arrest will not be admissible if an appropriate adult was absent.[22] The draft revised Codes of Practice retain this limitation on questioning vulnerable groups away from the station (Code C, 11.1). Of course, this does not mean that officers are unable to talk to and question juveniles except in police stations; the officer's task is to obtain the repetition, in the presence of an appropriate adult, of any admissions made.[23] The appropriate adult is temporarily unnecessary 'only in exceptional cases of need' (Annex C, note C1) when a senior officer considers that a delay in questioning 'will involve an immediate risk of harm to persons or serious loss of or damage to property' (Code C, annex C, 1). In our research, we did not encounter any such incidents, while the Home Office survey found two cases in 1000.[24]

The presence of an appropriate adult is the main device by which PACE seeks to prevent repetition of incidents occurring before 1986 in which young people 'confessed' to crimes of which they were innocent. The most notorious of these was, of course, the Confait investigation, in which a mentally handicapped adult and two juveniles were convicted, on the basis of their confessions, of crimes which they did not commit.[25] The failure of procedures based on PACE to prevent inaccurate confessions from a number of juveniles during the Broadwater Farm investigation illustrates the durability of the problem.[26]

The Code of Practice directs that the role of the appropriate adult should not be merely passive:

> The appropriate adult should be informed that he is not expected to act simply as an observer. The

---

22   [1989] Crim LR 141.
23   Dixon, *et al.* (1990).
24   Brown (1989) p. 39.
25   J. D. Baxter and L. Koffman 'The Confait inheritance - forgotten lessons?' (1983) 14 *Cambrian LR* 11, T. Thomas, 'The Confait Confessions' (1987) 3 *Policing* 214.
26   The investigation took place in late 1985, when the Tottenham police were operating as if PACE was already in force. Of ten juveniles who were charged, six were acquitted completely. In these and the adults' cases, confessions were predominantly the only evidence. See T. Gifford, *et al.*, *Broadwater Farm Revisited* (London: Karia Press, 1989) chapter 5.

purposes of his presence are, first, to advise the person being questioned and to observe whether the interview is being conducted properly and fairly; and, secondly, to facilitate communication with the person being interviewed. (Code C, Note 13C).

Officers are supposed to inform appropriate adults of this. However, the requirement to do so appears in a note of guidance rather than as a substantive section of the Code backed by the Discipline Code; this allows officers usually to ignore or overlook it. In the draft revisions of the PACE Codes, the obligation to explain the appropriate adult's role is included as a section of Code C (11.16). The decision in *DPP* v *Blake* should also be noted here. In this case, the 'appropriate adult' was the suspect's father, from whom she was estranged. The only communication between them was for him to ask if she was all right: she refused to speak to him. The court excluded from evidence a confession made in the father's presence, ruling that an adult must not just be present, but must be capable of fulfilling the role envisaged in 13C.[27]

This approach requires a major change in police practice and attitudes. Officers are prepared for third parties such as appropriate adults to attend interrogations, so long as they act simply as observers (unless there are special problems, e.g. of communicating with mentally ill suspects). At present, interruption of questioning by parents or social workers is likely to be, at best, resented by interrogating officers. (See e.g. the exclusion of a social worker from the interrogation of 'Juvenile C' during the Broadwater Farm investigation.)[28] While passive appropriate adults restrict officers to some extent simply by being there, they are also useful to them; they are witnesses whose presence means that it will normally be difficult to challenge the accuracy of the record or the propriety of questioning. For appropriate adults to take the more active role envisaged in the Code of Practice would require many officers to reconsider their style of questioning.

27   [1989] 1 WLR 432. See also revised Code C, note 1C.
28   Gifford, *et al.* (1989) p. 61.

Parents as appropriate adults

The Royal Commission explained the reasons for its recommendations on the interviewing of juveniles:

> It is . . . essential that a juvenile should have an adult present other than the police when he is being interviewed and it is highly desirable that the adult should be someone in whom the juvenile has confidence, his parent or guardian, or someone else he knows, a social worker or school teacher. Juveniles may not as readily understand the significance of questions or of what they themselves say and are likely to be more suggestible than adults. They may need the support of an adult presence; of someone to befriend, advise and assist them to make their decisions.[29]

There are a number of problems which juveniles and their appropriate adults encounter.[30] Parents are considered in this section, and social workers in the next.

First, when parents do attend the station, their helpfulness to their children varies. The Royal Commission recognised that 'parents may not always act in a supportive way and their presence may not necessarily solve the problem of the juvenile's suggestibility'.[31] As several researchers have found, this is a very mild account of some situations, in which parents see their role as being to assist the police in extracting 'the truth' from their children, often by means which police officers could not use in their presence.[32] However, it should be noted that the appropriate adult's activity (e.g. a mother striking a juvenile, as occurred in one case during observation) or inactivity (as in *DPP* v *Blake*) could lead to the exclusion of evidence under sections 76 or 78.

29   *Report of Royal Commission on Criminal Procedure* (1981) Cmnd 8092, para. 4. 103.
30   Irving and McKenzie (1989) pp. 163-4.
31   *Report of Royal Commission on Criminal Procedure* (1981) Cmnd 8092, para. 4. 103.
32   Dixon, *et al.* (1990), Irving and McKenzie (1989) p. 165 and Smith and Gray (1985) p. 476.

Like suspects, some parents can be disorientated, scared, and compliant to police requests. It should not be forgotten that, in the Confait investigation, the inaccurate confessions were countersigned by some of the suspects' parents (although they were not present at the original interrogations). Ronnie Leighton's mother commented;

> I can't explain it really, they just say sign. I mean when you've got a room full of detectives and . . . they look at you and they say 'sign', you naturally sign . . . I was just as scared as what Ronnie was.[33]

Most parents, for very understandable reasons, continue to act in this passive way. A solicitor reported a post-1986 incident in the rural sub-division in which a mentally handicapped juvenile 'made a statement in the presence of his parents and they had all signed it, which I wouldn't have allowed because I know . . . that he has an IQ which can't be measured'. Another told of a case in which the parent as well as the juvenile suspect was mentally handicapped.[34]

Some parents were observed being more helpful: examples were one father who told his son to think about what he was going to say, and another who made his son read the interview record carefully and told him to 'say if it is not what you meant'. While intelligent, aware parents can give this kind of commonsense advice, very few are able to deal with more technical or complex issues, such as leading questions, questions about intent, or questions which the suspect cannot answer properly (typically, 'Your pal says you were there; why would he say that if it isn't true?'), as well as other matters depending on legal criteria of 'fairness' or 'oppression' (PACE ss76,78). The PSI's pre-PACE observations remain valid:

> the adult usually has little or no knowledge of what kinds of approach or questioning are allowable and

---

33   Quoted Thomas (1987) p. 222.
34   These were surely the kind of circumstances envisaged in Code C, Note 1C: in dealing with the mentally handicapped and ill, it may 'be more satisfactory for all concerned if the appropriate adult is someone who has experience or training in their care rather than a relative lacking such qualifications'.

consequently says nothing or does not interfere with any questioning or behaviour by the officers that he [sic] disapproves of. Thus it is common for the adult to acquiesce in hectoring questioning, thinking it is 'normal' . . .[35]

Some knowledge of law and of police work is usually necessary to cope in such circumstances. The Royal Commission recognised this, and insisted that a parent's presence is 'no substitute for having access to legal advice'.[36] Irving and McKenzie argue that 'legal advice must . . . be available *in all cases* regardless of what juvenile or parent or guardian says'.[37] Similarly, Sanders *et al.* suggest that it should be presumed that all suspects want legal advice and that they should have to take a positive decision to refuse it.[38] The effectiveness of any such provisions would depend on the competence and commitment of legal advisers, which, at present, are not guaranteed.[39]

Secondly, some parents, particularly of juveniles who are often in trouble, are reluctant to attend the station, not least during the night; research for the Royal Commission found 'a third of parents of 50 juveniles unavailable or refusing to attend.[40] Now that an appropriate adult's presence is obligatory, increased efforts have to be made (by police officers or social workers) to persuade reluctant parents to appear. The result may well be delay in the investigation, a period in detention for the juvenile, and strained relations between police and social workers. This was illustrated by a typical observed example in which a juvenile's mother refused, at 0905, to attend the station. The custody officer then contacted the social services department, who said that they were unable to supply an appropriate adult because of understaffing. The angry custody officer insisted that social services should take responsibility for persuading the

35   Smith and Gray (1985) p. 476.
36   *Report of Royal Commission on Criminal Procedure* (1981) Cmnd 8092, para. 4. 103.
37   Irving and McKenzie (1989) p. 202, original emphasis.
38   Sanders, *et al* . (1989) p. 80.
39   See 'Legal Advisers' section below pp. 125-8.
40   *Report of Royal Commission on Criminal Procedure* (1981) Cmnd 8092, para. 4. 102, and cf. Brown (1989) p. 40.

mother to attend, which she eventually did at 1045. One alternative for the police in such circumstances is to call in a legal adviser, who can then act as an appropriate adult. Many of the legal advisers interviewed reported having assisted in this way. The propriety of this was in doubt (not least because of the potential conflict of role: see below), but the draft revisions to Code C note that 'a solicitor who is present at the station in a professional capacity may not act as the appropriate adult' (Note 1F. This does not entirely clarify the position of the solicitor's clerk, who in practice may well be allocated this task).

Delay, whether caused by parents, social workers, or legal advisers, is to some extent inevitable. However, it is vital that it should be minimised because of the effects of detention on juvenile suspects - notably, an inclination to tell the police what they want to hear in order to get out of the station.

Social workers as appropriate adults

To some extent, similar problems affect social workers, who may feel 'intimidated in a situation they are given scant training for, in a culture that is traditionally hostile to them, and on police "home territory"'.[41] There is a general lack of preparation for this kind of work, although the need for specific training has been recognised.[42] The extent of social workers' rights, responsibilities, and proper functions in police stations is not clear[43] and professional guidance[44] tends to restate the provisions of PACE rather than to deal with problems likely to be encountered in their implementation.

Social workers acting as appropriate adults are particularly likely to encounter the problem of contradictions in the task described

41 Thomas (1987) p. 222 and cf. S. Holdaway, 'Police and social work relations' (1986) 16 *British Journal of Social Work* 137.

42 H. Jones, 'Practice without precedent' *Community Care*, 9 July 1987, p. 22, and T. Thomas, 'The Police and Criminal Evidence Act 1984: the social work role' (1988) 27 *Howard Journal* 256, 262.

43 H. Giller, 'Processes and safeguards for "vulnerable persons"'. Paper presented to ESRC/Police Foundation Conference on PACE, Newcastle, 1989.

44 E.g. *Social Work Guidelines to the Police and Criminal Evidence Act 1984* (Birmingham: British Association of Social Workers, 1987) (BASW, 1987).

in the Code of Practice, Note 13C (see above). It is surprising that the British Association of Social Workers (BASW) considers that 'the role of the social worker in police interviews . . . is now clearly defined under the law'.[45] For example, the best advice to a suspect may be not to answer police questions, but this would, obviously, not serve 'to facilitate communication'. Some social workers do recommend silence in appropriate cases.[46] BASW tells social workers to inform suspects of their right of silence, but does not offer advice on when refusal to answer questions would be appropriate.[47] The extent to which a social worker can or should offer this or other legal advice is unclear; the Royal Commission's view was that a social worker acting as an appropriate adult 'should not attempt to act as (the juvenile's) legal adviser'.[48]

This neat division of function may not be sustainable in practice. BASW argues that social workers 'have a duty as individuals and professionals to ensure the detainee knows their rights, and is able to exercise them'.[49] As the following section will show, most juveniles do not ask for a solicitor: the appropriate adult will, in practice, be their only source of legal advice. As noted above, appropriate adults can order legal advice for the juvenile on their own initiative, but this is usually not done. While the additional delay involved is certainly an influential consideration, it is also the case that some social workers feel that they are more effective than legal advisers in protecting a suspect's (legal and other) interests. The social worker will have a particularly important task in the rare, but very serious cases, when police delay access to legal advice (PACE s. 56; Code C, Annex B). In such cases, the presence of an appropriate adult is still required and 'it is vital s/he gives the detainee proper advice'.[50]

This possible contradiction in the appropriate adult's ascribed

---

45   Ibid., p. i.
46   N. Kay and S. Quao, 'To be or not to be an "appropriate adult"?' *Community Care,* July, 1987, p. 22. This may also be a particular problem for legal advisers acting as appropriate adults.
47   BASW (1987) p. 27.
48   *Report of Royal Commission on Criminal Procedure*(1981) Cmnd 8092, para. 4.108.
49   BASW (1987) p. ii.
50   Ibid., p. 19, and cf. Gifford, *et al.* (1989) chapter 5.

purpose is the tip of a much larger issue, which is the tension between control and welfare in social work. The social worker may see him/herself as being in the station to help the juvenile, but may well be perceived by that juvenile as part of the system which is detaining and will probably punish him/her. (Legal advisers, particularly duty solicitors[51] and clerks who are ex-police officers, may be seen in the same way). This is exacerbated by some social workers' belief that they have:

> a duty not to encourage the juvenile to believe that he or she should try to evade responsibility for an offence committed and that part of the social worker's general duty is to inculcate moral responsibility in a juvenile.[52]

For a variety of reasons, most social workers will seek to maintain reasonable relations with the police.[53] The increasing emphasis on control in aspects of social work and the development of multi-agency policing strategies will increase the social worker's problem: he/she is asked 'to work alongside the police as colleagues and then to "challenge" them on their own territory'.[54] Appropriate adults who try to give legal advice, particularly during questioning, are likely to encounter problems in their relations with the police.[55]

The temptation is to act simply as a silent, passive witness of the interrogation: social workers thereby can 'collude with infringements' of the Code of Practice 'in the interests of establishing credibility', rather than acting as an 'advocate for a juvenile's rights'.[56] A common police attitude towards social workers' attendance at interrogations is illustrated by one officer's explanation to a social worker of his expected role: 'You are wallpaper, pal'.[57]

51   Sanders, *et al.* (1989) p. 76.
52   Kay and Quao (1987) p. 21.
53   Ibid.
54   Thomas (1987) p. 222.
55   Jones (1987) p. 24.
56   T. Thomas, *The Police and Social Workers* (Aldershot: Gower, 1986) p. 83.
57   M. Pinnock, paper presented to PACE Conference, Hull University, 1989. (1989a).

One product both of tape recording[58] and of investigating officers' familiarity with PACE[59] is more searching, intensive interrogation: in these circumstances, it is particularly important that social workers (and others, including legal advisers) do not take the easy choice of passivity and non-intervention.

Problems of attendance apply to social workers as well as to parents. Confirming disparaging police-cultural images of social workers,[60] particular difficulties can arise out of office hours, when more than half of requests to social services are likely to be made.[61] In some areas, a restrictive approach is taken, so that for example social workers normally attend only for juveniles in their own authority's care.[62] PACE s. 39 (5) creates a specific responsibility to provide such 'advice and assistance', but otherwise: 'The social services are not . . . obliged to furnish an appropriate adult . . . It is clear that there is no coherent policy throughout the country and that practices vary between areas'.[63] The department involved in the *Blake* case (see above) had a policy of only sending social workers to stations if parents could not be located or they refused to attend; the failure to consider the possible unsuitability of a parent was criticised by the court, which urged social workers to 'attend as promptly as practicable at an interview when requested to do so'. Such policies reflect views about parental responsibility, but they also have very significant economic roots.

Social services departments had to meet the demands resulting from PACE without any increase in their budgets. A circular issued by the Department of Health and Social Security (as it then was) at the introduction of PACE stated that it did not anticipate that the relevant PACE provisions 'which either replace existing legislation or consolidate existing good practice will have other than minor financial or manpower implications'.[64] This seriously

---

58   Dixon, *et al.* (1990).
59   Irving and McKenzie (1989).
60   Holdaway (1986) p. 150.
61   Giller (1989) p. 19.
62   Kay and Quao (1987) p. 20.
63   M. Haley and J. A. Swift, 'PACE and the social worker' (1988) 6 *Journal of Social Welfare Law* 357.
64   *PACE - Implications for Children and Young Persons*, Department of Health and Social Security, Circular LAC (85) 18, 1985.

understated the significance of PACE. Rights for vulnerable groups have been broadened and strengthened. Duties to provide and protect those rights have been placed legally on police and informally on other agencies. However, the resources (both financial and strategic) needed to make those rights into reality are inadequate.

Some social services departments have used existing resources to develop 24 hour provision for all juveniles. One operating in the main urban area of our research force receives, on average, three calls on each 'out of hours' shift. Duty workers aim to attend stations within 30 minutes (i.e. less than half the waiting time for appropriate adults elsewhere: see above, pp. 112-3). The benefits include reduction in detention lengths and accumulation of experience and expertise among specialised workers.[65] However, such provision is still relatively unusual.

Legal advisers

Potentially the most significant safeguard for all suspects provided by PACE is access to legal advice before and during interrogation. The weak provisions of the Judges' Rules have been replaced by clear obligations on the police to inform suspects that they have a right to legal advice; limitations on power to delay such access; provision for legal advisers' attendance at interrogations; and public funding of services for suspects in custody.

The result has been a substantial increase in the proportion of suspects who request legal advice, from less than 10% before 1986 to 25% nationally in 1987 (26% in the research force). Whereas many requests used to be refused, most suspects who ask for legal advice now receive it, with access being formally delayed for only a small minority.[66] In general, fewer juveniles than adults ask for or receive legal advice. In our research force, there was a significant increase between 1984 and 1987, with juveniles' requests rising from 2% to 17% and provision rising from 1% to 14%. The Home Office survey in 1987 reported a juvenile request rate of 11%,[67] while in 1988 Sanders *et al.* found 16%.[68]

---

65   M. Pinnock, 'Blues in the night' (1989) 4/7 *Social Services Insight,* 28 Feb., pp. 18-19 and (1989a).
66   Dixon, *et al.* (1990), Sanders, *et al.* (1989).
67   Brown (1989) p. 23.

While such increases are significant, most commentators point out that they still leave the vast majority of suspects in custody without legal advice. Many factors may influence a suspect against making a request.[69] It is reported that sometimes custody officers do not in fact offer access or fail to act upon requests.[70] In our research, we did not encounter charge room staff failing to offer legal advice to adult suspects on their arrival at stations. However, juveniles were treated differently. Some custody officers did not offer them legal advice; instead they routinely wrote 'Juvenile' in the section of the custody record which records the suspect's decision. The offer would be made to the appropriate adult at his/her arrival at the station. This practice, based on a misreading of PACE and misunderstanding of the financial consequences of receiving advice while in custody, meant that a juvenile could be detained for a considerable time without access to a lawyer (although, of course, interrogation could not normally begin before the arrival of the appropriate adult). As noted above, a request for legal advice at this point is made less attractive by the further delay which arranging it would entail. The draft revision of Code C (Note 3G) specifically disapproves of such treatment of juveniles, making clear that juveniles should be offered access to legal advice and any acceptance should be acted upon without waiting for the appropriate adult's arrival.

Some suspects are discouraged from asking for legal advice. Confirming the experience of our observations, Sanders *et al.* identify a number of 'ploys' which are used by officers for this purpose, some of which apply specifically to juveniles. Some custody officers do offer legal advice to juveniles, but suggest that a decision should be delayed until the appropriate adult's arrival. In turn, the adult may be discouraged from requesting advice at this point by being told that the juvenile had earlier declined an offer.[71] In conjunction with other

---

68   Sanders, *et al.* (1989) p. 34. As regards all these composite figures, one of
        the notable features is the inter-station variations which they conceal. Even
        when factors such as offence seriousness are controlled, it is clear that
        legislation which should have provided consistency is being applied in
        considerably different ways across the country: see Brown (1989) pp. 20-4,
        and further Sanders, *et al.* (1989) pp. 34-5.
69   Dixon, *et al.* (1990).
70   Sanders, *et al.* (1989) pp. 68-9.
71   Ibid., pp. 59, 61-3.

such ploys, this depresses the rate of requests for legal advice.

The fact that a significant increase in access to legal advice can be brought about is illustrated by a large rise in requests for legal advice made by one group of young suspects. In 1984, 4% of juveniles in our outer city sub-division requested legal advice: none received it. By 1987, 43% requested, with 37% receiving. This was apparently the result of the spread of information and experience among young people on the outer city estates and the practice of custody officers operating in the area's station. As Morgan has stressed, variation in request rates is 'the product of several local factors in combination - the quality of legal advice services, the nature of relations between the police and solicitors, standards of police behaviour and the nature of police-community relations'.[72]

The potential for such an increase suggests that it is wrong to concentrate unduly on police objections to or discouragement of legal advice. There are circumstances in which suspects are encouraged to obtain it. One, noted above, is when an investigation is delayed by inability to obtain an appropriate adult. In such cases, officers may turn to legal advisers to fill a dual role; these appropriate adults at least have a financial incentive for attendance. Two interviewed solicitors explained:

> Locally, the police are very grateful if they ring you and you go. They welcome you with open arms . . . Otherwise they are dependent on social workers.

> Parents won't turn up, social workers won't turn up . . . We are the last resort; the police are delighted to see you so they can get on with it.

More generally, such comments belie accounts in which police and solicitors' interests are always opposed. The effect of some legal advice is to assist the police, by encouraging confessions which come earlier than they might otherwise do and which cannot be challenged in court. While such advice may also be in the suspect's

---

72   R. Morgan, 'Detention in the police station'. Paper presented to the ESRC/Police Foundation Conference on PACE, Bristol, 1989, p. 3.

interest, we and other researchers encountered some cases in which (like the parents and social workers discussed above) legal advisers did little actively to assist suspects: some played a passive, non-interventionist role in interrogations, or failed to explain significant matters to their clients. Legal advisers often gave brief telephone advice rather than attending in person; while some solicitors were more likely to turn out in juveniles' than adults' cases, some were exasperated by calls during the night to advise those detained for minor offences. Critical attention needs to be directed as much at the quality as at the quantity of legal advice.[73]

Similarly, the police perspective on dealing with juvenile suspects is more complex than simplistic accounts would suggest. While investigating officers may give priority to securing admissions and convictions, custody officers have been made by PACE to accord at least equal importance to dealing with the suspect according to the rules, particularly those protecting his/her welfare.[74] This is especially so in the case of juvenile suspects: custody officers know that their treatment of such people may be the subject of particular scrutiny, with the possibility of disciplinary action and judicial exclusion of evidence as sanctions. While they will do what they can to assist their investigating colleagues, this must be balanced against their own interest in having the juvenile dealt with as expeditiously as possible and without creating grounds for subsequent complaint. For custody officers, juvenile suspects mean additional work and responsibility.[75] The comments of two solicitors reflect a widely held view:

> Most charge room staff just want to shift juveniles.

> The police are genuinely more co-operative in dealing
> with juveniles . . . they are anxious to deal with them
> quickly and get them away.

Far from the image of police and lawyers in irreconcilable conflict, the mundane reality is often a co-operation by these parties in the processing of suspects.

73   Dixon, *et al.* (1990), Sanders, *et al.* (1989).
74   Bottomley, *et al.* (1989) chapter 5, Dixon, *et al.* (1990).
75   Brown (1989) p. 38.

Conclusion

The conclusion must be a rather depressing one. It has been generally accepted that special arrangements have to be made in order to safeguard vulnerable suspects such as juveniles. However, such acceptance has not been followed by rigorous consideration of how to achieve this goal. It seems to be generally assumed that one person (parent, social worker, or legal adviser) is sufficient to protect a vulnerable suspect's various legal and welfare interests. This certainly is convenient in terms of resource allocation and fits with the strongly held police view that third party attendance during questioning should be minimised. However, the discussion above suggests that its justification is doubtful. Parents have a right, perhaps a duty, to attend. Juvenile suspects, even those accused of minor offences, also usually need welfare and legal support. Given the considerations discussed above, the best option would seem to be the establishment or expansion of specialist, legally competent social work teams.

In debates to date it has generally been assumed that an appropriate adult's presence is necessary without asking what an appropriate adult should do, who can best carry out this role, how it overlaps with the provision of legal advice, and what the implications are for public expenditure on social service and legal aid provision. In a system which has failed to address these questions, the potential exists for the recurrence of the problems which PACE was, in part, intended to prevent.

Finally, it should be stressed that these are not merely matters of civil-libertarian concern. The mishandling of suspects in, for example, the Confait and Broadwater Farm cases resulted in these investigations being so confused and misled by false confessions that people who had committed very serious crimes were never apprehended or punished. Effective safeguards for vulnerable suspects should be regarded as being in the public interest, in terms both of detecting crime and of protecting suspects' rights.

6

Care After 1991

M. D. A. Freeman

When I studied Family Law for the first time (in 1964-5) we were led to believe that there was no law of child care. Adoption apart there was little law relating to children at all. Of course this was a distorted perception but it was not uncommon at that time. Child law is one of the major developments of the 1970s. I cannot (I hope!) be alone in finding it difficult to keep abreast of developments in the case law or in the literature. But 25 years ago there was very little to read. It is Hugh Bevan who more than anyone has helped to foster this new climate. He is a true pioneer in constructing a science of child law: the first 'inaugural' to take as its theme child protection,[1] the first academic text,[2] an excellent commentary on the 'children's charter' of 1975 (with Martin Parry)[3] and his recent *magnum opus*, a second edition in name only of the text published in 1973.[4] They are all milestones in child law analysis. I am delighted to participate in this

---

1   *Child Protection and the Law* (Hull University Press: Inaugural Lecture, 1970).
2   *The Law Relating to Children* (London: Butterworths, 1973).
3   *The Children Act 1975* (London: Butterworths, 1976).
4   *Child Law* (London: Butterworths, 1989).

tribute to his career. I offer thoughts on what the law relating to care will look like after the implementation (we are told in October 1991) of the Children Act 1989.

This is a large undertaking. My focus accordingly concentrates on care proceedings, in particular the new ground (or minimum necessary conditions) for a care or supervision order. It will, of course, necessarily range wider than this as the new law on care is put into the context of other reforms in the structure introduced by the 1989 legislation. Differences between the old ground and the new minimum necessary conditions will be examined, difficulties will be uncovered, gaps pointed to and improvements suggested. Though the task is undertaken in a questioning and critical frame of mind, the primary aim is analysis and the model is Hugh Bevan's own work.

The new ground : some preliminary observations

For simplicity sake I will call the conditions which have to be satisfied before a care or supervision order can be made the new ground, though necessary minimum conditions or threshold criteria[5] may equally well be used to designate what must be proved to a court's satisfaction before such an order can be made.

The new ground is set out in s. 31(2). This states:

A court may only make a care order or supervision order if it is satisfied -
(a)   that the child concerned is suffering, or is likely to suffer, significant harm; and
(b)   that the harm, or likelihood of harm, is attributable to -
   (i)   the care given to the child, or likely to be given to him if the order were not made, not being what it would be reasonable to expect a parent to give to him; or

---

5   The Lord Chancellor has described them as the 'minimum circumstances' *Joseph Jackson Memorial Lecture* (1989) 139 NLJ 505.

(ii)   the child's being beyond
          parental control.

'Harm', 'development' and 'health' are defined by s. 31(9) and the same sub-section explains that 'ill-treatment' includes sexual abuse and forms of ill-treatment which are not physical. Section 31 (10) attempts an explanation of 'significant' in relation to a child's 'health' or 'development'. 'Significant' has to be seen in comparison with 'that which could reasonably be expected of a similar child'.

The new 'ground' is just that. It is very different from the grounds which developed with the 'fit person' order, became the grounds for a care order with the passing of the Children and Young Persons Act 1969 and took on accretions in 1975.[6] The new single 'ground' replaces the seven 'conditions' in the 1969 Act, as amended, and does away with the overriding condition which had to be satisfied before a care or supervision order could be made under the old legislation that the child 'is in need of care or control which he is unlikely to receive unless the court makes an order.[7] However, this removal of a welfare consideration is more apparent than real for it is clear that s. 1(1) applies to the making of a care order (it is a question with respect to the 'upbringing' of a child), so that the child's welfare is the court's 'paramount consideration'. In addition, the innovative provision in s. 1(5) applies, so that the court is not to make a care or supervision order, even where the ground is proved 'unless it considers that doing so would be better for the child than making no order at all'. All in all, it would be fair to say that the welfare consideration, far from being removed, has been strengthened. Indeed, since it was honoured in the breach, it would not be inaccurate to argue that the new legislation gives welfare a role in care proceedings that was formerly absent.

---

6   By the Children Act 1975, Schedule 3, para. 67.
7   See Children and Young Persons Act 1969, s. 1(2). After *Re S* [1978] QB
         120, the distinction between the primary conditions and general condition
         was blurred. See R. Dingwall, J. Eekelaar and T. Murray, *The Protection
         of Children* (Oxford: Basil Blackwell 1983) pp. 196-7. On the relationship
         between this and the order, and variability in practice, see (1986) 83 Law
         Soc Gaz. 2452.

One of the old 'conditions' (being 'beyond parental control') is now integrated into the single ground in s. 31(2). The education ground in the old law now becomes the ground for an education supervision order (see s. 36(3) and (4). To gild the lily, section 90 reiterates and emphasises that the 'offence condition' in s. 1(2)(f) of the 1969 Act is 'hereby abolished' (s. 90(1); the power to make, what were called, s. 7(7) orders is similarly abolished by the 1989 Act (see s. 90(2)(a)).

Two other preliminary points must be borne in mind. First, under the old law the legal framework of care was exceptionally complicated: there was a myriad of routes into care and the basis for care in the different cases was different (most obviously the grounds that had to be proved did not always coincide).[8] A child could go into compulsory care as a result of administrative action by a resolution assuming parental rights, an iniquity the removal of which will be mourned by few.[9] The new legislation abolishes this procedure, as it does all routes into care save that laid down in s. 31(2). The intention is to remove inconsistency and incoherence and to create unified framework under which 'parental responsibility' may be compulsorily vested in a local authority.[10]

Secondly, the new ground must be understood in the context of the provision (see s. 100(1) and s. 100(2)) which imposes restrictions on the use of wardship by local authorities. It will still be possible for a local authority to ward a child,[11] or rather to invoke the inherent jurisdiction of the court, but only in most restrictive circumstances. The trend, under which courts positively encouraged local authorities to seek the assistance of the wardship court,[12] is thus reversed. Under the new law, the local authority must first obtain leave (s. 100(3)) and may only clear this hurdle if the court is satisfied that 'the result which the authority wish to achieve could not be achieved through the making of any order of a kind to which

8   See M. D. A. Freeman (1982) 35 CLP 117; S. Maidment (1981) JSWL 21.
9   See S. Maidment in H. Geach and E. Szwed, *Providing Civil Justice for Children* (London: Edward Arnold, 1983) p. 71.
10   See s. 33(3). But parents remain parents, retain parental responsibility and do not lose it simply because a local authority also acquires it (see s. 2(5) and (6)).
11   See s. 100 and below, p. 168.
12   *Re D* [1977] Fam 158, 166 *per* Dunn J; *Re R* [1987] 2 FLR 400.

subsection (5) applies; and 'there is reasonable cause to believe that if the court's inherent jurisdiction is not exercised with respect to the child he is likely to suffer significant harm' (s. 100(4)).

The reformulation of the care ground, for example, its extension to prognosis of harm, will obviate the need to have as much recourse to wardship as was the case in the past, but the new restrictive approach to wardship will cause some problems, to which reference will be made later in this article. For the present, one further comment will be offered. The *volte-face* reflects a deliberate shift in policy away from coercive intervention into family relationships on broad welfare considerations and towards the establishment with the threshold criteria of standards of legality, of a doctrine of, what H. L. A. Hart called in another context, 'fair opportunity'.[13] Legislation could have gone the other way, requiring a local authority to have satisfied a court of nothing more than that the child's welfare would be promoted best by removal from his parents: in other words, by emphasising wardship rather than removing its sting. That this was not done, that the Act goes for autonomy rather than intervention, that intervention is limited by the threshold criteria as well as by s. 1(5), must be welcomed.[14]

The new ground analysed

The minimum threshold criteria for a care order consist of two elements:

> (i)   the child is suffering, or is likely to suffer significant harm, and

---

13   H. L. A. Hart, *Punishment and Responsibility* (Oxford: Clarendon Press, 1968).

14   The Lord Chancellor in his *Jackson* lecture referred to the 'integrity and independence of the family' as 'the basic building block of a free and democratic society'. Accordingly, he argued, 'unless there is evidence that a child is being or is likely to be positively harmed because of a failure in the family, the state, whether in the guise of a local authority or a court, should not interfere' (above, no. 5, p. 508). See also *Hansard*, HL vol. 502, col. 493. The Government's decision to restrict the scope of wardship was taken late in the day (see ibid., n. 5, p. 507).

(ii)   this is attributable either to the care given
or likely to be given, to the child or the
child being beyond parental control.

Each of these elements will require considerable judicial exegesis. Almost every word will require interpretation and analysis. Argument on the meaning of the language contained here (as filled out by later subsections) is likely to rage for as long as this legislation remains in force. A few comments to assist this process of debate and argument are, therefore, in order.

The temporal dimension

The ground is couched in the present continuous[15] and takes account also of the future. The original Bill contained the words 'has suffered' instead of 'is suffering'. The change was made by Government initiative during the Committee stage of the House of Commons to prevent an order being made 'on the basis of significant harm suffered several years previously, and which is not likely to be repeated'.[16] Thus, though historical evidence of harm may be relevant in assessing the future likelihood of harm, it will not be sufficient to satisfy the criterion set out above. It must follow that an isolated incident in the past, however serious, will not by itself ground proceedings.[17] Of course, abused children will continue to be removed, now using emergency protection orders,[18] before care proceedings are brought. Literally interpreted, such children are not suffering significant harm (unless they continue to suffer as a result of the pre-removal abuse). But the courts have held in the past that the words 'his development is being avoidably prevented' did not require the state to persist at the time of the hearing. They were, rather, descriptive of a category into which the child fell.[19] Such an

---

15   *Re D* [1987] AC 317.
16   *Per* David Mellor MP, col. 221.
17   But 'a child's development is a continuing process. The present must be relevant in the context of what has happened in the past, and it becomes a matter of degree as to how far in the past you go' *per* Butler-Sloss J in *M* v *Westminster CC* [1985] FLR 325.
18   Under s. 44.
19   See *H* v *Sheffield CC* [1981] JSWL 303.

interpretation is equally applicable to the new language.

The introduction of likelihood of suffering is an important innovation. It was clear under the former legislation that an order could not be made on the basis of perceived risk of future harm to the child.[20] The removal of a newborn baby (in particular, the first child) where it was feared the mother would be unable to cope was thus of dubious legality.[21] The place of safety order obtained in respect of 'Baby Cotton', the surrogacy *cause célèbre* which hit the headlines in January 1985, was similarly tainted.[22] Protection in such cases had to be sought in wardship. The effect this limitation had on local authorities was particularly felt when it was approached to receive into care an abused child. If it did so, it found itself in a difficult position if it subsequently wanted to commence care proceedings on the basis of prognosis of harm should the child be returned. All these cases are now covered.

Ante-natal harm

One of the most controversial of cases in recent years is the so-called 'heroin addict mother' case of *Re D*.[23] The House of Lords sanctioned the removal of a baby born with foetal drug syndrome because the harm done to her before her birth was continuing at the time compulsory measures of care were initiated. This is not the place to criticise the decision, though I remain unrepentant in my belief that it was wrong in law and undesirable as a matter of social policy.[24] It is, however, worth asking whether similar action taken by a local authority under the new legislation will succeed (though perhaps I should say 'should succeed', since it is equally likely that

---

20   See *Essex CC* v *TLR and KBR* (1978) 9 Fam Law 15.
21   M. D. A. Freeman (1980) 10 Fam Law 131.
22   *Re C* [1985] FLR 846. See also M. Hayes and V. Bevan, *Child-Care Law - A Practitioner's Guide*, (Bristol: Jordan, 2nd ed., 1988) p. 49.
23   [1987] AC 317.
24   See M. D. A. Freeman (1988-1989) 27 J Fam L 101, 105-9.

the courts will stretch[25] the 1989 language). Early commentators on the new legislation seem in no doubt that the same result may be achieved as in *Re D*. Masson, indeed, notes that the decision in *Re D* 'did not permit orders in relation to all children local authorities sought to protect'.[26] If the implication of this is that the new law is even more efficacious than the old (as construed by the Lords) in tackling the problem of the child harmed before birth, then I cannot agree. Bainham argues that the 'straining'[27] of the 1969 legislation (which is not, I think, how he interpreted it in an authoritative note in the *Modern Law Review*)[28] will no longer be necessary: 'Should the facts of the *Berkshire* case recur, it will now be possible for the court to make an order based entirely on the risk of harm to child. In assessing this risk it would be open to the court to have regard to the mother's behaviour during pregnancy'.[29] But is this analysis correct? I do not think so. The new provision only bites where the harm the child is suffering or is likely to suffer is 'attributable to the care given to the child . . . not being what it would be reasonable to expect a parent to give to him'. The Act is, however, clear in defining a child as a 'person under the age of eighteen'.[30] The child born with withdrawal symptoms as a result of the ingestion of drugs (or other harmful substances) during pregnancy is suffering significant harm (that is not contested), but it is harm attributable to the care given to him when he was not a child but a foetus. That, after birth, a child has a right of action in respect of a pre-natal injury was long the matter of controversy and is now the law because of legislative intervention.[31] But, as Sir George Baker P said in the *Paton* case (and this has been approved by the Court of Appeal),[32] 'the foetus cannot, in English law, have a right of its own at least until it is born

25   Lord Brandon thought the statutory provision should receive 'a broad and liberal construction which gives full effect to [its] legislative purpose' (p. 347). *Sed quaere*.

26   See Masson's *Current Law Statutes Annotation*, 1990 (comment on s. 31 at p. 69).

27   A. Bainham, *Children - The New Law* (Bristol: Jordans, 1990) para. 5. 12.

28   50 MLR 361 (1987).

29   Bainham, n. 27.

30   Section 105(1).

31   Congenital Disabilities (Civil Liability) Act 1976. See also J. Eekelaar and R. Dingwall (1984) JSWL 258.

32   *Re F* [1988] 2 FLR 307.

and has a separate existence from its mother'.[33] I conclude that, if the facts of *Re D* were to recur, a care order could not legitimately be made.

This leads to the thorny question of the protection of the unborn.[34] The question is fraught with conflict because it raises issues of civil liberties and the control of pregnancy[35] and the extent to which these considerations should trump whatever protection we would wish to accord the child *en ventre sa mère*. The new legislation has not shifted the balance. Care proceedings cannot be used as an instrument to protect the unborn: they are not 'persons' under the age of eighteen. It was, further, held before the passage of the 1989 Act that a foetus cannot be made a ward of court.[36] The restrictions on wardship in the Act are thus only relevant insofar as it could be anticipated that *Re F* might be reviewed by the House of Lords. But, though the argument for allowing the warding of a foetus is substantial, as Bevan points out[37] and the *Tameside* case[38] in particular illustrates, this is a remote contingency.

What is 'significant harm'?

To activate care 'significant' harm (or its likelihood) is required. The DHSS *Review of Child Care Law* explained this thus:

> Having set an acceptable standard of upbringing for the child, it should be necessary to show some substantial deficit in that standard. Minor shortcomings in the health

---

33   *Paton v British Pregnancy Advisory Service Trustees* [1979] QB 276, 279.
34   An issue which has, hitherto, had greater impact in the USA See M. A. Field (1989) 17 *Law, Medicine and Health Care* 114 and V. Kolder, J. Gallagher and M. Parsons (1987) *New England J. of Medicine* 1192. Cf. J. A. Parness (1986) 20 Fam LQ 197.
35   But the questions are not new: see M. Becker (1986) 53 *Univ of Chicago L Rev* 1219.
36   *Re F* [1988] 2 FLR 307. See also the California Court of Appeals case of *Reyes v Superior Court* 75 Cal App 3d 214 (1977). Cf. Lyon and Bennett (1979) 9 Fam Law 35, 36.
37   *Child Law*, n. 4, p. 337.
38   *The Times*, 11 Nov. 1987.

and care provided or minor defects in physical, psychological or social development should not give rise to any compulsory intervention unless they are having, or are likely to have, serious and lasting effects upon the child'.[39]

'Significant' suggests 'substantial', 'considerable', 'noteworthy'. It imposes a lesser standard than might have been required. The equivalent ground for intervention in Goldstein, Freud and Solnit's *Before the Best Interests of the Child*, the philosophy of whose book has clearly influenced the Act, is the infliction of 'serious bodily injury'.[40] Ignoring the limitation to 'bodily injury', it is, I think, clear that 'significant' is a lesser standard than serious. It is also a lesser standard than 'severe'. Harm may be 'significant' in a number of ways: in amount, in effect, in importance. Where physical harm is concerned the estimation of significance may cause less problem than where emotional trauma is in issue and where there will clearly be need for psychological evidence. Physical injury tends to be associated with 'non-accidental injury' but it will be appreciated that an accident attributable to poor care can cause significant harm. But this should not necessarily lead to a care order: the criteria in s. 1 take on particular significance in this context. Drawing the line between 'significant' harm and harm not to be so designated will not be easy. Nor should we forget that insignificant harm may also be of importance, particularly where a series of such relatively insignificant harms have occurred for they may well betoken risk of significant harm in the foreseeable future.

Harm explored

'Harm' itself is broadly defined in the Act. 'Harm' means 'ill-treatment' or 'the impairment of health and development'. Lord Mackay explained 'ill treatment' thus: it 'is not a precise term and would include, for example, instances of verbal abuse or unfairness

---

39   Para. 15 (15).
40   (New York: Free Press, 1979), p. 72. See, further, M. D. A. Freeman, *The Rights and Wrongs of Children* (London: Frances Pinter, 1983) pp. 253-5.

falling a long way short of significant harm'.[41] The examples he gives may be instructive, but this statement cannot be taken at face value. If the acts fall short of significant harm, they cannot form the basis of a care application. What Lord Mackay may be adverting to is the reference in s. 31(10) to significant harm being located in the context of similar children, but this only applies when the question of significance turns on the child's health or development. The health of a timid child may well be affected deleteriously by action which objectively falls short of that which could be expected to lead to significant harm in a sturdy, resilient child. This will be pursued further when 'similar child' is discussed.

The problem of sexual abuse

'Ill-treatment', the Act prescribes, 'includes sexual abuse and forms of ill-treatment which are not physical'.[42] This, it is suggested, in no way changes the existing law. Emotional abuse clearly came within the umbrella of 'being ill-treated' in s. 1(2)(a) of the 1969 Act.[43] The specific inclusion of sexual abuse is welcome. As recently as 1980 a DHSS Circular on child protection registers did not extend its purview to sexual abuse.[44] The 1989 Act does not go on to define sexual abuse or indicate what comes within it. In a recent case a father was said to have indulged in 'vulgar and inappropriate horseplay' with his daughter.[45] Where is the line to be drawn? Some sexual abuse (certainly rape and arguably other forms) is gross physical abuse in addition to being sexual abuse. All sexual abuse is without question severe emotional abuse. Is exposing a child to pornographic material sexual abuse? And, if so, how is pornography to be defined? A high percentage of households take newspapers which have the potentiality to deprave and corrupt vulnerable minds.

---

41   *Hansard*, HL vol. 503, col. 342.
42   Section 31 (9).
43   *F* v *Suffolk CC* (1981) 2 FLR 208.
44   LASSL (80) 4 Aug. 1980. Criticised at the time by BASPCAN, *Child Sexual Abuse*, 1981. See also M. D. A. Freeman, above, n. 40, p. 132. An early article on sexual abuse is M. D. A. Freeman (1978) 8 Fam Law 221.
45   *C* v *C* [1988] 1 FLR 462. New forms emerge: see the revelations about 'satanic' or 'ritualistic' abuse in the *Guardian*, 10 Sept. 1990.

There is not surprisingly no universally accepted definition of what constitutes child sexual abuse.[46] The intention of the abuser is crucial so that the inclusion within the definition of sexual abuse of anything that gives him sexual gratification is meaningful. It is critical to stress this element for two reasons: first, there are actions (for example, voyeurism) of which the child is unaware and, secondly, by emphasising what it does for the perpetrator, child sexual abuse can be seen as a wrong that reduces the child to a sexual object - her person is not the subject of, what Dworkin has called, 'equal respect and concern'.[47] It is difficult then to define sexual abuse. A useful working definition, put forward by the Standing Committee on Sexually Abused Children in 1984, is:

> Any child below the age of consent may be deemed to have been sexually abused when a sexually mature person has, by design or by neglect of their usual societal or specific responsibilities in relation to the child, engaged or permitted the engagement of that child in any activity of a sexual nature which is intended to lead to the sexual gratification of the sexually mature person. This definition pertains whether or not this activity involves explicit coercion by any means, whether or not initiated by the child, or whether or not there is discernible harmful outcome in the short term.[48]

Proof of harm will in many cases be the ultimate stumbling-block.

The Act also does not define what is meant by ill-treatment. We know what it includes (at least in part) and we know it is wider in scope than physical abuse. Failure or refusal to obtain medical treatment for the child would probably have been considered as 'neglect' under the old legislation (though I note Bevan slots it

---

46   See, for example, D. Finkelhor, *Child Sexual Abuse* (London: Sage, 1984) pp. 23-4. I have considered this in (1989) 42 CLP 85, 88-91.

47   *Taking Rights Seriously* (London: Duckworth, 1977 pp. 180-3. See also M. D. A. Freeman (1988) 1 *Children and Society* 299.

48   SCOSAC, 1984. See also D. Glaser and S. Frosh, *Child Sexual Abuse* (London: Macmillan, 1988) p. 9.

equally into ill-treatment),[49]   There is, I think, little doubt that, with
the demise of 'neglect', such failure or refusal would be regarded as
ill-treatment.   The line between legitimate corporal punishment and
ill-treatment is difficult to draw.[50] Each generation draws it
differently: what it sanctions as legitimate becomes narrower and
narrower.

Corporal punishment

But, when is corporal punishment itself to be regarded as ill-
treatment? As a matter of policy it would make sense to acknowledge
that all hostile force against a child is wrong: only children may be
hit; they are the only legitimate victims of violence now left.[51] The
lessons of history and the experience of other countries point
inexorably to a time when hitting children will be regarded as wrong
and unlawful.   As Peter Newell puts it: 'children are people too'.[52]
The four Nordic countries[53] and Austria[54] have banned corporal
punishment and we, belatedly, have gone a long way to outlawing it
outside the home,[55] though amendments to the Children Bill to make
it unlawful for parents and for foster parents to administer physical
chastisement not surprisingly failed.[56] It was the links with child
abuse that were prominent among the reasons for Sweden's decision

---

49   *Child Law*, n. 4, p. 626.
50   See P. Newell, *The Independent*, 15 May 1989.
51   See Michael Freeman, *Childright*, no. 51 (Oct. 1988), p. 5. See also D.
      Herman (1985) 19 *Family Law Q 1*.
52   In a book, published by Bedford Square Press in 1989, with that title.
53   In Sweden in 1979 (IYC), in Finland (in 1983), Denmark (in 1986) and
      Norway (in 1987). See, further, P. Newell, *Children are People Too*
      (London: Bedford Square Press, 1989) chapter 3.
54   In 1989: the Youth Welfare Act states that 'using violence and inflicting
      physical or mental suffering is unlawful'.
55   It was abolished, as from 15 Aug. 1987, in state schools and for pupils with
      assisted places in independent schools by the Education (No. 2) Act 1986 s.
      47 (s. 48 for Scotland). See also Residential Care Homes (Amendment)
      Regulations 1988, S.I. 1988/1192.
56   See debates in the House of Lords, 23 Jan. 1989, 16 Feb. 1989, 16 Mar.
      1989.

to ban physical punishment. As the Ministry of Justice in Sweden put it;

> There are still great risks that a parent who is used to chastising his child will gradually increase the degree of violence and, one day, will beat the child badly. Most parents who are prosecuted for maltreating their children defend themselves by saying "I didn't mean to hurt him, I just administered physical punishment which I am entitled to do.' As long as it is not totally clear that a parent may not use physical violence when bringing up a child, it will be difficult to stop or reduce child assault.[57]

The Lester Chapman case is most instructive.[58] Lester (aged eight) died of exposure after running away from home for the fourth time. On one occasion, when he ran away after being beaten, he was taken to Reading police station. 'According to the police officer the injuries would have amounted to the offence of causing actual bodily harm, had they not been in the cause of chastisement by a mother of her son'.[59] A doctor observed 'eight weals on the right buttock and three on the left, with the skin broken within some of the lesions'.[60] In his opinion the injury was 'trivial' but 'a more severe punishment than one would expect to be given to a child of his age'. After a social worker arrived, she, the police officer and the doctor agreed that there was no justification for seeking a place of safety order to remove Lester from home, though he made it clear that he didn't want to go home and would run away again. As Newell comments: 'Lester, his parents, and the professionals who failed to act were all affected by the current social norm, namely, the acceptance of hitting children, including hitting them hard and with implements. Lester was the only person to be affected fatally'.[61]

57   Quoted in Newell, n. 53, pp. 24-5.
58   *Inquiry into the Death of Lester Chapman: Report of an Independent Inquiry*, Berkshire CC, 1979.
59   Ibid.
60   Ibid.
61   Op. cit., n. 53, p. 26. See also now EPOCH, *Child Abuse and Physical Punishment* (London: EPOCH, 1990)

English law attempts to draw the line by permitting moderate and reasonable chastisement.[62]   These are vague and value-laden epithets and subject to differing interpretations. In the *Chapman* case it would appear that inflicting what amounted to ABH was not, in the minds of three professionals, ill-treatment when the victim was the perpetrator's child. The problem is especially acute when families originate from cultures where the norms appear to be different. The Newsons note that parents of Afro-Caribbean origin 'punish their children still more frequently and severely than do indigenous white parents'.[63] Historically, these values can be explained as deriving from a social system which institutionalised slave labour and the physical beating of slaves. The Newsons believe that this, plus the commitment to a revivalist religion (also imported from Britain) that emphasises that pain to the body is of far less concern than damnation of the soul, at least in part explains the stress on physical chastisement which is believed to be so prevalent among Afro-Caribbean parents.

Two cases are worth briefly noting. In *R* v *Derrivière*,[64] a father of West Indian origin punched his twelve-year-old in the face, causing him to suffer bruises, swellings and lacerations. Charged with causing actual bodily harm, he was convicted and sentenced to six months' imprisonment. The attack was described by the Deputy Chairman of the Inner London Quarter Sessions as a 'brutal assault'. The Criminal Division of the Court of Appeal upheld the decision and set out the broad principle thus:

> Standards of parental correction are different in the West Indies from those which are acceptable in this country; and the court fully accepts that immigrants coming to this country may initially find that our ideas are different from those upon which they have been brought up in regard to the methods and manner in which children are to be disciplined. There can be no

62   *R* v *Hopley* (1860) 2 F and F 202, 206, *per* Cockburn LCJ.
63   'Parental Punishment Strategies with 11-year-old children', in N. Frude
        (ed.), *Psychological Approaches To Child Abuse*, (London: Batsford, 1980)
        p. 73.
64   (1969) 53 Cr App Rep 637.

doubt that once in this country, this country's laws must apply; and there can be no doubt that, according to the law of this country, the chastisement given to this boy was excessive . . . Nevertheless had this been a first offence, and had there been some real reason for thinking that the appellant either did not understand what the standards in this country were or was having difficulty adjusting himself, the Court would no doubt have taken that into account and given it such consideration as it could.[65]

This was not Derrivière's first conviction for assaulting a child of his. He had previously received a suspended sentence and so a clear warning of the unacceptable nature of his behaviour in England. The implication is that cultural difference may mitigate a sentence but does not afford any defence to the charge itself.[66] In the context of care, this could be interpreted to mean that the threshold condition of 'ill-treatment' is satisfied by conduct like Derrivière's but in itself it might not be an appropriate case for removing the child from the parent (applying the principles set out in s. 1).

Re H centred around a family of Vietnamese boat people.[67] There were repeated instances of neglect, ill-treatment and bizarre cruelty on the part of the mother towards her children. She beat the children with sticks, hit the three-year-old across his face with a flip-flop and, on one occasion, placed him naked from the waist down outside in the snow as a punishment. The judge held that the case had to be considered against the 'reasonable objective standards of the culture in which the children have hitherto been brought up, so long as these do not conflict with our minimal acceptable standards of child care in England'.[68] He found evidence that 'in Chinese culture, as applied to the lower social and cultural levels of society, in some rurally based societies, such as North Vietnam . . . chastisement with sticks . . . is practised'.[69] But, he found the mother's cruelty grossly

---

65   Ibid., pp. 638-9.
66   And see S. Poulter, *English Law and Ethnic Minority Customs,* (London: Butterworths, 1986) p. 148.
67   [1987] 2 FLR 12.
68   Ibid., p. 17, *per* Judge Callman (sitting as an additional High Court judge).
69   Ibid., pp. 17-18.

excessive by any standards. In the circumstance, he decided, it would be in the children's best interests for them to remain with long-term foster parents with a view to adoption. But, supposing the mother's conduct had only flouted English standards and not those of both cultures? I agree with Bevan[70] that it would have justified intervention by the court, and probably in our context a care order being made, after full consideration of the principles in section 1.

The original Children Bill drafting would have caused difficulties in both these cases (on the assumption that there were care cases). In assessing standard of care the court was required to compare that provided with what it would be 'reasonable to expect the parent of a similar child' to provide.[71] The intention behind the inclusion of the ambiguous phrase 'similar child' was to enable the particular attributes of the child (for example, physical, mental, emotional characteristics) to be taken into account so as to compare the child with other children with similar characteristics. The provision was, however, remodelled (as we shall see) because it was not clear whether cultural considerations (and the child's social background) should be taken into account or not. In *Re H,* for example, should the question of whether the children were being ill-treated be assessed by comparing their treatment with that experienced by the children of other boat people or other Chinese children or should the comparator be other children living in this country? Although the final drafting surmounts this problem, the issue remains and is likely further to fuel the debate between those who advocate cultural pluralism and those who argue, here in the name of protecting children, for a unified moral standard. The difficulty with the latter view is that, even ignoring ethnic minorities, there is no consensus on what constitutes acceptable disciplinary measures. The Newsons found practices in Nottingham that would be unacceptable in Haiphong.[72]

70   *Child Law,* n. 4, p. 17.
71   See M. D. A. Freeman, 'The Politics of Child Care', in M. D. A. Freeman, *Critical Issues in Welfare Law,* (London: Stevens, 1990) p. 103. 105-106.
72   *Four Years Old in An Urban Community* (London: Allen and Unwin, 1968).

The 'similar child'.

Section 31(10) states: 'Where the question of whether harm suffered by a child is significant turns on the child's health or development, his health or development shall be compared with that which could reasonably be expected of a similar child'. This provision is far from easy to interpret and could give rise to argument in litigation. It should be noted, first, that the reference is to 'a similar child' and not a child of 'similar parents'. Secondly, the standard of care below which parents must not fall is that which can be reasonably expected to be given to similar children. It follows that only rearing below this threshold level may attract state intervention.

But, what is a similar child? According to Lord Mackay,[73] it is a child with the same physical attributes as the child concerned, and not a child of the same background. The development of a two-year-old has, accordingly, to be compared with that of other two-year-olds, and not with other two-year-olds from similar backgrounds. On this test a child from a deprived background is expected to achieve intellectual growth and emotional maturity comparable to children who come from well-ordered, well-heeled and stimulating environments. By emphasising the physical or 'personal' attributes of the child, the social and environmental context of the child's life is being ignored. But to ignore the impact of poverty, for example, on intellectual development is to take a myopic view of what can be achieved in circumstances of deprivation.[74]

What the phrase does, however, achieve is the comparison of *this* child with children like him: that is to say, children who have the same attributes. The development of a deaf four-year-old (who may only speak a few words) is to be compared with what is to be expected of other deaf four-year-olds, and not with other four-year-olds. But the value of this may be apparent rather than real. First, even within the context of a physical disability like deafness, it is not apparent what the appropriate comparators are. Is a four-year-old, whose deafness was only diagnosed late, to be compared with a four-

---

73   *Hansard*, vol. 503, col. 354.
74   See H. Wilson, 'Families in Poverty' in R. N. Rapoport, M. P. Fogarty and R. Rapoport, *Families in Britain* (London: RKP, 1982) ch. 12. See also P. Wedge and J. Essen, *Children in Adversity* (London: Pan Books, 1982).

year-old who was being appropriately treated before he reached his first birthday? And what is appropriate treatment? Is the deaf child to be integrated into the hearing world or specially educated at a school for the hearing impaired?[75] Should he be taught to speak or encouraged to sign? Intense conflicts rage over these matters. When comparing deaf children, how much account should be taken of the amount of their hearing loss (there is a wide spectrum of deafness ranging from moderate through serious to severe), of the type of deficiency (is it conductive hearing loss or sensori-neural, caused by infections or as a result of genetic factors?), or even of the particular type of loss they have (high, lowtone etc.)?[76] Is a deaf child of deaf parents a similar child to a deaf child of hearing parents? If we take account only of the characteristics of the child, as the statute requires and as the Lord Chancellor indicates we should, then a deaf child of deaf parents is like a deaf child of hearing parents. But is he? He will be reared in a different environment. His parents may well have attitudes to deafness and to the education of the deaf very different from parents who have not themselves experienced the disability.

Even with such a clearly defined condition as Down's Syndrome[77] there is, as Janet Carr,[78] a research psychologist' notes, 'enormous variability, from near-normal intelligence to profound mental handicap, from the amiable, outgoing and cooperative person to one who is difficult and destructive'. Similarly with epilepsy. Under the umbrella of epilepsy 'lies a wide range of disorders with the only unifying characteristic being that every now and again the child will have a seizure of some sort',[79] And Asthma.[80] The underlying cause is still not fully understood and there is still argument about the definition of the condition. Nevertheless, children with asthma 'may range from very mild cases with only occasional

75   See M. Nolan and I. G. Tucker, *The Hearing-Impaired Child and the Family* (New York: Souvenir Press, 1983). Cf. H. Lane, *When the Mind Hears* (New York: Random House, 1984) and O. Sacks, *Seeing Voices* (London: Picador, 1989)

76   See I. Tucker, 'Deafness', in S. Curtis (ed.), *From Asthma to Thalassaemia* (London: BAAF, 1986) chapter 6.

77   See A. Gath, 'Down's Syndrome' in ibid., chapter 8.

78   'Helping Parents of Mentally Handicapped Children' in ibid., chapter 1 (p. 13).

79   See E. Ross, 'Epilepsy' in ibid., chapter 9 (p. 86).

80   See J. O. Warner, 'Asthma' in ibid., chapter 2.

episodes of minimally distressing wheeze . . . to the very severe chronic asthmatic with very frequent attacks of distressing wheeze, limited exercise tolerance, stunted growth and deformed chest'.[81]

The goal of the 'similar child' notion may be laudatory in that it tries to emphasise the special needs of children with handicaps. But, as we have seen, it uses language that obfuscates and overlooks the essential individuality of families and their problems. By concentrating on the child it also ignores the impact of interaction between the child and his parents, the effect such interaction can have even on physical handicaps and on the parents. Thus, there is evidence that mothers of Down's Syndrome children suffer disproportionately from depression[82] and that the birth of a Down's Syndrome child can turn a moderately successful or shaky marriage into a poor or dysfunctional one,[83] with obvious concomitant effect on the child's development and health. It also ignores those cases (the emotionally frozen child may be an example)[84] where the source of a child's problems may lie in early family history.

The quality of care

A care order may only be made if, in addition to the child suffering significant harm (or likely to suffer significant harm), the harm (or its likelihood) is 'attributable to' one of two factors: (i) the care given to the child, or likely to be given to him if the order were not made, not being what it would be reasonable to expect a parent to give to him or (ii) the child's being beyond parental control. These two prerequisites may be described as 'the quality of care' and 'parental control'. Each will be looked at separately, the 'quality of care' in this, and the 'beyond control' in a later, section.

First, the 'quality of care' provision must be examined. It will be noted that the linking phrase is 'attributable to'. This suggests a linking of harm to quality of care or a relationship between them.

---

81   Ibid., p. 42.
82   A. Gath, *Down's Syndrome and the Family: the Early Years* (London: Academic Press, 1978). See also O. Rowlands, 'Down's Syndrome and the Family' in *Adoption and Fostering*, vol. 6, no. 1 (1982) p. 21.
83   Ibid.
84   See B. Jefferies, *Adoption and Fostering*, vol. 5, no. 1 (1981) p. 9. See also C. Del Priore, *Adoption and Fostering*, vol. 8, no. 4 (1984) p. 38.

Parliament does not use the words 'caused by' or 'the result of', each of which would imply a direct causative link. Bainham thus misleads when he says of the second element that it is 'a causative one'.[85] Harm must be linked to the care given by the parent but it need not be caused by it. The mother who does not prevent her boyfriend sexually abusing her daughter has harmed the daughter and that harm is attributable to the care she has given the child not being what it would be reasonable to expect a parent to give to her. This is the case whether she knows her boyfriend to have such abusive tendencies or not. Of course, it does not follow in such a case that a care order will be made or the child removed from home. Neither the order, nor this action, may be necessary, particularly if the relationship has failed or he is in prison.

The provision would be clearer if 'care' had been defined. Given the problems that failure so to do caused under previous legislation,[86] this may surprise. But it should not do so. There it was important to know whether a child was 'in care' because being in care was a pre-condition to the passing of a parental rights resolution.[87] In this context 'care' has no such consequences: it does not imply a status but deliberately embraces a range of activities from day-to-day interaction at one end of the spectrum to failure to discharge obligations at the other.

The meaning of 'care' becomes clearer when the child is not living with the parent. This situation is worth focussing upon because it is the one which could cause problems. Take the following example. The local authority is providing accommodation for the child and has boarded him out with foster parents. The parents request the child's return. Under the new legislation there is no requirement to give notice[88] and no waiting period.[89] Moving the child, who is well-settled, will cause emotional disturbance. The local authority accordingly wants him to remain where he is. There is

85   Bainham, n. 27, p. 101.
86   See M. D. A. Freeman (1976) 6 Fam Law 136.
87   See Child Care Act 1980 s. 3 and *London Borough of Lewisham* v *Lewisham Juvenile Court Justices* [1980] AC 273.
88   As there was previously when the child had been in care for six months (see s. 13(2) of the Child Care Act 1980).
89   The old law provided for a waiting period of 28 days.

no difficulty about proving the likelihood of the child suffering significant harm. But to obtain a care order it will be necessary to prove that the harm will be 'attributable to' the parents' care. If 'care' were interpreted literally and thus narrowly, it would be impossible to sustain a link. The parents are not looking after the child and they can now do so (let us assume this is not contested): the harm is attributable to the move (perhaps the child has been with the foster parents a considerable period of time). But 'care' must be seen to embrace a wider range of activities than the day-to-day interaction involved in child-rearing. Questions such as: what contact have they had with the child? did they keep access appointments? did they communicate with the child? did they send birthday and Christmas presents? If they have done that which can be expected of reasonable parents, who are themselves prevented from looking after their child, then their 'care' cannot be impugned and a care order cannot be made. The court in those circumstances might well still make a residence order in favour of the foster parents,[90] but this would not result in a forfeiture of parental responsibility.[91] It should be added that a parent who does not 'care' in the sense just adumbrated for reasons which are beyond her control (for example, she is in a psychiatric hospital) will not be able successfully to defend a care order application, if moving the child will cause significant harm, for this will be attributable to her lack of 'care' falling below that of a reasonable parent, such a hypothetical parent not being psychiatrically ill.

Quality of care - and social inequality

The quality of care to activate a care order must fall below what it is reasonable to expect of a parent. The Lord Chancellor, commenting on this provision, said that it 'seems to centre more on the needs of the child whose case is before the court rather than on some hypothetical child and the hypothesis is transferred to the parent'.[92] This poses an objective standard: what it would be reasonable to

90   Under s. 8.
91   Nor would a care order (see s. 2(6)).
92   *Hansard*, HL vol. 512, col. 756.

provide for the child in question. The emphasis is on *this* child, given this child's needs. If he has asthma or brittle bones[93] he may need more care, or a different type of care from 'normal' children. The standard is objective: the parents' quality of care must equal that of hypothetically reasonable parents. Nevertheless, as in the adoption process, it must be assumed that there is a band of reasonableness[94] and not a single right answer. The reasonableness criterion makes no allowance for parents who, for one reason or another, are incapable of meeting the reasonableness hurdle. The feckless, the unintelligent, the irresponsible, the poor, the disadvantaged must compete in the same race as those more fortunately endowed. The problem arose under the old law with the requirement that, for example, the 'juvenile's proper development [was] being avoidably prevented' (in s. 1(2)(a)). The better view was that the fact that the parent had no control over his disability did not make any consequent harm to the juvenile unavoidable.[95] I agree with Bevan's view[96] that *Salford CC v C*,[97] which appeared to decide to the contrary, was wrong. Parliament has now also adopted this view. Reasonable parents do not suffer from disability, any more than they suffer from alcoholism, drug addiction or, for that matter, poverty. All parents come to the judgment seat of care proceedings on an equal footing, however unequal they are in the world outside the court.

Quality of care - and cultural pluralism

The extent to which this provision admits of cultural pluralism is not entirely clear.[98] Bainham's view is that the different situations of ethnic minority groups become relevant at a point where, the ground having been proved without reference to cultural difference, s. 1 comes into play. He points to the checklist of factors in s. 1(3) which includes the 'background' of the child.[99] Thus, using the *Mohamed* v

---

93   *Re Cullimore, The Times*, 24 Mar. 1976; *Re P* [1988] 1 FLR 328. See also the *Guardian*, 20 Dec. 1974.
94   *Re W* [1971] A.C. 682; *Re L* [1990] 1 FLR 305.
95   See Hayes and Bevan, n. 22, pp. 47-8.
96   *Child Law*, n. 4, p. 626.
97   [1981] 3 FLR 153.
98   See generally, S. Poulter, n. 66.
99   Bainham, n. 27, p. 101.

Knott[100] decision, he argues that the girl was suffering significant harm but 'at the second stage . . . the court would need to consider carefully whether the right course of action would be to make an order plucking [her] from her "matrimonial home" and placing her in care'.[101] White, Carr and Lowe state, rather ambiguously, that 'while the new criteria will require the child's circumstances to be put in context, they do not invite unnecessary comparisons'.[102] They do not elaborate upon which circumstances are relevant, what context they are to be placed in, or what is to be deemed a necessary and what an unnecessary comparison. Nor is it, I think, right to assume that the Act looks at social inequality and cultural pluralism identically. Race and culture are identified in the Act as matters to which a local authority which is looking after a child must give 'due consideration'.[103] The ideology of this legislation is committed to cultural pluralism. This should be borne in mind when seeking the true meaning of the provision being analysed. Is cultural difference, then, significant in assessing reasonableness of care? It must be remembered that, although the standard is objective, we are looking at *this* child and his needs. Looked at thus, Muslim children, Rastafarian children, the children of Hasidic Jews may be different and have different needs from children brought up in the indigenous, white, nominally Christian culture. I would that this interpretation were not that favoured by Parliament, but that is because I would prioritise children's rights and because suffocating, inward-looking cultures stunt growth and thwart the development of autonomy. Remember Justice Douglas's eloquent dissent in *Wisconsin* v *Yoder*, when speaking of the education of Amish children, he said that the child 'may want to be a pianist or an astronaut or an oceanographer. To do so he will have to break from the Amish tradition. It is the future of the student, not the future of the parents, that is imperilled by to-day's decision'.[104]

100   [1969] 1 QB. 1.
101   Bainham, n. 27, p. 102.
102   R. White, P. Carr and N. Lowe, *A Guide to the Children Act 1989* (London: Butterworths, 1990) p. 81.
103   See s. 22(5) (c).
104   406 US 205, 244-5 (1972). See also Freeman, above, n. 40, pp. 268-9.

But Parliament, it seems to me, is saying that we must not ignore cultural difference when examining the reasonableness of care. This is not to adopt total relativism: certain standards of care (not permitting a blood transfusion, for example)[105] cannot be countenanced. But, within limits which it would be difficult to define precisely, what constitutes reasonable care will differ in different communities. The Act seems to recognise this.

How, then, would a case like *Mohamed* v *Knott*[106] be decided after the Act comes into operation? The case centred around the question whether a thirteen-year-old from Northern Nigeria, lawfully married under her personal law, could be said to be 'in moral danger' when, it seems, forced to have intercourse before she reached puberty by a man almost twice her age with venereal disease.[107] The justices thought the continuance of such an association 'repugnant to any decent-minded man or woman'.[108] But the Divisional Court did not think this was the test. Said Lord Parker CJ:

> it could only be said that she was in moral danger if one was considering someone brought up and living in our way of life . . . to hold that she is in moral danger . . . can only be arrived at . . . by ignoring the way of life in which she was brought up . . .[109]

The ground of being 'in moral danger' has been removed by the 1989 Act. To sustain a care order it will thus be necessary to prove significant harm attributable to a standard of parental care falling below that which is reasonable. There can be little doubt that a girl in Mrs Mohamed's situation is suffering 'significant harm'. But two further hurdles need to be surmounted. First, can it be said that this harm is 'attributable' to a shortcoming in parental care? Parents in this country who allow their thirteen-year-old daughter to live with

---

105   Cf. *Re T* [1981] 2 FLR 239. See also *Jane* v *Jane* [1983] 4 FLR 712. On scientology see the vigorous indictment of Latey J in *Re B and G* [1985] 1 FLR 134.
106   [1969] 1 QB 1.
107   Though he was desisting from intercourse until his venereal disease was cured.
108   *Mohamed* v *Knott*, p. 15.
109   Ibid., pp. 15-16.

(or marry abroad) any man, let alone the 'bad lot' that Mr Mohamed seems to have been, would indubitably be failing to fulfil their parental responsibilities. But what of parents in Nigeria who, we are led to believe, merely followed the customs and practices of their society? It can still, I think, be said that the harm their daughter was suffering was attributable to their allowing her to marry and leave the home environment for an alien culture where she was likely to lack protection. The harm, it will be remembered, needs only to be linked to failings in parental care, not caused by it. Secondly, did the parents' care fall below that which it is reasonable to expect parents to give to a pre-pubescent daughter? Again, were this a purely domestic case, there would be no doubt whatsoever. But, it is not, and, as I have argued, it is consistent with the ideology of this Act to take account of cultural difference when examining the reasonableness or otherwise of parental care. That could lead us to the conclusion that *Mohamed* v *Knott* would be decided the same way (albeit, obviously, by a different route) as it was by the Divisional Court in 1968. But such a conclusion is not inevitable. Certain standards of parental care, whatever the cultural context, are beyond the pale - and, perhaps, *Mohamed* v *Knott* provides one such example. If so, a law that was not capable of protecting a thirteen-year-old in 1968 may now be a more effective instrument to-day. In a society now sensitised to the problem of child sexual abuse[110] such a conclusion might be both expected and welcomed. This leaves out of account the impact of s. 1. The question is whether such a girl should be removed from her husband. With hindsight we are right to suspect that Mrs Mohamed might well have been better off in care: she divorced her husband within a relatively short time of the case.[111] But it would be wrong to judge a case by what we discover subsequently. No general conclusion on the application of s. 1 can be offered, since each case has to be considered individually. 'Background' is, however, clearly relevant.[112]

---

110 Though it took the *Cleveland* affair in 1987 to do this.
111 With his other wife, they were the first, and so far as is known, the only, wives to divorce the same husband on the same day.
112 See s. 1(3) (d).

Beyond parental control

Under the old law being beyond parental control was one of the primary conditions for a care order. Care proceedings on this ground could be activated, indirectly at least, by a parent. There are thus changes, both substantive and procedural, in the new legislation.

First, the procedural change. No longer will parents be able to request the local authority to bring their child before the court or to apply by complaint to a juvenile court for an order directing an authority to do so, where the authority refuses or fails to comply with the request within 28 days. Conflicting views were expressed to the Ingleby Committee,[113] some 30 years ago, on the desirability of this parental right. On the one hand, it was suggested that it might lead to an irreparable breach of relationship with the child; on the other, that it might have a salutary effect and might strengthen the relationship.[114] Until now, the latter consideration has prevailed. The new legislation seems to be influenced more by the former, though there was all-party support for an amendment that would have allowed an application for a care order by any person with parental responsibility.[115] It is difficult to estimate the significance of this change. Although the number of care orders made on the ground of 'beyond parental control' was quite high,[116] it is not clear what percentage of these orders stemmed from parental initiative. The wardship route is also now closed to parents.[117] They can still, however, request that the local authority provides accommodation for a child with whom they cannot cope.[118] This may cause problems with adolescents, particularly where authorities have adopted policies not to use voluntary receptions for children over a particular age.

113   See Cmnd 1191.
114   See paras 120-34.
115   See HC Debs, 23 May 1989, Standing Committee B, cols 218-22.
116   In 1980 10% of the orders made were on this ground.
117   *A v Liverpool CC* [1982] AC 363.
118   See s. 20.

Reference was made during debates at the Committee stage of the House of Commons to one London authority which has a policy of not receiving children over thirteen into voluntary care.[119] But this fetters discretion and is thus potentially amenable to challenge by judicial review.[120] This is the ultimate remedy upon which parents may have to fall back.

The substantive change is that being beyond parental control survives as a ground only where there is significant harm to the child, or its likelihood, and this is attributable to the child's being beyond parental control. Children who are beyond parental control often harm others (for example, nine-year-olds who burgle), but that will not satisfy the threshold conditions of s. 31(2)(ii), unless it can be shown that the child himself is also likely to suffer significant harm. Proving that the sexually promiscuous teenager or the glue-sniffing child is suffering significant harm will not be difficult, but courts may have to stretch a point to attribute this to their being beyond parental control. A difficulty may also arise over the concept of control. It is not entirely clear whether this is an objective standard (is the child beyond the control of a *reasonable* parent?) or a subjective one (is he beyond the control of *his* parents?) The point is not unimportant because different parents exercise, and believe in, different standards of control. There are class and cultural differences. To what extent is it permissible to take cognisance of these? Since this limb of the section makes no reference to reasonableness, it has to be assumed that the subjective test applies. Most children who are beyond an objective standard of parental control and are suffering, or are likely to suffer, significant harm will probably fit into the parental upbringing limb. A few, however, will not do so. Perhaps this *lacuna* is inevitable: it might not be thought to be right to impose objective standards of control on parents.

A final point to note concerns the meaning of 'parental'. It must be assumed, given the nature of this legislation, that the epithet is wide enough to embrace all those who are exercising parental functions and responsibilities. If that is not so, we have a *lacuna* in the legislation of some importance. For example, if a mother who

119   *Per* R. Sims MP, Standing Committee B, col. 227.
120   *A-G (on the relation of Tilley)* v *Wandsworth LBC* [1981] 1 All ER 1162.

cannot cope asks the child's grandparents to care for the child and the grandparents cannot control the child such that he associates with drug-takers or steals, the possibility of recourse to care proceedings ought to be open. There is some support for my interpretation in Masson's commentary.[121] But this assumes the retention of the ground itself can be justified.

As a matter of policy we must be left with the nagging doubt that being beyond parental control is not just a relic of the old law (as White, Car and Lowe observe),[122] but a hangover from a pre-*Gillick* era.[123] It is a status 'offence'[124] and may well interfere with a child's civil liberties. The child who breaks the law may deserve to be punished but how does one who is troublesome and refractory deserve to be treated?

The new ground - the gaps

The new unified ground has now been analysed. It will be apparent that a number of the primary conditions found in the 1969 legislation have no place in the new structure. Have gaps been created and, if so, intentionally or unintentionally?[125] Are there situations in which a care order could previously have been sought but where that possibility is now foreclosed? References have already been made to some differences: others will now be explored.

(i) bringing an offender into the household

The New Act contains no 'Kepple' clause.[126] This was added by the Children Act 1975 in the wake of the Maria Colwell case.[127] It was an imperfect instrument for, although the list of offences in Schedule

---

121   Masson, n. 26 (comment on s. 31 at p. 70).
122.   White, Carr and Lowe, n. 102, p. 81.
123   *Gillick* v *West Norfolk and Wisbech Area Health Authority* [1986] AC 112.
124   I discuss these in *The Rights and Wrongs of Children*, n. 40, pp. 79-81.
125   See *Re Y* [1988] 1 FLR 299 and *Re L, The Independent*, 23 Mar. 1990.
126   William Kepple was Maria Colwell's stepfather. He was found guilty of her murder, but the Court of Appeal substituted a finding of manslaughter. See, generally, *Report of the Committee of Inquiry into the Care and Supervision Provided in Relation to Maria Colwell*, HMSO, 1974.
127   Sch. 3, para. 67.

1 of the 1933 Act were wide in range, these were limited to earlier offences against juveniles under 16. William Kepple himself, the nominal target of the clause, had many convictions, including a number for violent offences, but none came within the schedule.[128] It is arguable that the provision ought to have embraced all offences of violence and arguably sexual offences against adults (particularly, as Bevan argues, against mentally defective women).[129] Further, proving someone who was not a member of the household might become so was a heavy burden to discharge, though it may be that courts did not over-trouble themselves with evidentiary niceties. The provision was not much used and its demise should not cause problems. If the bringing of a child molester into the house is likely to put the child at risk of suffering significant harm and this risk is attributable to failing in parental care (as it must be because a reasonable mother would put her child's welfare before the relationship with the molester), a care order will be made. The new unified ground also overcomes problems in the 'Kepple clause'. There is no restriction to Schedule 1 offences and the interpretational problems associated with 'household'[130] do not have to be confronted.

(ii) another child of the household

It was possible under the old law for a care order to be made in respect of C2 when the primary condition in paragraph (a) (but only that one) is or was satisfied in the case of C1 who is or was a member of the household to which C2 belongs. It made no difference that C1 was no longer a juvenile or was dead[131] or that care proceedings were never brought in respect of C1. The condition would not operate, however, if C1 were, to use Bevan's example, a 20 year old son who is mentally infirm.[132] The meaning of 'household' was liberally

---

128 But the *Auckland* case, roughly contemporaneous with Colwell, would have been caught by the so-called 'Kepple' clause. See *Report of the Committee of Inquiry into the Provision and Co-ordination of Services in the Family of John George Auckland*, HMSO 1975.

129 *Child Law*, n. 4, p. 631.

130 See *R v Birmingham Juvenile Court ex parte N* [1984] 2 All ER 688.

131 See *Surrey CC v S* [1974] QB 124.

132 *Child Law*, n. 4, p. 628.

construed in *R* v *Birmingham Juvenile Court, ex parte N* [133] where the mother of the two children was the same, but they had different fathers. Again, the new unified ground covers this situation, and avoids the problems associated with the meaning of 'household'. It should also enable a care order to be made (subject, of course, to s. 1) where 20-year-old mentally infirm siblings are ill-treated.

(iii) truancy

Truancy is no longer a ground for a care order. It is possible (though not I think, intended) that it may come within s. 31(2) where the blame for non-attendance lies with the parents. The parent who keeps the child off school so that he can help in the shop or so mollycoddles the child that he seldom attends school clearly comes within the new unified ground. But these are not the paradigmatic cases, nor is it intended that non-attendance at school will be tackled in this way. Instead, s. 36 provides education supervision orders as the main method for dealing with children who truant from school. In addition, it will remain possible to prosecute parents under the Education Act [134] though the sanction of imprisonment of parents has now been removed.[135]

Some concern has been voiced that it will no longer be possible to make care orders on truants. But the concern centres mainly on the new inability to continue the so-called 'Leeds experiment' under which applications for care orders were continually adjourned, so that the threat is constantly hung over the heads of children who had records as persistent truants.[136] The system is said to have worked, though the evidence is equivocal, but the practice was of dubious legality.[137] The new legislation's timetabling provisions (in s. 32) would have brought the practice to an end (or

---

133   [1984] 2 All ER 688. The width of the interpretation is drawn attention to by S. Cretney, *Principles of Family Law* (London: Sweet and Maxwell, 1984) p. 530.

134   Education Act 1944, s. 37 (5), 39 (1).

135   Schedule 15.

136   See I. Berg *et al.* (1978) 18 *Br J of Criminology* 232, discussed by M. D. A. Freeman, *Legal Action Group Bulletin,* June 1980, p. 135, 137.

137   For agreement see Hayes and Bevan, n. 22, p. 54.

unduly constrained it). But the removal of the freestanding condition of truancy as a ground for a care order cuts off the life blood of the practice. Whether education supervision orders will work remains to be seen. Many will regret the demise of the 'Leeds system'.

(iv) moral danger

The removal of the moral danger condition should not cause problems because the extension of the new unitary ground to cover prognosis of harm should cover most, if not all, cases for which it was used. But problems may occur where attribution to failings in parental upbringing are difficult to establish (for example, the sixteen-year-old boy involved in homosexual activities, where no exploitation is involved) and where, possibly as in the previous example or where promiscuity is involved, s. 1 considerations militate against the making of an order. This they will clearly do if it is likely that the making of a care order will only make a bad situation worse.

(v) the juvenile offender

Under the previous law it was possible to make a care order where a juvenile was guilty of an offence (but not homicide).[138] Had the possibility of prosecuting juveniles for criminal offences been removed, as was intended,[139] this procedure would have become the norm. But prosecutions remained possible, were preferred by the police, magistrates and even social workers and were, as a result, used to the almost total exclusion of care proceedings (where, in addition to proof of the offence, it was also necessary to prove the juvenile was in need of care or control). So few cases were brought under this ground that the publication of statistics failed to distinguish between juveniles committed to care under this primary ground and those for whom care orders were made in the course of criminal proceedings (under s. 7(7) of the 1969 Act).

138   Children and Young Persons Act 1969, s. 1(2)(f).
139   See A. Morris *et al., Justice For Children* (London: Macmillan, 1980), D. H. Thorpe *et al., Out of Care: The Community Support of Juvenile Offenders* (London: Allen and Unwin, 1980) chapter 1.

The Act specifically abolishes both the power to make a care order on proof of the offence condition under s. 1(2)(f) (see s. 90(1)) and the powers of the court to make care orders under s. 7(7) and s. 15(1) of the 1969 Act (where a supervision order was discharged) (see s. 90(2)).

It may still be possible to secure a care order where a child commits a criminal offence, but only where the threshold conditions of s. 31(2) are proved. It will not be easy to establish that the child either is suffering, or is likely to suffer, significant harm attributable to failing in parental upbringing or, more likely, being beyond parental control. It may, however, be possible where the criminal activity is itself dangerous (for example, involvement in violent activities or drug-taking).

The s. 7(7) care orders in criminal proceedings are abolished and replaced by supervision orders with a residence requirement (with a maximum of six months) under s. 12AA of the 1969 Act (see Schedule 12, paras 22-5). This new sentence can only be imposed where a further serious offence, punishable by imprisonment for someone over 21, is committed by someone already subject to a supervision order with a requirement under 12A(3) of the 1969 Act or a residence requirement. The court must also be satisfied that the behaviour which constituted the offence was due, to a significant extent, to the circumstances in which the offender was living (see s.12AA(6) of the 1969 Act).

We are told the intention is to:

> put another step on the escalator of criminal penalties
> . . . to prevent (young offenders) from reaching the
> point on the escalator which amounts to custody. One
> can draw a clear distinction. Being required to live in
> a residential accommodation will not involve the total
> deprivation of liberty that would be involved in being
> placed in a custodial institution.[140]

The Government's motives are apparent enough but the use of care as punishment stigmatises the whole care system. One of the supposed

---

140   *Per* David Mellor MP, Standing Committee B, cols 502-3 (13 June 1989).

objectives of the new legislation is to destigmatise care. A feared unintended consequence of this provision may be a reluctance to recommend supervision powers because of their triggering effect. There is also the danger that care provision will become saturated with offenders to the detriment of children in need of care. Coupled with this is the worry that inappropriate placements will have to be made where there are suitable ones. All in all, it would not be unfair to say that this provision wreaks of the regressive and retributive, and seems to pay scant attention to the exigencies of children's lives.[141] It is a sad reflection of this Government that its concern for children (if indeed it is real, which is dubious) has to cede to its blinkered commitment to 'law and order' policies.[142] Its refusal to grasp the nettle of corporal punishment, in a measure concerned to protect children from abuse, is also part of this dissonance.

On the other hand, it is possible that the new order may be seen as too lenient with the result that those who, in the past, might otherwise have been committed to care will be pushed up the tariff to a custodial sentence.

A final problem with the new order concerns the question as to whether it may be made on an offender who is already being looked after by a local authority, either as a result of accommodation being provided or by reason of a care order. There is nothing in the Act to prevent such an order being made but it may look incongruous and could lead to such children being pushed up the tariff. If it does, it will have the effect of discriminating against the disadvantaged children who will continue to make up the bulk of the 'care' population.[143]

(vi) cases under section 3 of the Child Care Act 1980

Local authorities will no longer be able to assume parental rights in respect of children in their voluntary care. Where they are providing accommodation for a child and wish to retain that child, it will now be necessary to use care proceedings and prove the minimum conditions

---

141   See, further, my 'Children's Charters and Children's Acts' in *IRCHIN Newsletter*, Nov. 1989.
142   See M. D. A. Freeman (1984) 37 CLP 175.
143   See *Rights and Wrongs of Children,* n. 40, pp. 148-50.

in s. 31(2). Are there grounds in s. 3 of the Child Care Act 1980, upon which parental rights could be assumed by virtue of resolution, that do not fit within the new unitary ground?

Several, it would seem, are problematic. Where parents are dead or have abandoned a child (s. 3(1)(a) and (b)(i)), it is difficult to see s. 31(2) being satisfied, in the first case because there is no parental shortcoming and, in the second, because although in paradigmatic cases of abandonment (leaving in a bus shelter, etc.) the statutory test will clearly be satisfied, most cases of abandonment are 'statutory abandonment', that is to say parents not notifying their address to the local authority for twelve months (see s. 3(8) of the Child Care Act 1980) and this provision is repealed by the new legislation and no equivalent presumption is substituted. The second case is obviously of greater concern but it is difficult to see how an order can be obtained if the parents can provide appropriate care.

The controversial three years ground (s. 31(1)(d)) introduced in 1975 and reported to be in frequent use,[144] is not covered in the new legislation. It was introduced to alleviate the problem of children who 'drifted' in care[145] and to assist long-term planning. The whole rationale of the three years' provision was to assist decision-making for children in care where there was no parental fault. It is difficult, accordingly, to see how (or why) s. 31(2) should be satisfied. Of course, if Adcock *et al.*'s finding[146] can be generalised there should be no problem. They found that in all but four of their 71 'three years children' another ground could have been used. The problem then may be more apparent than real, though a residue of cases would not have fitted into another s. 3 ground and, it is submitted, will accordingly slip through the s. 31(2) net.

The three years plus child is likely to be with foster parents. They will be able to apply for a residence order under s. 8 and s. 10(5)(b), where the child has lived with them for a period of at least three years, and under s. 10(5)(c)(iii), with the consent of those with

---

144		H. Cain, *Adoption and Fostering*, vol. 5, no. 4 (1981) p. 17 and M. Adcock
		et al., *The Administrative Parent* (London: BAAF, 1983) p. 48.
145		The so-called 'children who wait' (see J. Rowe and L. Lambert, *Children
		Who Wait* (London: ABAA, 1973).
146		Adcock, *et al.*, n. 144, pp. 48-50.

parental responsibility. If the child has not lived with the foster parents for three years then, unless they are relatives, the consent of the local authority is a pre-requisite for an application for a residence order (see s. 9(3)).

(vii) care and matrimonial proceedings

Under the previous legislation it was possible to commit a child to care in the course of a plethora of other proceedings, of which one further example will be singled out for discussion: namely, matrimonial, and in particular, divorce, proceedings.[147] The ground for the care order was that there were 'exceptional circumstances making it impracticable or undesirable' for the child to be entrusted to the care of a parent or other individual. An order directing that children in care remain in care made in the course of s. 41 certificate of satisfaction proceedings is not a care order.[148]

It will remain possible to make a care order in course of divorce proceedings but only where the threshold conditions of s. 31(2) are satisfied. There can be little doubt that in some cases they will be satisfied but in others, though the broad discretion in s. 43 of the Matrimonial Causes Act 1973 would have allowed for a care order to be made, the more carefully circumscribed conditions in the 1989 Act will not be met. A good illustration is afforded by *R* v *G (Surrey CC intervening)*.[149] An order was made (and upheld by the Court of Appeal) where it was the intention of the local authority to leave one of the two children with the father. It was said that a valuable purpose of the procedure under s. 43 was to enable a local authority to see whether a child could be rehabilitated with a parent. If this failed, the child could be removed promptly without the expense and delay of further recourse to the court. A supervision order would not allow this to be achieved. Sir John Arnold P interpreted 'entrusted' to mean clothed with total responsibility for the child's upbringing. 'Nothing short of that . . . amounts to entrusting the child to that parent or individual'.[150] This father could

---

147   Under s. 43 of the Matrimonial Causes Act 1973.
148   *Re W* [1989] 1 FLR 47.
149   [1984] 3 All ER 460.
150   Ibid., p. 467.

not have total responsibility entrusted to him because he was unable or unwilling to arrange access to the mother. This broad interpretation to s. 43 and its flexible use will now, it is thought, be lost, somewhat ironically given the emphasis the new Act gives to parental responsibility,[151] with the repeal of s. 43 and the new overarching unitary ground. If the child is likely to suffer significant harm it is difficult to see how he can be entrusted even partially to a parent: if he is not likely to suffer significant harm, there is no scope for a care order. Although a supervision order would have the disadvantage, already referred to, it may be that it would be the more appropriate order (particularly in the light of s. 1(5)) but it has to be stressed that the minimum conditions of s. 31(2) need to be satisfied equally and, in the absence of fear of significant harm, it will not be possible to do so.

(iv) wardship

With another contribution to this volume on wardship,[152] it is only necessary here to offer a few comments on the future interaction of care and wardship. The restrictions on the use of wardship are controversial, and justifiably so. They are, however, at one with the philosophy and structure of the Act: without imposing restrictions on inherent jurisdiction the establishment of a single standard of intervention (the 'significant harm' test in s. 31(2)) would have been rendered nugatory.[153] Accordingly, the Act restricts the local authority's recourse to wardship in three ways.

First, the High Court's powers to commit a child to care in s. 7 of the Family Law Reform Act 1969 are abolished (s. 100(1)). The High Court will still be able to make a care order but only where the grounds in s. 31(2) are satisfied.

Secondly, the inherent jurisdiction of the High Court cannot be exercised to require a child to be placed in care, supervised by a

---

151   See s. 3.
152   That by Martin Parry (see Chapter 10).
153.   Though the decision to restrict its use was a late decision (see Lord Mackay's *Jackson Lecture* (1989) 139 NLJ 505, 507). But problems will occur: see, for example, *Re P* [1987] 2 FLR 467 (wardship used where there was suspected child sexual abuse which it was difficult to prove). See also the Wayne Brewer case in 1977.

local authority, or accommodated by or on behalf of a local authority. In addition, it cannot be exercised to make a child subject to a care order a ward. Wardship and local authority care are incompatible. These provisions (in s. 100(2)(a)(b) and (c)) are clear but s. 100(2)(d) is not so straightforward. It prevents the High Court from exercising its inherent jurisdiction[154] 'for the purpose of conferring on any local authority power to determine any question . . . in connection with any aspect of parental responsibility for a child'. Three cases must be distinguished. If there is a care order, the local authority will already have 'power' since parental responsibility will vest in it. Thus, if a fourteen-year-old in its care is pregnant, then it, subject to the *Gillick* principle,[155] may consent to an abortion: it cannot, as in *Re P*,[156] divest itself of this responsibility by warding the girl and letting the court take the decision. If there is conflict with the girl's parents, the option of a neutral decision-maker is removed. Where there is no care order then, if the local authority is providing accommodation, it may do what is reasonable in all the circumstances of the case for the purpose of safeguarding or promoting the child's welfare (s. 3(5)). Consenting to an abortion would, it is submitted, fall outside the reasonableness criterion (in the context of medical treatment this extends to that which is routine, and no further).[157] The authority can neither make the decision itself, nor ask the High Court to give it power to make the decision. In the third case, the child is as yet outside the local authority's ambit of authority. It cannot invoke the inherent jurisdiction of the court in order to protect the child (unless the case fits within s. 100(4) and (5) and it cannot apply for a specific issue order (see s. 9(5)(b)).[158] One result of the latter two examples (provision of accommodation and being outside authority control) is

154 And note Lord Mackay's comment (ibid.) that:
  wardship is only one use of the High Court's inherent *parens patriae* jurisdiction . . . it is open to the High Court to make orders under its inherent jurisdiction in respect of children other than through wardship.

155 That is, following Lord Scarman's reasoning, rather than Lord Fraser's.

156 [1986] 1 FLR 272 (a 1981 case).

157 For agreement (on this point) see Bainham, n. 27, p.20.

158 Masson, n. 26, expresses a different view (commentary on s. 100 at p. 171).

that local authorities may feel pressurised into seeking care orders. In the sorts of situations envisaged here they may fail to secure them, not because they cannot satisfy a court of the minimum conditions in s. 31(2), but because of s. 1(5). It may come to be seen that removal of the option of wardship was shortsighted.

Thirdly, if the local authority wishes to apply to the court for an order under the inherent jurisdiction it must obtain leave (see s. 100(3)) and satisfy the conditions in s. 100(4) and (5). Leave will only be granted if the result could not be achieved by the local authority applying for an order other than by exercise of the court's inherent jurisdiction, *and* there is reasonable cause to believe that the child will suffer significant harm if the jurisdiction is not exercised. The first of these pre-requisites will make it difficult for a local authority to obtain leave where the child is not in its care, because the Act provides a range of orders for which the authority may apply (from care and supervision orders to prohibited steps and specific issue orders). The second requires there to be, in the court's view, 'reasonable cause' to believe that the child will suffer 'significant harm'. Whilst it may be that Parliament thought that the insertion of 'reasonable cause' posited a lower standard of intervention than that required for a care order, I doubt if it will be so interpreted. This means that a local authority will have to satisfy the same 'significant harm' test, even though it does not wish to acquire parental responsibility. There was surely a strong case for arguing that a lower standard should need to be satisfied for intervention on a single issue of upbringing.[159] It is unfortunate that a legislature sensitive to gradations in other areas should, on this question, resort to thinking in terms of black (a transfer of parental responsibility by means of a care order) and white (no state intervention).

There are a few situations in which s. 100(4) and (5) should be satisfied. It must be assumed that Parliament does not wish to gainsay Lord Templeman's *dictum* in *Re B*,[160] so that a local authority must seek the leave of the High Court before consenting to a sterilisation operation on a child in its care. Following a change in

---

159   For agreement see Bainham, n. 27, p. 202. See also N. Lowe (1989) 139 NLJ 87 and J. Eekelaar and R. Dingwall (1989) 139 NLJ 217.

160   [1989] AC 189, 205. See also Heilbron J in *Re D* [1976] Fam 185.

Government thinking, clearly emphasised in Lord Mackay's *Jackson* lecture, what the authority must seek to invoke is inherent jurisdiction rather than wardship.[161] The difference is more than one of verbiage: by seeking inherent jurisdiction the authority will be asking the court to rule on one question only and not, as with wardship, transferring parental authority to the Court so that all major decisions[162] have to be taken by it.

Other examples where the use of inherent jurisdiction may remain possible are (i) to seek an injunction to prevent someone molesting a child (as in *Re B*)[163] or to prevent someone, for example a violent father, from discovering a child's whereabouts (as in *Re JT*)[164] and (ii) to restrain harmful publicity about a child (as, for example, in *Re L*).[165] More troublesome is the thorny problem of the defective neonate.[166] Whether such a child should live or die has twice been taken to English wardship courts. In the 'Baby Alexandra' case in 1981[167] the Court of Appeal ruled that a life-saving operation, to remove an intestinal blockage on a Down's Syndrome baby, should be performed. It upheld the right of life where it could not be shown that such life was demonstrably awful. In *Re C*,[168] where the local authority had decided to make the child a ward before she was born for reasons unconnected with her medical condition, the child suffered from massive handicap and no treatment could alter the hopeless prognosis. She was 'terminally ill before she was even born'.[169] It was inconceivable that she would develop any appreciable skills: she was blind, probably deaf, had spastic cerebral palsy of all four limbs and was severely mentally handicapped. The Court of Appeal agreed with the first instance judge who held that life-prolonging treatment should be withheld. It also stated that the

161   See *Jackson Lecture*, above, n. 154.
162   *Re CB* [1981] 1 All ER 16.
163   [1975] Fam 26.
164   [1986] 2 FLR 107.
165   [1988] 1 All ER 418. See also *Re C* (No. 2) [1990] 1 FLR 263; *Re M and N* [1990] 1 FLR 149.
166   See the discussion in *Rights and Wrongs of Children*, n. 40, pp. 259-63.
167   [1981] 1 WLR 1421.
168   [1990] 1 FLR 252.
169   Ibid., p. 254.

public interest required 'the court's decision and the reasons for it should be open to public scrutiny'.[170] Will cases like *Re B* and *Re C* get public scrutiny at all when the Children Act comes into operation? The two cases have to be distinguished. The criterion for leave (in s. 100(4)(b) is satisfied in *Re B* (if the court's inherent jurisdiction had not been exercised Alexandra would have suffered significant harm - death). But this is only so because it was decided that her life could not be shown to be demonstrably awful. Does this mean that the court should err on the side of opening jurisdiction when taking the leave decision? I should have thought so, if for no other reason than that life and death decisions should be publicly scrutinised. In *Re C*, however, it is difficult to see how the 'significant harm' criterion would be met, but much would depend upon what was meant by harm. The baby in *Re C* was dying and would die within months rather than years whatever the court did. Could it, therefore, be said that she would be likely to suffer 'significant harm' if leave were not granted? It is unfortunate that decisions like that in *Re C* may now be taken without the opportunity for a court to supervise them. Other methods of accountable review are accordingly required.[171]

One final example of where inherent jurisdiction will not be possible where wardship has previously been invoked is the sort of situation which arose in the colourful case of *Re SW*.[172] An unruly, 'beyond control' adolescent approaching her eighteenth birthday was, of course, beyond the protective jurisdiction of care but she could be, and was, warded. I am not alone in thinking that this was an inappropriate use of wardship. It was an infringement of civil liberties and a circumvention of legislation which limited care applications (as under the new legislation) to those under 17.[173] It was also a temporary stop-gap action. Even were the facts of *Re SW* to satisfy the leave requirement in the new legislation (and how could invoking inherent jurisdiction prevent 'significant' harm?), s. 1 would now make it virtually certain that no action under children's legislation be taken. Criminal proceedings, which were in any event

---

170   Ibid., p. 260.
171   See I. Kennedy and A. Grubb, *Medical Law* (London: Butterworths, 1989) pp. 498-528.
172   [1986] 1 FLR 24.
173   See J. Eekelaar (1986) 28 *Childright* 9, 10.

being taken in *Re SW*, would be the likeliest alternative, though the possibility of action under mental health legislation cannot be totally ruled out.[174]

These restrictions on wardship were, and are, controversial. Problems may occur, as Lord Mackay acknowedged, in 'difficult borderline cases where at present wardship . . . would offer a remedy'.[175] It is to be expected that these cases will be taken by the High Court and much will depend on how it interprets the minimum conditions in s. 31(2). But, as a matter of policy, it is surely right that state intervention into the lives of families should be circumscribed by grounds and not left to depend on notions of welfare.

Conclusion

The new structure has to be accounted an improvement upon the old. It is more coherent, better-geared to the needs of families and fairer. But, as I hope I have shown, it is replete with interpretational problems, complexities remain and uncertainties abound.

If I may end, as I began on a personal note. Some three years ago (at Hong Kong 'Sevens' time) Hugh Bevan gave a paper at Hong Kong University on the 'Jeanette' case.[176] 'If Michael Freeman were present' he is reported to have said, 'he would disagree with me'. Unbeknown to Hugh I was actually 100 yards away. Not that he can reasonably have been expected to anticipate this! I don't know what Hugh said about *Re B* but it is a fair bet that I would have disagreed with him since on that case I seem to disagree with almost everyone.[177] He, I am sure, will disagree with things I say in this article. But, fortunately, he is not far away. I hope in the years to come he will continue to participate actively in academic debate. I look forward to reading what *he* has to say about the shape of 'care' to come.

---

174   If there were 'mental disorder' under Mental Health Act 1983.
175   See the *Jackson Lecture,* above n. 153, at p. 507.
176   *Re B* [1988] AC 199.
177   See 'Sterilising the Mentally Handicapped' in M. D. A. Freeman, *Medicine, Ethics and the Law* (London: Stevens, 1988) p. 55.

7

Children's Education and the European Court of Justice

Mark Gould

Discussion of educational rights in English law has traditionally concerned the provision of particular types of education.[1] Rights in European Community law have tended to come about as a result of economic factors.[2] Children do not usually play a major part in the economy, but European Community law has become increasingly involved with those aspects of education which fall within the competence of the Community. In particular, EC law requires a reduction of inequality between certain Community citizens in some educational matters. The extent to which such inequalities may be

I am grateful to my colleague Nigel Lowe for reading and giving extensive comments on an earlier draft of this essay. However, responsibility for all remaining errors is mine.

1   H. K. Bevan, *Child Law* (London: Butterworths, 1989) chapter 11. More generally, see K. P. Poole, *Education Law* (London: Sweet and Maxwell, 1988).

2   Particularly in relation to the 'four freedoms': freedom of movement of goods, persons, services and capital.

reduced by reference to Community law depends *ratione personae* on the status of the particular individual and *ratione materiae* on the type of education concerned. My aim here is to assess the impact of Community law on children's educational rights. In what ways and to what extent does European Community law extend educational rights to children? To answer this question it is convenient to distinguish between those educational rights which accrue to the children of migrant workers within the Community and those which apply more generally to all Community citizens.[3]

Educational rights for the children of migrant workers

The right to free movement for workers is one of the fundamental freedoms of the Treaty of Rome. The basic principle is found in Article 48 EEC, with Article 49 EEC providing for Community legislation to eliminate obstacles to this freedom of movement. As a matter of logic it would seem that only those obstacles which *prevent* free movement should be the subject of legislation. It is not clear that educational discrimination against Community nationals already resident in another Member State constitutes a barrier to the free movement of workers. In this context, then, it must be argued that social and cultural inequality would have the effect of deterring workers from migrating. If this argument is accepted, Community law may be utilised to combat such inequality. However, this approach may be problematic.

The Treaty of Rome is virtually silent as to the advantages to be afforded to the families of migrant workers. Article 51 EEC allows the extension of particular social security rights to migrant workers and their dependants.[4] More detailed provisions on the rights accruing to workers' dependants were included in later legislation adopted pursuant to Articles 49 and 51 EEC. Most important for our purposes is Regulation 1612/68 on freedom of movement for workers

---

3   I shall be concentrating on the developments of these rights by the European Court of Justice since the legislation in this area generally creates opportunities for non-national education rather than rights.

4   This provision was given a broad interpretation by the European Court of Justice in Case 44/65, *Hessische Knappschaft* v *Maison Singer* [1965] ECR 965.

within the Community.[5] The preamble to this Regulation refers to the fundamental right of free movement for workers and their families and to the need to eliminate obstacles to this mobility 'in particular as regards . . . the conditions for the integration of [the worker's] family into the host country.' The connection between these objectives and the aims of Articles 48 to 51 EEC are clear and uncontroversial. My argument here is that the European Court of Justice has interpreted the provisions of Regulation 1612/68 so broadly in the creation of educational rights as to strain the connection with the fundamental Treaty principle of free movement of workers.[6]

Casagrande and Article 12 of Regulation 1612/68

Article 12 of Regulation 1612/68 allows the children of migrant Community workers access to education in the host State on the same terms as nationals of that State. The plaintiff's father in *Casagrande* v *Landeshauptstadt München*[7] was an Italian migrant worker who died in 1971. The plaintiff (a life-long resident of Munich) relied on the right conferred by Article 12 of Regulation 1612/68 to claim a means-tested grant so that he could continue at school into the 10th class in the academic year 1971/72. The federal German law on educational grants only provided aid to those children in the classes above the 10th. The Bavarian law, however, made funds available to those pupils in the 5th to 10th classes who satisfied certain conditions. One of those conditions was that the claimant be a German national, a stateless person or an alien who had been given political asylum. Because Casagrande did not fall into any of these categories, his application was refused. He appealed to the Bavarian Administrative Court, which made a reference to the European Court of Justice under Article 177 EEC. The Bavarian law clearly discriminated against

5   JO 1968 L 257/2 (OJ Eng. Spec. Ed. 1968 (II) p. 475).
6   The Court does not see its interpretative task in strict legal terms; preferring teleological or purposive methods of interpretation. See H. Kutscher, 'Methods of Interpretation as seen by a Judge at the European Court of Justice' *Reports of the Judicial and Academic Conference* (Luxembourg: Court of Justice of the European Communities, 1976).
7   Case 9/74 [1974] ECR 773.

Community nationals, but it was argued that this was not contrary to Community law because the Community had no competence in the field of educational policy. The Court of Justice dismissed this argument. Whilst accepting that educational policy itself was not a matter for the Community, it stated that 'it does not follow from this that the exercise of powers transferred to the Community is in some way restricted if it is of such a nature as to affect the measures taken in the execution of a policy such as that of education and training.'[8] The fact that Community policy may infringe upon an area of national competence does not, therefore, inhibit that policy. In the result, therefore, the plaintiff had a right to consideration for a maintenance grant on the same basis as a German national. This case was closely followed by *Alaimo* in which the judgment was succinctly stated: 'Article 12 of Regulation No. 1612/68 must be interpreted as ensuring for the children referred to an equal position with regard to all the rights arising from admission to educational courses'.[9]

To further the aim expressed in the preamble to Regulation 1612/68 (that of integrating the worker's family into the host country) Article 12 provides that:

> the children of a national of a Member State who is or has been employed in the territory of another Member State shall be admitted to that State's general educational, apprenticeship and vocational training courses under the same conditions as the nationals of that State, if such children are residing in its territory.

Secondly:

> Member States shall encourage all efforts to enable such children to attend these courses under the best possible conditions.

There is immediately apparent a distinction between the two paragraphs of this Article. The first confers a right to equal treatment as regards the formal conditions for entry into education. The second

8   [1974] ECR 773 at 779 (consideration 12).
9   Case 68/74, *Alaimo* v *Préfet du Rhône* [1975] ECR 109 at 114.

refers to the problems that might arise from the substantive inequalities existing between children. This latter provision does not require the elimination of these inequalities, however. Were one to take a legalistic view of these provisions, Casagrande's claim to a maintenance grant should have failed. On this analysis, the discrimination in considering students for such funding falls within the second paragraph; not being a condition for access to education *stricto sensu.*[10] The Court did not take such a robust view. Instead it seemed inclined to conflate the two paragraphs of Article 12.[11] Reading the Article as a whole it then concluded that:

> in providing that the children in question shall be admitted to educational courses 'under the same conditions as nationals' of the host state, Article 12 refers not only to rules relating to admission, but also to general measures intended to facilitate educational attendance.[12]

Article 12 after *Casagrande*

Following *Casagrande* it would appear that the main function of the Court in interpreting Article 12 is to determine exactly which children are included in this provision. Since the clear intention of the Court is that *ratione materiae* the Article includes virtually everything affecting admission to education, its extent *ratione personae* must be considered. In *Brown* v *Secretary of State for Scotland*[13] the petitioner was born and educated in France and his parents had not worked in the United Kingdom since before he was born. It was held that these circumstances did not entitle him to education in the United Kingdom on the same footing as if he were a UK resident or his parents had worked in the UK during his lifetime.[14] Similarly, in

---

10   In fact the maintenance grant was an important condition of access, as was evidenced by the fact that Casagrande did not continue in school when the grant was refused.
11   [1974] ECR 773 at 79 (consideration 8).
12   [1974] ECR 773 at 779 (consideration 9).
13   Case 197/86 [1988] 3 CMLR 403.
14   He did have rights under other aspects of Community law than Article 12 of Regulation 1612/68, however. See below and Mark Gould, 'Equality of Access to Education?' (1989) 52 MLR 540.

Humbel,[15] the Court ruled that the child of a French migrant worker resident in Luxembourg was not entitled to remission of educational fees payable in respect of his schooling in Belgium. The question arose because Luxembourg nationals were not required to pay these fees, irrespective of their status. The Court was unable to ascertain why this was so. Arguably, if it resulted from a bilateral agreement between Belgium and Luxembourg, Humbel should have been able to succeed.[16]

In *Echternach and Moritz*[17] both plaintiffs had been refused student allowances as they did not hold the residence permits required by the Dutch authorities to classify them as foreign students entitled to be treated as nationals. They claimed that their right to equal treatment arose from EC law, rather than Dutch law. The Dutch authorities argued that Echternach was not the child of a Community worker, since his father worked for the European Space Agency, an international organisation governed by a special statute under international law, and that Moritz was not the child of a worker from another Member State as his father had returned to his State of origin after having been employed in the Netherlands. The Court held that:

> a Community national working in a Member State other than his State of origin does not lose his status as a worker within the meaning of Article 48(1) of the Treaty by occupying a post in an international organisation, even if the conditions of his entry and residence in the State in which he was employed were specifically governed by an international agreement concluded between the international organisation and the State in which it had its seat.[18]

---

15   Case 263/86, *Belgium* v *Humbel* [1989] 1 CMLR 393.
16   See Case 235/87, *Matteucci* v *Communauté Française Belgique* [1989] 1 CMLR 357, and below, n. 51, and associated text.
17   Joined Cases 389 and 390/87, *Echternach and Moritz* v *Netherlands Minister for Education and Science* (judgment of 15 Mar. 1989, not yet reported).
18   *Ibid.*, consideration 11 (my translation).

As a result such a worker's child could rely on the same rights as the child of any other Community migrant worker. As regards the child of a returning migrant worker, the Court looked simply at the wording of Article 12 which extends to the child of a national of another Member State who 'is or has been employed' in the host State. It could be argued that this phrase was intended to apply only to those workers who had lost their jobs but still remained resident in the host State, but in the absence of any words to the contrary the Court of Justice held that the plaintiff Moritz was clearly included.[19]

Having held that the plaintiffs fell within the ambit of Article 12, the Court commented:

> The Court has already decided that a grant made for maintenance or for education with a view to the pursuit of secondary or post-secondary level studies should be considered as a social advantage within the meaning of Article 7(2) of Regulation 1612/68, to which migrant workers are entitled under the same conditions as nationals of the host State. The same principle should be applied to the children of these workers where they are admitted to education in the host State by virtue of Article 12 of this Regulation since any other interpretation would often deprive the Article of all effect.[20]

Given that *Casagrande* provides adequate justification for the extension of Article 12, it may be wondered whether this more fully reasoned justification was necessary. It may be that the Court wished to base that decision *ex post facto* on a firmer, more rational, base. If this is so then the decision in *Echternach and Moritz* has little additional importance, except insofar as a clearer analysis makes the task of the Court of Justice and of national courts easier. On this basis the case could be equally restrictive or liberalising. More plausibly, if

---

19   This case is different to that of *Casagrande*, not least in the fact that the student had left the territory of the host State only to take up residence later. It is disappointing to see little made of these differences by the Court of Justice.

20   *Echternach and Moritz*, consideration 34 (my translation).

only because the *Casagrande* formula has already been stated in the previous paragraph of the judgment, the Court may have had in mind a restatement of the effect of Article 12. Interestingly, although Article 7(2) of Regulation 1612/68 is mentioned, no real emphasis is placed on it. At this point it is appropriate to give an outline of the effect of this provision on children's and educational rights.

Social advantages and children: *Michel S.*

Regulation 1612/68 is concerned primarily with creating a Community-based framework within which workers may exercise the right of free movement. As such, the majority of its provisions apply to workers themselves rather than to their dependants. Superficially only provisions such as Articles 10-12 of this Regulation, which are specifically directed to the families of migrant workers, seem to extend rights to people who are not workers. Such an interpretation would require that Article 7 could only apply to workers themselves.[21] In early cases regarding the concept of 'social advantages' in Article 7(2) the Court of Justice followed this strict interpretation. In *Michel S.*[22] it rejected a claim that Article 7 could extend to workers' families by reference to the wording of the Article itself and to the fact that Regulation 1612/68 divided the provisions affecting workers from those regarding their families and other

21   Article 7 reads, in part, as follows:
        1.   A worker who is a national of a Member State may not . . . be treated differently from national workers by reason of his nationality in respect of any conditions of employment or work, in particular as regards remuneration, dismissal, and should he become unemployed, reinstatement or re-employment.
        2.   He shall enjoy the same social and tax advantages as national workers.
        3.   He shall also . . . have access to training in vocational schools and retraining colleges.

22   Case 76/72, *Michel S.* v *Fonds national de reclassement social des handicapés* [1973] ECR 457. In this case no great injustice was done since the Court held that the benefit sought (specialised training and rehabilitation for a mentally handicapped young person) fell within the scope of Article 12 of the Regulation.

dependants by placing them in separate Titles within the Regulation. Following this and other early cases, it seemed that the rules for applying Article 7(2) were clear: 'The social advantages within the meaning of [the Article] should be connected with employment, they should benefit the workers themselves, and they should not benefit family members.'[23] In order to extend the concept to encompass educational rights for workers' children, it would appear to be necessary to break at least two, if not all, of these rules.

Expanding Article 7(2): *Cristini*

In *Cristini*[24] Article 7(2) was given a broad interpretation. Here the plaintiff, the widow of an Italian migrant worker and resident in France, applied for a card entitling her and her four children to reduced price travel on French national railways. The application was refused, and the plaintiff appealed. During the hearing of the appeal, the European Court of Justice was asked to consider whether the reduction card was a social advantage within the meaning of Article 7(2). If the three rules outlined above were to be followed, there would be no possibility of including such a benefit within this provision. The card was not connected with employment: it was intended as a mainly demographic measure to ensure that those with large families were not disadvantaged in the state provision of transport.[25] In this case it could not benefit the worker on whom the claim was based, since he was dead; consequently, it benefitted only members of the worker's family.[26]

The Court first considered the concept of 'social advantages' in the context of the other provisions of Article 7. It noted that not all

---

23   David O'Keefe, 'Equal Rights for Migrants: The Concept of Social Advantages in Article 7(2), Regulation 1612/68' (1985) 5 *Yearbook of European Law* 93 at 99.

24   Case 32/75, *Cristini* v *SNCF* [1975] ECR 1085.

25   See also a later case where a childbirth allowance was held to constitute a social advantage: Case 65/81, *Reina* v *Landeskreditbank Baden-Württemberg* [1982] ECR 33.

26   *Quaere* what the position would have been if the worker had still been alive? There would clearly have been a benefit to him as he would have had to spend less on travel with the card than without it. This consideration may have informed the Court's decision.

those provisions concerned rights arising out of a contract of employment: provisions on reinstatement and re-employment,[27] for example, have nothing to do with such a contract. Having made this point, the Court obviously felt that the term 'social advantages' could not be interpreted restrictively, and therefore had to include almost all social and tax advantages to which a national worker has access. This broad interpretation also enabled workers' families to benefit on the same terms as the families of national workers. Since the worker in this case was dead, the Court relied again on the comparison with a national worker and on Regulation 1251/70,[28] which confers a right of residence on the families of deceased Community workers who had themselves acquired such a right, and extends the right to equality of treatment established by Regulation 1612/68 to such families.[29]

It is difficult to see how the two years between *Cristini* and *Michel S.* (even when coupled with a more detailed examination of Article 7(2)) could result in such a change in the Court's position. Outside the Court, however, a definite (although slight) change in the Community's goals may be discerned. A summit conference of Heads of State or Government held in Paris in October 1972 affirmed that the economic expansion encouraged by the Treaties was not an end in itself, but should also have the effect of improving the quality of life and (more importantly) the standard of living of Community citizens. As one of its formal conclusions the conference emphasised that as much importance was attached to vigorous action in the social field as to Economic and Monetary Union.[30] This initiative followed publication by the Commission of 'Initial guidelines for a social policy programme' in 1973.[31] The first concrete result of all this was the Council Resolution of 21 January 1974 concerning a social action programme.[32] These developments took place (for the most part) between the Court's judgments in *Michel S.* and *Cristini*. It would be surprising if this subtle change in emphasis went unnoticed by the

---

27   Article 7(1).
28   JO 1970 L 142/24 (OJ Eng. Spec. Ed. 1970 (II) p. 402).
29   Article 7, Regulation 1251/70.
30   See Bull. EC 10-1972 pp. 14-23 for the complete text of the 16-point declaration.
31   Bull. EC 5-1971 pp. 5-10 and 13-19. The Guidelines are in Bull. EC Supp. 2/71.
32   OJ 1974 C 13/1.

Court of Justice and, whilst it may not fully explain the change of heart between these cases,[33] such a change may be symptomatic of a more general alteration in the Community's objectives.[34]

The effect of *Cristini* is to change the criteria for determining the extent of entitlement to social advantages. Now the test is whether a particular advantage is granted to workers generally by virtue of their status as workers or by the fact of their residence in the national territory irrespective of any link with a contract of employment. If this is so, and it therefore seems appropriate to extend them to Community workers in order to facilitate the free movement of workers within the Community, then such advantages will fall within Article 7(2).[35] As the Court stated in *Deak*,

> a worker anxious to ensure for his children the enjoyment of the social benefits provided for by the legislation of the Member States . . . would be induced not to remain in the Member State where he had established himself and found employment if that State could refuse to pay the benefits in question to his children because of their foreign nationality.[36]

Now the important question for the Court to answer is whether denial of a particular advantage would induce a migrant worker not to

---

33   A number of other factors may have come into play, such as the fact that the plaintiff in *Cristini* may have been perceived as being 'deserving'.

34   Contemporaneous changes within the Community included the accession of three new Member States, with a concomitant expansion in the personnel of the European Court of Justice.

35   This definition is taken from Case 249/83, *Hoeckx* v *Openbaar Centrum voor Maatschappelijk Welzijn Kalmthout* [1985] ECR 973 at 988 (consideration 20) and Case 122/84 *Scrivner* v *Centre Public d'Aide Sociale de Chastre* [1985] ECR 1027 at 1036 (consideration 24), but has been used on a number of occasions by the Court of Justice.

36   Case 94/84, *Office National de l'Emploi* v *Deak* [1985] ECR 1873 at 1886 (consideration 23). In this case the Court of Justice held that Article 7(2) could extend to all Community migrant workers' children irrespective of the child's nationality.

remain in the host State.[37] To what extent do educational advantages fall within the ambit of Article 7(2)?

Education as a social advantage

Before *Echternach and Moritz* only three cases decided by the European Court of Justice had considered the concept of 'social advantages' in the context of education.[38] In two of these cases the plaintiff claimed the social advantage as a migrant worker rather than as such a worker's dependent. In the third, the plaintiff's status was uncertain.

In *Lair* the Court of Justice had no difficulty in finding that a grant for maintenance during university studies fell within Article 7(2) because such grants were available to national workers and on the ground that such a course was intended to improve vocational qualifications and promote the individual's career advancement.[39] Clearly this is a case of 'levelling the playing field' for all workers. However, the Court tied the provision of a maintenance grant as a social advantage to courses which were related to the worker's previous work activity.[40] This was done so that these students could retain their worker status and therefore continue to rely upon Article 7 (2).[41] The plaintiff in *Lair* had clearly established herself in the host

37 This question is tempered somewhat by the existence of directives regarding the transferability of specific benefits; most notably Directive 1408/71, JO 1971 L 149/2 (OJ Eng. Spec. Ed. 1971 (II) p. 416). Article 7 (2) may be seen, therefore, as a kind of safety net.

38 Case 39/86, *Lair* v *Universität Hannover* [1989] 3 CMLR 545; Case 197/86, *Brown* v *Secretary of State for Scotland* (above n. 13) and Case 235/87, *Matteucci* v *Communauté Française Belgique* (above, n. 16).

39 [1989] 3 CMLR 545 at 564 (considerations 18-28).

40 Thus implicitly overruling the judgment of Dillon J. in *MacMahon* v *Department of Education and Science* [1982] 3 CMLR 91 at 96.

41 [1989] 3 CMLR 545 at 566 (consideration 39). This need to connect the course with previous employment is at odds with the Court's broad interpretation of Article 7(2) earlier in the case. How, for example, can a worker wishing to effect a career change rely on Article 7(2)? Such a course would plainly not be connected with previous employment, but with that envisaged for the future. Further, in consideration 37, the Court envisaged a suspension of the need for a link with previous employment in cases where a plaintiff has become involuntarily employed and needs to undergo retraining in another field of activity. This gloss was not added to the operative part of the judgment.

State, having lived in the Federal Republic of Germany for over five years and working sporadically for periods amounting to almost three years before starting a course at University there. The petitioner in *Brown*, however, worked in the host State for only eight months before going to University. Further, he only obtained this employment by virtue of already having gained a place at University. In these circumstances, the Court held that such a person could not be considered to be a 'worker' within the terms of Regulation 1612/68 and therefore could not claim a grant for maintenance as a social advantage.[42] In neither of these cases could the Court consider the position of a migrant worker's child.[43]

In *Matteucci* it was not clear if the plaintiff was a worker or whether she was dependent on her father, an Italian migrant worker resident in Belgium. She had worked as a teacher of eurhythmics whilst still studying in Brussels. By a bilateral agreement between Belgium and the Federal Republic of Germany, a number of scholarships were made available for Belgian nationals to study in Germany. Matteucci applied for one of these scholarships in order to undertake a course in Berlin. Her application was not forwarded to the German authorities for consideration on the ground that she did not have Belgian nationality. The plaintiff claimed that Articles 7, 48 (as implemented by Regulation 1612/68), 59, 60 and 128 EEC gave her the right to consideration for these discretionary awards on the same terms as Belgian nationals. As the scholarship was intended solely for the student's maintenance, the Court had to choose whether to apply Article 7(2), 7(3) or 12 of the Regulation.[44] In his Opinion the Advocate General, Sir Gordon Slynn, confirmed that the scholarship could fall within the ambit of each of these provisions.[45]

---

42   [1988] 3 CMLR 403 at 423 (consideration 27).

43   Brown did attempt, unsuccessfully, to rely on Article 12: see above, n. 14, and associated text.

44   The question whether education is to be considered a 'service' in Community terms (Articles 59 and 60 EEC) was ignored in this case, but in *Humbel* the Court found that it was not. The use of Articles 7 and 128 EEC is restricted solely to questions of access to education, the limitations of which will be seen in the next section.

45   The Advocate General assists the Court by making reasoned submissions on the cases before it: Article 166 EEC. These Opinions are not binding on the Court.

He then turned his attention to differences in result arising out of the alternative determinations of the plaintiff's status.[46] This is important because different criteria apply to those rights accruing to migrant workers and to those which may be relied upon by their children. We have already seen how Article 7(2) requires a course to be related to previous employment. Article 7(3) only allows equal consideration in respect of courses in 'vocational schools', a term which the Court of Justice interpreted narrowly in *Brown*.[47]   As a worker the plaintiff could rely on Article 7(2) and/or Article 7(3). As a worker's child she could rely on Article 7(2) and/or Article 12. An additional complication arises out of the fact that her rights under Article 7(2) are not the same whatever her status. If she were a worker, the course to be undertaken would have to be related to her previous employment (following *Lair*) for her to be able to claim equal consideration for the scholarship under this provision. However, as a worker's child, she could obtain the same result whether or not the course were related to any particular type of work. Slynn AG regarded it as possible that she could be deemed to be dependent on her father, despite her part-time employment, and so be eligible to be considered under Article 7(2).

In order to rely on Article 7(2) the migrant worker's child must still be dependent on the worker. Article 12 may not require such dependence,[48] but if it may be prayed in aid by all children of Community migrant workers, whatever their state of independence, some anomalies may result:

> It may seem strange that a child of a migrant worker who is an adult should . . . acquire rights to education not open to workers in the light of the Court's judgments in *Lair* and *Brown* that the rights to

46   The question of the plaintiff's status is one for the national court to decide, relying at least in part on definitions laid down by the European Court of Justice.

47   'The term vocational school . . . refers solely to establishments which provide only instruction interposed between periods of employment or else closely connected with employment.' [1988] 3 CMLR 403 at 421 (consideration 12).

48   This was the opinion of the European Commission, expressed in its submissions to the Court of Justice in this case.

education under Article 7(2) are limited to courses
where there is a link between the previous occupation
and the studies in question.[49]

Balancing this problem with the need to encourage 'mobility
and integration of workers and their families', Slynn AG was of the
opinion that Article 12 should apply if the child is ineligible under
Article 7. Thus, a migrant worker who is herself the child of a
Community migrant worker and who wishes to undertake an
educational course may fall foul of the stringent requirements of
Article 7 but still acquire educational rights denied to other
community migrant workers through the operation of Article 12.[50]
The Court neatly avoided this question by basing its judgment on the
assumption that the plaintiff was a worker and therefore only
considering Article 7.[51] It thus tacitly presaged the increased
importance of Article 7(2) in *Echternach and Moritz*.

Article 7 or Article 12?

The position now for the educational rights of migrant workers'
children is unsatisfactory. The Court of Justice has shifted its
emphasis from Article 12 of Regulation 1612/68 to Article 7(2) of the
same Regulation. This change of emphasis has raised a number of
unresolved problems. What is the practical difference (if any) for
dependent children between these two provisions? After *Matteucci*,
are migrant workers who are also children of migrant workers
precluded from pursuing claims under Article 12? The sole guidance

---

49   Case 235/87 [1989] 1 CMLR 357 at 366 *per* Slynn AG.
50   Slynn AG was aware of the problems this could cause as successive
      generations of migrant workers spread throughout the Community, see
      [1989] 1 CMLR 357 at 366.
51   Since the plaintiff's claim appeared to fall within the narrow constraints of
      Article 7, and bearing in mind the Court's apparent reluctance to say any
      more than is necessary to decide a case, this course of action is not
      particularly surprising. However, it means that direct comparison between
      this case and *Humbel* is made more difficult; especially as regards the
      arrangement whereby Belgium did not impose the *minerval* (a tax on
      foreign students) on Luxembourgeois students.

is the Court's dictum in *Echternach and Moritz* that the effects of Article 7(2) in respect of educational rights should extend to migrant workers' children. This, taken with the *Matteucci* decision, seems to indicate a move away from reliance in this respect on Article 12.[52] Justification for this may be found in the potential extent of Article 12 (as outlined by Slynn AG in *Matteucci*), and in the fears expressed by the Member States about the economic, social and constitutional implications of the Community's foray into the educational sphere.[53] Article 12 would allow a larger number of people to claim educational rights than would Article 7(2). What remains to be seen is how, and whether, the Court will continue the move away from reliance on Article 12.

General Community educational rights

Article 128 EEC provides that 'the Council shall . . . lay down general principles for implementing a vocational training policy.' Those general principles are to be found in Council Decision 63/266.[54] Community law thus may have a direct influence on educational policy.[55] This influence is, however, restricted to vocational training. Further, it may be argued that since Decision 63/266 does not actually establish such a policy then the Community's influence is all the more limited.[56] However, through the operation of Article 7 EEC, the Community may exert a more real, although indirect, influence on the provision of vocational training by the Member States. Article 7 EEC forbids all discrimination on the ground of nationality within the scope of the Treaty. It is by invoking Articles 7 and 128 EEC that individuals who are neither migrant workers nor migrant workers' dependants may claim limited educational rights under Community

52   See also *Humbel*, decided on the same day as *Matteucci*.
53   These misgivings have been expressed in the submissions by various Member States (particularly the Federal Republic of Germany and the United Kingdom) to the Court in a number of the 'education cases' and, more generally, over the LINGUA and ERASMUS programmes instituted by the Community in the late 1980s.
54   OJ Eng. Spec. Ed. 1963/4 p. 25.
55   Although it has no competence to formulate such a policy.
56   Decisions of the Council are not generally binding on the Member States: Article 189 EEC.

law. The first case in which the European Court of Justice considered such rights was that of *Forcheri*.[57]

A right to education or vocational training: *Forcheri*

Mrs Forcheri was the wife of a Community official of Italian nationality and resident in Belgium. She undertook a three year course in Brussels, for which she had to pay an enrolment fee (called the *minerval*) in addition to the tuition fees. The *minerval* was levied only on foreign students whose parents were not resident in Belgium (with the exceptions of some French and all Luxembourgeois students). In challenging the apparently discriminatory *minerval*, Forcheri sought to rely on Articles 7, 48 and 49 EEC, Article 12 of Regulation 1612/68 and the Protocol on Privileges and Immunities of the European Communities.[58] In the proceedings for a preliminary ruling, Rozès AG's opinion was uncompromising. Community officials are not regarded as migrant workers for the purposes of Articles 48 and 49 EEC and Regulation 1612/68, and thus the only connection with Community law is through the Protocol on Privileges and Immunities. Relying on Case 208/80,[59] she noted that the Member States must refrain from impeding the internal functioning of the Community. She did not regard the imposition of the *minerval* as being sufficiently general or direct to constitute such an impediment.[60]

The Court ignored these problems, instead producing Article 128 EEC like a rabbit from a hat.[61] Analysing this Article and Decision 63/266, the Court noted that 'the opportunity for [educational and vocational] instruction falls within the scope of the Treaty,'[62] Its final judgment was brief and potentially far-reaching:

57   Case 152/82, *Forcheri* v *Belgium* [1983] ECR 2323.
58   Despite the fact that Article 12 refers specifically to children, the Court could have interpreted this broadly to include all dependants of migrant workers (or at least spouses). Were the question to arise now with the spouse of a migrant worker, it is more likely that the Court would utilise Article 7(2) as detailed above.
59   Case 208/80, *Lord Bruce of Donnington* v *Aspden* [1981] ECR 2205.
60   [1983] ECR 2323 at 2341.
61   [1983] ECR 2323 at 2335 (consideration 14).
62   [1983] ECR 2323 at 2336 (consideration 18).

> If a Member State organises educational courses relating *in particular* to vocational training, to require of a national of another Member State *lawfully established* in the first Member State an enrolment fee which is not required of its own nationals in order to take part in such courses constitutes discrimination by reason of nationality, which is prohibited by Article 7 of the Treaty.[63]

After *Forcheri*, then, it would appear that all Community citizens who are lawfully established in Member States other than their own have a right to equal access to educational courses (not just vocational training).[64]

Vocational training: *Gravier* and after

The plaintiff in *Gravier*[65] was a French national, resident in France, who registered for a course in strip-cartoon art in Belgium. She applied for exemption from the *minerval*, but was refused it. The question for the Court of Justice was whether she had a right to equal access to this course. The Court ignored the question of lawful establishment, central to the *Forcheri* decision. The student in this case was the holder of a residence permit solely by virtue of her status as a student; when she refused to pay the *minerval*, she was refused enrolment and that permit lapsed. The question of establishment was bound up with the point at issue here. It is also difficult to contemplate systematic controls for Community nationals at the point of entry.[66] Thus, it is probably in the interests of equity and

63   [1983] ECR 2323 at 2337-8 (operative part of the judgment) (my emphasis).
64   Anne de Moor has expressed concern that the requirement of lawful establishment contradicts the apparently general application of Articles 7 and 128 EEC: 'Article 7 of the Treaty of Rome Bites' (1985) 48 MLR 452 at 455-6.
65   Case 293/83, *Gravier* v *City of Liège* [1985] ECR 593.
66   Indeed the Court has ruled that such controls, if intended to determine whether nationals fall within the free movement provisions of the Treaty, are forbidden by Community law: Case 157/79, *R* v *Pieck* [1980] ECR 2171.

practicability that the benefits of equal access to education are left open to all Community citizens.

Having broadened the *Forcheri* principle in one regard, the Court then apparently narrowed it in another.[67] In *Forcheri*, the Court of Justice appeared to forbid discrimination between Community nationals in the provision of all types of education. In *Gravier*, however, the Court concentrated on conditions of access to vocational training. It seems that this concentration on vocational training is a restriction of the *Forcheri* principle, but this is not certain. The Court did not make this distinction, but only used the phrase that had been used by the national court in the questions it had referred. However, successive cases have concerned 'vocational training' rather than general education, and so it may be accepted that the *Gravier* principle is the better one. An indication that the Court in Gravier intended to restrict the extent of the *Forcheri* decision may be found in the definition of 'vocational training' which it provides:

> Any form of education which prepares for a qualification for a particular profession, trade or employment or which provides the necessary training and skills for such a profession, trade or employment is vocational training, whatever the age and the level of training of the pupils or students and even if the training programme includes an element of general education.[68]

This is clearly very wide, although it is narrower than the *Forcheri* definition, and may in some measure supplant that definition. Can it still be argued that *Forcheri* still applies when a plaintiff is not caught by *Gravier*?[69]

Before deciding whether *Forcheri* is still good law, it is necessary to ascertain the precise boundaries of *Gravier*. This case

---

67   This argument is made by James Flynn, '*Gravier*: Suite du Feuilleton' in Bruno de Witte (ed.) *European Community Law of Education* (Baden-Baden: Nomos, 1989) 95 at 99.

68   [1985] ECR 593 at 614 (consideration 30). It is for the national court to determine whether a particular course falls within this definition.

69   This question will be considered below.

left a number of questions unresolved. Does the decision apply only to discrimination in the level of fees charged for vocational training or, more broadly, to all factors which determine whether or not a student takes up a place at an educational institution? How much of a particular course may be general education before it falls outside the *Gravier* definition? Does the right to non-discrimination mean that non-workers gain the same or similar advantages as migrant workers and their dependants? Some of these questions have been addressed in more recent cases.[70]

Refining the *Gravier* principle

In *Blaizot, Lair* and *Brown* the Court of Justice had to consider whether the *Gravier* definition of vocational training could include university-level education. *Commission* v *Belgium* (Case 293/85) was also concerned with this point, but was dismissed by the Court on procedural grounds. Slynn AG did, however, consider the substantive point and concluded that university-level studies could be regarded as vocational training. As with any other level of training, such university courses would have to prepare for a qualification, or provide the necessary skills and training, for a profession, trade or employment. Courses which were intended to provide only a general education are not vocational:

> Thus, courses which essentially are intended to increase knowledge or cultural awareness or 'develop the mind' would ordinarily be excluded. A course in literature, mediaeval history or classics may be invaluable for the successful career diplomat, the politician or the clergyman but they do not have a

70   Since *Gravier* the Court has considered discrimination between
Community nationals in the provision of vocational training in seven cases:
Cases 293/85, *Commission* v *Belgium* [1989] 2 CMLR 527; 309/85, *Barra*
v *Belgium* [1988] 2 CMLR 409; 24/86, *Blaizot* v *University of Liège*
[1989] 1 CMLR 57; 39/86, *Lair* v *Universität Hannover* (above, n. 38);
197/86, *Brown* v *Secretary of State for Scotland* (above, n. 13); 263/86,
Belgium v *Humbel* (above, n. 15) and 42/87, *Commission* v *Belgium* [1989]
1 CMLR 457.

sufficiently direct link with the skills needed in those particular professions.[71]

In *Blaizot* the Court agreed that excluding university courses from the *Gravier* definition could lead to disparities between Member States, as there was no common definition of the concept of university-level education, and vocational training in the narrowest sense may be carried out at this level in some Member States but not in others.[72] Finally, in *Brown*, the Court of Justice turned the definition round; now all university courses can be considered to be vocational, except for general courses:

> In general university education fulfils [the conditions for vocational training], with the exception of certain special courses of study which, because of their particular nature, are intended for persons wishing to improve their general knowledge rather than prepare themselves for an occupation.[73]

The Court's definition of 'vocational training' is not concerned with the level of the institution or the career intentions of the student, but with the content of the course. Is this satisfactory? If, for example, a student wished to become a translator, a modern languages course (at any level) would be vocational in the general sense of the word; for a different student on the same course whose intention was to become a language teacher, the course would be similarly vocational; for a student who wished to pursue some career entirely unconnected with language skills, such a course would not be vocational. Slynn AG's response to this type of argument is to avoid it: if a course is specifically geared to training translators or teachers then it is vocational, otherwise not.[74] This cannot be an equitable solution, since it could lead to students choosing particular courses

71   [1989] 2 CMLR 527 at 540, *per* Slynn AG. In *Lair*, however, the national court apparently accepted that a degree course in Romance and Teutonic languages and literature was vocational.
72   [1989] 1 CMLR 57 at 66 (consideration 18).
73   [1988] 3 CMLR 403 at 420 (consideration 10).
74   [1989] 2 CMLR 527 at 540.

purely because they had been deemed to be vocational rather than because of their actual merits.[75] The alternative, however, would be to throw away the *Gravier* definition altogether and open up all types of education to free access for all Community students. This kind of 'academic tourism' would be unacceptable to a large proportion of the Member States.[76]

In *Humbel* the Court was asked, in effect, whether the *Gravier* definition extended to general secondary education. The course at issue here was one of six years' duration; divided into three 'degrees' of two years each. In the fourth year during which the defendant's son studied general subjects, he was charged a *minerval*. The final 'degree' was clearly vocational, as was conceded by both the parties, and no *minerval* was charged. The defendant's argument was that, since completion of the fourth year of study was necessary in order to proceed to the vocational stage, that year (and presumably all those previous) should also be considered to be vocational. The Court clearly saw the logic of this argument, but was concerned not to extend the definition of vocational training to include all types of education:

> The different years of a programme of instruction should not be viewed as separate parts but must be considered in the framework of the entire programme and in particular its purpose, provided that the programme constitutes an indivisible whole and that it is not possible to distinguish one part which does not constitute vocational training and another part which meets this definition.[77]

---

75 This could lead in turn to a kind of ghettoisation, with non-national students taking only 'vocational' courses, while national students had a full choice of courses.

76 See, however, Case 242/87, *Commission* v. *Council* (judgment of 30 May 1989, not yet reported) where the Court upheld the legal basis of the ERASMUS Decision (Articles 128 and 235 EEC), ruling that most ERASMUS activity in universities would be concerned with vocational training, and that that small proportion which was not could not take the programme as a whole outside the bounds of Article 128 EEC (consideration 27).

77 [1989] 1 CMLR 393 at 404-5 (consideration 12).

National courts must therefore determine whether a particular course leads inexorably to another, vocational, course.

Once a course is deemed to fall within the Court of Justice's definition of vocational training, what benefits may non-national students claim equally with national students? In *Gravier* the Court was concerned with a financial barrier to access to training for non-national students. However, it accepted 'that the conditions for access to vocational training fall within the scope of the Treaty',[78] and therefore that discriminatory application of these conditions of access as between Community nationals is prohibited by Article 7 EEC. No cases have yet arisen of discrimination in the application of non-financial conditions of access, but *Lair* and *Brown* raised the question of grants for maintenance, which were only payable to non-national students who fulfilled particular conditions not applied to nationals.[79] The plaintiffs did not fulfil these conditions, and argued that they were discriminatory and that a maintenance grant was a condition of access to vocational training. The Advocate General was sceptical:

> Though of course I realise that if a student cannot eat or have a bed he cannot study, it does not seem to me that the means of subsistence have a sufficiently direct link with access to the course itself to fall within the principle of non-discrimination spelled out in *Gravier*.[80]

The Court agreed that maintenance grants were excluded, but for slightly different reasons. Following submissions made by the government of the Federal Republic of Germany, it held that the provision of maintenance grants was a matter of the Member States'

---

78   [1985] ECR 593 at 613 (consideration 25).

79   In *Lair*, s. 8(2) of the German Federal Act on Training Grants only allowed educational grants to be payable to non-nationals who had been engaged in full-time employment in the Federal Republic for at least five years (excluding periods of unemployment). In *Brown* the law required applicants to have been ordinarily resident in the British Isles for at least three years, or resident in the EC for the same period and employed in Scotland for nine of the preceding twelve months, or to be the child of an EC national employed in Scotland.

80   [1988] 3 CMLR 403 at 413.

educational policy and thus outside the Community's competence.[81] In addition, such provision is an aspect of social policy which was not included in the EEC Treaty.[82] This legalistic argument can be criticised, since the Court has been dabbling on the fringes of educational policy in many of the cases already discussed. The decision appears to be symptomatic of the way in which the Court pragmatically limits the effects of its earlier cases (*Gravier* in this instance) in its successive judgments.[83]

Education as a service?

One question raised in the *Gravier* reference, but not answered by the Court of Justice is whether education is a service. This is important because of the Court's ruling in *Luisi and Carbone*:

> The freedom to provide services includes the freedom, for the recipients of services to go to another Member State in order to receive a service there, without being obstructed by restrictions, even in relation to payments . . . tourists, persons receiving medical treatment and persons travelling for the purpose of education or business are to be regarded as recipients of services.[84]

This was a case where the restrictions were applied by the home State, rather than that in which the services were received, and may thus be limited in its effect. It was, further, argued by the plaintiff in *Gravier* and, later, the defendant in *Humbel* that education was a service within the meaning of Articles 59 and 60 EEC.[85]

81   [1988] 3 CMLR 403 at 421 (consideration 17).
82   [1988] 3 CMLR 403 at 421 (consideration 18). See Joined Cases 281, 283-5 and 287/85, *Germany* v *Commission* [1987] ECR 3203.
83   For a more detailed analysis of this aspect of the case see Gould (1989) 52 MLR 540 at 548-50.
84   Joined Cases 286/82 and 26/83, *Luisi and Carbone* v *Ministero del Tesoro* [1984] ECR 377 at 403 (consideration 16).
85   Article 60 (1) EEC provides that 'services shall be considered to be "services" within the meaning of this Treaty where they are normally provided for remuneration.'

Is education 'normally provided for remuneration'? In order
to answer this question in the affirmative it was argued in both cases
that reliance should be placed on the Opinion of Warner AG in
Debauve.[86] He stated that the broadcasts in question were a service
'no matter from whom in any particular case payment may come or
may not come.'[87] If education were to be included within Articles 59
and 60 EEC then discrimination in the provision of education would
be caught by Article 7 EEC.[88] Slynn AG was not convinced by the
Debauve argument:

> [Warner AG] was . . . concerned in that case with
> television programmes financed either by licence fees
> paid by those who had television sets or by fees for
> advertisers. It does not seem to me that he had in mind
> the present question where the State pays for what is
> said to be a service out of State taxes.[89]

The Court in *Gravier* was content to rest on Article 128 EEC and
therefore ignored the question of education as a service. In *Humbel*,
however, it had no such choice. With the minimum of discussion, the
Court followed Slynn AG:

> Firstly, by establishing and maintaining [a national
> education] system the State does not engage in
> activities for which remuneration is received, but is
> fulfilling its duty to its people in the social, cultural
> and educational fields. Secondly, the system in
> question is generally financed by the public budget
> and not by pupils or their parents.[90]

86   Case 52/79, *Procureur du Roi* v *Debauve* [1980] ECR 833.
87   [1980] ECR 833 at 876.
88   This would provide a wider base than Article 128 EEC, since there would
      be no need to distinguish between vocational and other forms of education.
89   [1985] ECR 593 at 603.
90   [1989] 1 CMLR 393 at 405 (consideration 18).

By losing any real link with remuneration, education cannot be regarded as a service for the purposes of Articles 59 and 60 EEC.[91]

Gravier or Forcheri ?

The state of development of the educational *jurisprudence* of the European Court of Justice has come to a natural break. Arising out of the conjunction of Articles 7 and 128 EEC there is a general Community right to non-discrimination in the conditions of access to vocational training, as defined in the cases from *Gravier* to *Brown*. These conditions of access only encompass direct measures taken to restrict or impede entry to such courses: they do not include indirect measures such as maintenance grants. Education is not a service in Community law. But what of *Forcheri*? Has this case been overruled or just ignored? The rights conferred by this decision were simultaneously wider and narrower than those in *Gravier* and its successors. Has the Court retreated from this position? It could be argued that *Forcheri* is still good law and that *Gravier* was in fact only a slight redefinition of the *Forcheri* principle occasioned by the particular facts in that case. The plaintiff in *Forcheri* was already lawfully established in the host State, whereas those claiming rights in subsequent cases were resident solely for the purposes of undertaking vocational training.[92] It seemed to be accepted by the Court in later cases that residence for the purpose of vocational training was a Community right.[93] However, cases may arise where the plaintiff is seeking clearly non-vocational training (thus falling outside *Gravier*), but is lawfully established in another Member State. If this lawful

---

91   The Court has not ruled on the *Luisi and Carbone* argument, but it is most likely that that case does not extend to restrictions applied by the host State.

92   Unless they were workers, as in *Lair*.

93   Julian Lonbay points out that:

> in 1985, after *Gravier*, the Commission amended the [proposed Right of Residence Directive (OJ 1979 C 207/14 amended by OJ 1985 C 171/8)] to exclude from its scope those seeking vocational training. Clearly they were of the view that *Gravier* implicitly gave such a right, and thus its inclusion in the proposal would be otiose.

('Education and the Law: The Community context' (1989) 14 EL Rev 363 at 381).

establishment does not arise from the plaintiff's relationship with a worker, then it could be contended that *Forcheri* applies. The situation would be comparable to that in the United States of America, where the Supreme Court has ruled that a state statute restricting financial assistance for higher education to nationals or aliens who have applied for US citizenship, or who have filed a statement of intent so to apply, discriminates unconstitutionally in breach of the Fourteenth Amendment.[94]

Forcheri would therefore be a safety net for those who fall between the *Gravier* line of cases and the worker-related provisions.[95] However, such an interpretation would require two conflicting interpretations of Article 128 EEC. In *Forcheri* the Court held that through this Article and Decision 63/266, 'the opportunity for [educational and vocational] instruction falls within the Treaty.'[96] In *Gravier*, however, these provisions only encompassed vocational training. There is nothing in the Treaty to suggest that one class of Community citizens (those lawfully established in another Member State) should acquire a right denied to the commonality.

Concluding remarks

The answer to the question 'In what ways and to what extent does European Community law extend educational rights to children?' may be simply stated. Those children who can rely on the worker-related provisions of EC law enjoy equal access to all aspects of education, including grants for their maintenance. However, those children who wish to travel abroad for their education cannot necessarily rely on these provisions and must, therefore, ensure that the course which they wish to attend is one of vocational training, as defined by the Court of Justice.

---

94   *Nyquist* v *Mauclet* 432 US 1 (1977).
95   Some little support for this argument is provided by the Opinion of Slynn AG in *Gravier*. He appears to distinguish the *Gravier* situation (Community citizen moving in search of vocational training) from that in *Forcheri* (pre-established Community citizen wishing to undertake course in host State); [1985] ECR 593 at 600.
96   [1983] ECR 2323 at 2336 (consideration 18).

This simple answer is inadequate since it gives only a partial view of the situation at present, and gives no indication of possible directions of the law in the future. Judging from the changes in the position of the Court of Justice on this issue in the past, it would be illogical to assume that the extent of children's educational rights in Community law is now settled. In some respects the Court has based its judgments on shaky ground, in others it has created artificial distinctions which may ultimately be difficult to sustain.

The use of the worker-related provisions of Community law to extend rights to workers' children seems attractive, but may be criticised. The rights which accrue to workers are not and should not be the same as those applicable to their children because of the limits placed on the Community's competence by the Treaty of Rome. The rights that workers have result directly from their economic position as workers. Certainly the requirement of free movement for workers may necessitate the extension of particular advantages to children and other family members, but in the absence of legislation the Court is not empowered to create new rules. In its expansion of Articles 7 and 12 of Regulation 1612/68, the Court has usurped the legislative function. The barriers to free movement that were alleged in these cases should have been the subject of legislative rather than judicial intervention if existing legislation was deficient.[97]

Having taken the apparently irrevocable step to expand Community law into the field of education, through the use of Regulation 1612/68 and Articles 7 and 128 EEC, the Court of Justice has created a number of anomalies which can only make further litigation inevitable. The distinction between Articles 7 and 12 of the Regulation has only recently been made, and there is no indication yet that it will be pursued to its logical conclusion. It would be irrational of the Court to prefer Article 7 to Article 12, but that is the end of the path on which it started in *Matteucci* and *Echternach and Moritz*. The use of the term 'vocational training' forced by Article 128 EEC has resulted in difficulties for national courts which try to apply the

97   See, however, Bruno de Witte, 'The Scope of Community Powers in Education and Culture in the Light of Subsequent Practice' in Roland Bieber and Georg Ress, (eds), *Die Dynamik des Europäischen Gemeinschaftsrechts* (Baden-Baden: Nomos, 1987) 261.

broad *Gravier* definition. It is unlikely that simple reiteration of this principle will suffice for long. At some point the Court of Justice will have to narrow its definition or find a new one that is simpler to apply. Similarly, it must be decided whether or not *Forcheri* is still good law. European Community law on education is far from settled.

Despite the Court's apparent reluctance to encroach on the Member States' competence, the 'education cases' and successive legislative measures in this area have affected the execution of national education policy. The Court has ruled on the financing of education in Belgium,[98] and the Council has instituted a Community-wide programme for language tuition in higher education and, implicitly, schools.[99] The extent to which this is acceptable to member States depends, they claim, on the extent to which their cultural values are undermined. This has been challenged by Jean-Claude Scholsem, who sees this resistance as being based in financial considerations, and suggests a kind of 'fiscal federalism' (such as that used in the United States) as a means to eliminate the problem.[100] Are the cultural arguments used by the Member States really to be reduced to financial expediency? I think not. Despite a rich common heritage, the Member States of the Community have developed in very different ways. This is nowhere more evident than in education. The way a nation educates its children is fundamental to that nation, and determines its future health and orientation. Is it any wonder that this is a domain closely guarded?

---

98 Case 42/87, *Commission* v *Belgium* (above, n. 70).
99 The LINGUA programme: Decision 89/489/EEC, OJ 1989 L 239/14.
100 Jean-Claude Scholsem, 'A propos de la circulation des étudiants: vers un fédéralisme financier européen' (1989) 25 *Cahiers de Droit Européen* 306.

8

Children and Divorce

J. C. Hall

Divorce is often seen by the parties to the proceedings as a means of re-acquiring one's freedom: the legal shackles fall away, and even the former on-going financial obligations will now disappear provided that the court is willing to make a clean break order.[1] Thus the joy of the glorious single status of youth is recaptured. Life becomes again (it is fondly hoped) what it was always meant to be.

No such benefits, real or imagined, accrue to any minor children of the marriage; and almost invariably they suffer. Adults, it is widely believed (at least by adults), have a right to human happiness, but children must take second place. Of course the parents consider that their offspring will derive direct benefit from their own happiness and thus have little difficulty in persuading themselves that a desired divorce will be good for the children. But will it? The authors of a recent book which deals with the effect of divorce on children,[2] one of them a distinguished retired Lord Justice

---

1   Matrimonial Causes Act 1973, s. 25A(3).
2   Jacqueline Burgoyne, Roger Ormrod and Martin Richards, *Divorce Matters* (Harmondsworth: Penguin Books, 1987).

of Appeal with particularly wide experience of family litigation,[3] are of the opinion that 'Despite what some parents might prefer to believe, it is rare for a child to welcome a separation',[4] and observe that 'Children usually retain the fantasy of their parents getting back together again for years after a separation.'[5]

It is only fair to record that many parents who divorce are of course deeply conscious of the harm which may befall their offspring and thus do their utmost to minimise it. Some there are, indeed, who with great nobility actually decide to postpone the whole process of divorce - and thereby sacrifice their own personal happiness - until the children have finished their school education. How many parents fall into this worthy category is not known, but one suspects that such parents are heavily outnumbered by those who decide to press ahead.

It is hardly surprising, therefore, that the question has sometimes been asked whether the law should not place divorce beyond the reach of couples with children under school-leaving age (or even under the age of majority); but not much support has emerged for so drastic a solution. An alternative, more moderate solution, is to confer on the court a discretion to refuse to grant a decree where it thinks that this would be in the interests of the children. Such a suggestion was made to the Royal Commission on Marriage and Divorce, 1951-55, (chairman Lord Morton of Henryton),[6] but it was firmly rejected. The Royal Commission pointed out a major difficulty and a major objection: how in practice would the court decide whether or not to refuse a decree for this reason; and would the children's interests 'be best served if they could be regarded by their parents as the reason for the failure of the divorce proceedings'?[7]

It is significant, however, that in the years that followed the Report of the Royal Commission two prominent judges with extensive divorce experience revived the proposal for banning

---

3   Sir Roger Ormrod.
4   p. 125.
5   Ibid. See, however, p. 127, where the authors point out that the 'overt distress of children when their parents separate and eventually divorce . . . is generally short lived'.
6   Cmd 9678.
7   Para. 219.

divorce by parents (or parents of a particular kind) of dependent children. In 1965 Sir Jocelyn Simon P suggested that divorce on the ground simply of mutual consent be introduced, but that such a reform be coupled with a ban on divorce on this or any other ground if the couple had any children under sixteen.[8] This proposal he repeated when giving the Riddell Lecture for 1970, pointing out that procreation of children is generally an advertent act, so that it might well be thought reasonable to hold that parents owe their child 'a paramount duty to preserve its family background.'[9]

Sir Jocelyn (by then Lord) Simon's successor as President of the Family Division (as the PDA Division had been renamed), Sir George Baker P, suggested that one particular category of parent, namely the parent who had acquired that status through the medium of an adoption order, should be debarred from petitioning for divorce throughout the adopted child's minority. Presumably this proposed restriction was based on the fact that to adopt a child is an even more well-considered act than physical procreation. (One wonders whether Sir George Baker P would have regarded parenthood resulting from *in vitro* fertilisation or one of the other scientifically assisted methods of achieving that status as falling into the same category.) But neither the general restriction on divorce proposed by the first President of the Family Division nor the more limited restriction proposed by the second seem to have attracted any significant degree of support.

In *Putting Asunder,*[10] the Report of the Group which had been appointed by the Archbishop of Canterbury in 1964, any proposal to differentiate between categories of petitioners for divorce received pretty short shrift. 'We cannot think it just,' said the Group, '. . .that there should be one law of divorce for those with children and another for those without.'[11] Furthermore the Group, just like

---

8   Address to the West Midlands regional conference of The Law Society, entitled 'The Seven Pillars of Divorce Reform'. Sir Jocelyn was then President of the Probate, Divorce and Admiralty Division of the High Court, which a few years later was renamed the Family Division. Sir Jocelyn later became a Lord of Appeal, as Lord Simon of Glaisdale.

9   *The Times*, 21 Feb. 1970.

10 *Putting Asunder* (London: SPCK, 1966).

11 Para. 57.

the Morton Commission a decade earlier, considered it unlikely that it would invariably prove to be of benefit to children to live with parents who had been refused a divorce on their account. The Law Commission responded swiftly to the proposal in *Putting Asunder* for a radical change in the basis of English divorce law[12] in their *Reform of the Ground of Divorce: The Field of Choice*,[13] in which they specifically echoed the second reason put forward by the Archbishop's Group for opposing discrimination against parents in respect of divorce, by pointing out that 'the children would come to be regarded as the main obstacle to their parents' happiness'.[14]   The Law Commission also felt that public opinion would not accept a total ban on divorce by parents of dependent children, and they referred to the result of a survey in 1965 which had been conducted by National Opinion Polls Ltd for the *Daily Sketch* in which only 33% of a representative sample of just over a thousand adults who had been interviewed supported the suggestion (most of the 33% being people belonging to 'the older age groups').[15]   As for the suggestion of introducing a discretionary principle, whereby a petitioner with children would only receive a decree if he or she could show that the children's welfare would actually be advanced by a divorce, the Law Commission were again not in favour, because of the risk of pressure being placed on children who were sufficiently old to give evidence to come forward and state that they would welcome the granting of a divorce.   More generally it would certainly be undesirable 'to make the children the fulcrum on which their parents' hopes of a divorce would turn.'[16]

As mentioned earlier two Presidents of the Family Division subsequently revived the proposal for restrictions, appearing thereby to be in disagreement with the Law Commission, but the weight of opinion seems to be against it.   Two Working Papers of the Law

---

12   Namely the substitution of the ground of irretrievable breakdown, to be established only after an inquest into the failure of the marriage, for the doctrine of the matrimonial offence.
13   Cmnd 3123 (1966).
14   Para. 51.
15   Ibid., n. 74.
16   Para. 51

Commission which appeared in 1980 and 1986[17] mentioned the question again, but attracted little if any enthusiasm for change; and in the Discussion Paper on The Ground for Divorce, *Facing the Future*, published in 1988[18] the Law Commission was once again firmly dismissive of the idea, pointing out quite correctly that restrictive divorce laws do not necessarily make parents stay together and that it is the fact of parental separation rather than divorce which is usually damaging to the children.[19]   What is more 'there must always be some cases, perhaps where physical or sexual abuse has occurred, when it will be better for the children if their parents are divorced and others in which it is impossible to tell which course will be best.'[20]   Sadly, therefore, one is obliged to admit that restrictive grounds for divorce in the case of those with dependent children do not necessarily safeguard the latter's interests.

*   *   *

Instead of placing special restrictions on the ability of a parent to launch divorce proceedings, English law, since soon after the Second World War, has adopted a different approach to the problem. Following a recommendation by a Committee under the chairmanship of Denning J (as he then was) the Matrimonial Causes Rules 1947 required every petitioner with children under sixteen, and irrespective of whether there was a prayer for custody, to include a statement in the petition giving details of their ages, their present and proposed homes, their education and the arrangements for their maintenance. This requirement, however, did not prove successful, because no sanctions could be imposed by the court if, as frequently happened, only sketchy information was included.   In consequence, this modest reform was soon abandoned and in the Rules of 1950 no mention was made of any obligation to acquaint the court with plans for the children's future.

---

17   *Time Restrictions on Presentation of Divorce and Nullity Petitions,* Law Commission Working Paper, No. 76 (1980) at paras 84-7; and *Custody,* Law Commission Working Paper, No. 96, at para. 4-14.
18.   Law Com. No. 170.
19   Ibid., para. 3.37.
20   Ibid.

However the Royal Commission on Marriage and Divorce, 1951-55,[21] returned to the question and advocated a much bolder approach than that enshrined in the Rule of 1947. The court must be given teeth, said the Morton Commission, and accordingly no decree *nisi* should be made absolute until the court had satisfied itself as to the children's welfare.[22] Parliament accordingly passed the Matrimonial Proceedings (Children) Act 1958 to implement this recommendation.

An outline of the proposed arrangements for the children was included at first in the petition itself, and the question of whether they met the statutory criteria was dealt with in open court when the petitioner gave evidence in support of the petition. Within a few years it became apparent that some judges seemed content to 'rubber-stamp' the petitioner's proposals; and certainly it was only in a small minority of cases that the court exercised its power to adjourn the hearing for a court welfare officer to make enquiries and then report on the situation.

Consequently the Law Commission decided that an investigation of the system was needed to ascertain whether it was itself satisfactory (or the 'best which could be devised in the circumstances'); and in 1966 the present writer volunteered to conduct some research which included a small piece of field work, financed by a grant from the Cambridge Law Faculty. The result of this survey, coupled with those of a smaller survey in Birmingham by Mr John Tiley, then of that University's Law Faculty, and with an analysis of replies to questionnaires on the subject which had been sent to judges of the PDA Division, special commissioners for divorce, registrars, divorce court welfare officers, and a sample of children's officers, as well as responses from the public to an invitation to comment on the scheme which, with the help of the John Hilton Bureau appeared in the *News of the World,* was published as

---

21　　　Cmd 9678.
22　　　Paras 366-81. The actual recommendation (para. 373) was that (i) 'in every divorce case the court must be satisfied that the arrangements proposed for the care and upbringing of any children under sixteen . . . are the best which can be devised in the circumstances' and (ii) 'that, until the court is so satisfied, the decree *nisi* must not be made absolute' (subject to a proviso for the taking of an undertaking in certain circumstances to bring the question back to the court within a specified time).

Law Commission Working Paper, No. 15 (1968). The general conclusion was that, although the system had obvious limitations and weaknesses, it was worth preserving and could well be improved even within the limits of available resources. (Although the court could withhold its approval of the proposed arrangements, once this was granted there was no way of ensuring adherence to them unless, as occurred in only a minority of cases where the statutory criterion of 'exceptional circumstances' was fulfilled, the court made a supervision order.[23] Yet there was generally a psychological value in requiring the submission of proposed arrangements as it showed the divorcing public, provided the question did not receive perfunctory treatment from the judge as sometimes unfortunately happened, that society was concerned with the fate of the innocent victims of their broken marriages.)

A disturbing discovery of the survey, however, was the ease with which a court could be grossly misled. Thus in one case which was investigated the following story emerged: the petitioner had stated to the court that the child was living at a certain address, whereas what transpired when enquiries were made many months after the court had expressed its satisfaction with these arrangements was that, far from living at this address, which included a fictitious street in a real town, the child had lived throughout in another town some forty miles away. Whether this monstrous deception of the court had been accidental or deliberate, and whether that child was at risk or was perfectly well cared for will never now be known; but a discovery like this seriously undermined confidence in the operation of the principle of scrutiny of proposed arrangements.

Over the following years the scope of this principle and its method of implementation were both modified. The scheme was extended to include sixteen and seventeen year olds still in receipt of education or training; all aspects, including financial support and education, of the child's welfare were brought within the ambit of the judicial scrutiny; and the consequence of an omission by the court to make the necessary order under the section were stiffened by providing that the final decree which was subsequently pronounced should be totally void.[24] Consideration of the proposed

---

23 Under what is now Matrimonial Causes Act 1973, s. 44.
24 Now s. 41 of the MCA 1973.

arrangements, now required to be set out in a separate document instead of in the petition itself, was transferred from open court to the judge's chambers, thus facilitating a more informal discussion. (This of course has become the only occasion since 'special procedure' became the norm for undefended cases that the petitioner actually has to attend court. The respondent's attendance, though encouraged, has never been made compulsory.)

A good deal of research has gone into the effectiveness of the machinery embodied in the Act,[25] and criticism has been plentiful.[26] The Law Commission devoted no less than fifteen pages of its Working Paper on Custody, which was published in 1986, to a thorough appraisal of the arguments for and against the whole system, before proceeding to set out in a further four pages what appeared to be the options for reform.[27] The Commission's preference, subsequently put forward as a recommendation in its Report (No. 172) on *Guardianship and Custody* in 1988, was for the replacement of the present duty for the court to satisfy itself concerning the arrangements (withholding decree absolute as a sanction) with a much more modest duty, akin to that placed on a magistrates' domestic court when hearing an application for a financial provision order under the Domestic Proceedings and Magistrates' Courts Act 1978,[28] of deciding what if any order need be made for the children.[29] Only in exceptional circumstances would the court be empowered to direct that the decree should not be made absolute until leave to do so had been granted.[30]

The need to remind parents of their responsibilities was to be met by 'improving' the present form of the statement of arrangements which the petitioner has to file (but the Report did not say how);[31]

---

25   Ibid.
26   For a very helpful bibliography see Law Commission Working Paper, No. 96 (1986) p. 90, n. 34. There is a particularly valuable article by Davis, Macleod and Murch (1983) 46 MLR 121.
27   See paras 4.8 to 4.10 and 4.11 to 4.16.
28   s. 8.
29   Para. 3.9.
30   Ibid.
31   Para.. 3.10.

and the respondent was to be 'encouraged' to join in the petitioner's statement or to file his own (but how?).[32] The statement(s) would be considered at an earlier stage of the proceedings than at present, when the judge usually takes the children's appointments (as they are generally known) on the same day as, and immediately after, the decrees *nisi* are pronounced.[33] The Law Commission envisaged that scrutiny of the statement(s) of arrangements would be handled by the registrar, though preferably with the assistance of a court welfare officer, rather than the judge as at present, though with power to refer the case to the judge 'if need be'. The petitioner would not normally need to attend, but there would be power to call the parties for an interview.[34] The Law Commission gave as its reason for dropping the present obligation for a petitioner always to attend, the fact that this 'could be seen as singling out parents who divorce as necessarily more irresponsible than others';[35] but is this really so? Is the law branding them as 'irresponsible' when all that it is saying is: if you wish to be released from a legal obligation which you freely entered into for life you must first give the court some assurance that you are endeavouring to minimise the inevitable disruption of your children's lives?

*   *   *

The Children Act 1989 embodies the Law Commission's recommendation on this matter.[36] It accordingly replaces (once it is in force) the existing section 41 of the Matrimonial Causes Act 1973 with a quite different version. This requires the court to consider not, as hitherto, whether the arrangements proposed for the children are satisfactory (or the best that can be devised) but merely whether the

32   Ibid.
33   Ibid.
34   Ibid.
35   Ibid.
36   Very surprisingly the draftsman departed from the terms of the draft Bill annexed to Law Com. No. 170 and included the change, in the form of a substituted s. 41, not in the main body of the Bill where one would expect to find it, but in Schedule 12 under the heading of 'Minor Amendments'. Surely, whatever its merits, it constituted more than a 'minor' change in English Law.

court should exercise any of its 'powers' under the Act in respect of them. The powers include of course the making of a residence or contact order under section 8, but the court will be governed by the general principle in section 1(5) that no order is to be made under the Act unless to do so will be positively advantageous for the child. Thus in contrast with the present position when a court almost invariably makes a custody and access order if there is a child under sixteen, the Act establishes a virtual presumption against the making of any such order.

It is only in 'exceptional circumstances' rendering this necessary in the child's interests that the court will now have power to place an embargo on applying for the decree to be made absolute. Yet a further curtailment of the scope of the provision is that it ceases to apply to a child of sixteen or more who is still being educated or trained (though in a particular case the court can direct that it shall apply). No longer is there any reference in the section to the child's welfare; and no longer of course does a decree absolute which is inadvertently granted without following the procedure laid down by the section become void.

The upshot is that we have now seen the abandonment by Parliament of the ideal promoted (unanimously) by the Royal Commission of 1951-55. Perhaps then the time has come to turn to alternative mechanisms for reminding divorce petitioners of their obligations as parents.

There are some countries which have adopted provisions designed to make it more difficult for parents to obtain a divorce than non-parents. Thus the West German Civil Code[37] enables a court to refuse to grant a decree if in the circumstances of the particular case this would be in the children's interests. This principle, it will be appreciated, is considerably more far-reaching than even our former-style section 41, because it enables a court to say that, despite the presence of a ground for divorce, the petition must be dismissed because the respondent wishes to save the marriage and the children would benefit from its preservation.

Poland has a similar principle. The Polish Family and Guardianship Code of 1964 provides that 'although a complete and

37   Article 1568.

permanent disintegration of matrimonial life [the ground for divorce] has been stated, the divorce shall not be granted if it is contrary to the interests of common minor children'.[38]

Sweden adopts a different approach: its astonishingly liberal divorce law which was introduced in early 1974 imposes a delay on the obtaining of a dissolution if a parent petitions - presumably in the hope that during that time wiser counsels may prevail. Thus, whereas a childless couple enjoy the luxury of immediate divorce by consent, a waiting period of six months has to elapse before the marriage is dissolved if there are children under sixteen.[39]

One should also notice two other legal systems which, while not imposing restrictions of a substantive nature, nevertheless discriminate at a procedural level against a petitioner with children. In the USSR the option of a ZAGS divorce, namely one granted administratively by the Registry for Acts of Civil Status, is denied to those with minor children, the parties here being required to attend a hearing in court.[40] A parallel distinction obtains in a part of the world which does not in general have much of a similarity to the Soviet Union, namely California, whose Civil Code excludes the possibility of utilising what is called 'summary dissolution procedure' if the parties have children.[41]

In England divorce reform is once again in the air. In 1988 the Law Commission published a Discussion Paper on the Ground for Divorce[42] in which it reached the conclusion that the two proposals for reform which are the most realistic are divorce after a period of separation and divorce by a 'process over time', the second of these being the one which the Law Commission provisionally prefers. Now that Parliament, by passing the Children Act, has dismantled the machinery for judicial scrutiny of the proposed arrangements for the children's welfare, there is surely a great deal to be said, whichever

38   See The International Society on Family Law's *Annual Survey of Family Law*, 1985, p. 209.

39   See H. D. Krause, *Family Law*, (West Publishing Co.: St. Paul, Minn., 2nd ed.1983), pp. 419-20.

40   See *Annual Survey of Family Law*, 1987, p. 316.

41   Art. 4550. See Krause, p. 420.

42   Law Com. No. 170. See also the observations of Lord Mackay of Clashfern L C at the conference of the NSPCC on 14 Mar. 1990 (reported in *The Times*, 15 Mar. 1990).

ground for divorce is adopted by English law, for differentiating in the length of time which must elapse on the basis of absence or presence of children. Thus if the ground is to be separation then this could, for example, be for a period of either twelve or eighteen months, and if it is to be process over time it could be nine or fifteen months, respectively.

This might not be popular with parents generally. If therefore Parliament considered it to be too drastic a solution, attention might instead be turned to the Russian/Californian model. Divorce jurisdiction, whether it be based on separation or on process over time (or indeed remains as it is today) could be vested in magistrates' domestic courts in the case of childless couples, while in the case of others it would remain the exclusive preserve of county courts. This should not be thought to imply that the former are second-class citizens entitled to only a lower grade of justice, but rather that society is emphasising that the dissolution of a marriage where there are dependent offspring is of a different order of seriousness and necessitates the presence of a professional judge. After all, more is at stake here than the happiness of two adults (important to society though that undoubtedly is) and the difference should be made plain for all to see - and ponder.

9

Controversy about Children's Rights

W. N. R. Lucy

This essay, unlike the others in this volume and unlike Hugh Bevan's own work,[1] is not concerned with the analysis of children's institutional rights. Rather, it examines the controversy which institutional and non-institutional right claims seem inevitably to generate. What is said here is thus not solely and uniquely applicable to the issue of children's rights: it is applicable to the discourse about rights in general. Yet the account offered as to why that whole discourse is controversial applies, *ceteris paribus*, to the particular segment of it concerned with children's rights. Moreover, the issue of children's rights impinges on the general claims made in this essay in two particular ways. First, the argument is made with an eye to its implications for the formulation and interpretation of any institutional statement of children's rights such as that contained in the UN

The author wishes to thank Hillel Steiner and Alastair Edwards; the former having read and commented on the whole draft, the latter having read and commented on some sections of an earlier draft. Obviously, they are not to blame for anything said here.

1   The most recent example being *Child Law* (London: Butterworths, 1989).

Convention on the Rights of the Child.[2] Second, the pretext for my discussion is a number of claims made in Professor MacCormick's influential article on Children's Rights.[3]

The initial claim of the essay is that before we can properly understand, formulate and interpret particular rights claims and the controversy they usually generate, we need to understand the deep structure of the controversy about the nature of rights in general. What I offer here is one seemingly plausible account of the structure of that controversy. It is not the only and perhaps ultimately not the best account.[4] It holds that controversy about rights is explicable because the concept of a right is essentially contested. Such contestability affects the whole of what we may call rights discourse, which embraces the disputes about the foundations of rights (covering their distribution, content and justification), the elucidation of rights language (Hohfeldian ostensive definition), and theories of rights (will and interest theories). The relationship between theories of rights and our rights language is understood thus: the former aim to tell us what is common to the latter and how it is best understood. Thus both will and interest theories offer competing accounts of what, if anything, holds our rights language together. On the one hand, the will theory holds that the link between all facets of rights talk is found in the fact that rights are agents' options or powers of waiver over the enforcement of a duty.[5] On the other hand, the interest theory claims, obviously, that all spheres of rights language are connected because they protect agents' interests through the imposition of a duty. In this context the essential contestability claim goes to the relationship between theories of rights and foundational justifications, holding that different theories of rights, which are supposedly discrete conceptual analyses of the nature of a right in general terms, exist and compete

---

2   For text, see pp. 294 ff. below.

3   Chapter 8 of his *Legal Right and Social Democracy* (Oxford: Clarendon, 1982), referred to hereinafter as *Children's Rights*.

4   The controversy could, for example, be understood as one between competing real definitions.

5   This characterisation of the will theory, and the characterisation of the interest theory which follows, are heavily indebted to N. E. Simmonds, *Central Issues in Jurisprudence* (London: Sweet and Maxwell, 1986), hereinafter *Central Issues*

because they are influenced - in a sense to be explicated - by different foundational accounts of the rights we have and why we have them.

If this is true it will be the case that those who disagree on the contours of the concept of a right cannot agree, contrary to MacCormick's view, on 'the substantive moral tenet involved in ascribing [rights] to children'[6] or, *a fortiori*, to anyone else. MacCormick's point here is that *disagreement* between 'morally acute and clear sighted people'[7] about how to answer the conceptual question 'is it true to say children have rights?' co-exists with *agreement* on the reasons which show why children are foci of moral concern, itself a substantive or foundational question. In Section I it is argued that this cannot be so because the conceptual arguments for and against the competing theories or analyses of rights are inconclusive. The arguments do not within their own terms compel us to choose one theory over another. If that is indeed the case we are left with the question 'what criteria do morally acute and clear-sighted people follow in making that choice?' for they do in fact make it. The answer I offer, as already suggested, is that this is determined by the foundational theory one accepts. That, at least, is what Section III is designed to show.

This diagnosis of the controversy about rights is not radical, though it is not explicitly accepted by writers like MacCormick[8] and would probably be opposed by old style linguistic philosophers whose demise is celebrated by some.[9] I say MacCormick in particular does not explicitly accept this diagnosis because I believe it is implicitly adopted by him in Children's Rights. This can be seen if we note the starting point of his argument there - it is that the assertion that children have rights is 'barely contestable' and that those who deny it suffer from 'moral blindness'.[10] This moral claim is not merely rhetorical for it provides the basis, perhaps even determines the

---

6   MacCormick, *Children's Rights* p. 155.

7   Ibid.

8   Some do, however, recognise that the conceptual dispute between competing theories of rights is not one resolvable in purely conceptual terms: see L. W. Sumner, *The Moral Foundation of Rights* (Oxford: Clarendon, 1987) p. 53; N. E. Simmonds, 'Rights, Socialism and Liberalism', (1985) 5 *Legal Studies*, pp. 1-9 at p. 4.

9   T. Campbell, *The Left and Rights* (London: RKP, 1983) preface.

10   MacCormick, *Children's Rights*, p. 155.

structure and assumed success, of the subsequent conceptual argument. Hence the truth of the moral claim that children have rights provides a test case which shows the 'untenability of all forms of will theory'.[11] If this is not an example of the choice between competing theories or conceptual analyses of rights being determined by an accepted foundational theory, then it is difficult to know what such an example could ever look like. Moreover, if it is indeed an example of the determination of conceptual analyses by foundational theory it shows us what is wrong with MacCormick's observation that 'in relation to their substance, rights belong to the class of essentially contested concepts'.[12] For if this is true of the substance of rights (or foundational theories) it must be true, I argue, of their form (the way they are analysed). MacCormick's observation is therefore wrong because it contains only a partial truth.

Three preliminary points need be made before I turn to the substance of the argument. First, in diagnosing controversy about rights by reference to the essential contestability thesis (hereinafter 'the thesis' or 'ECT'), I offer a composite picture of the thesis drawn from writers whom I call 'friends' of the thesis.[13] The motivation here is to give an account of the thesis which captures its strengths and avoids some of the difficulties manifest in some versions of it. To that end I have necessarily selected what I take to be compelling in the friend's account of the thesis and rejected, for reasons stated below, what is weak. Moreover, I cannot here offer a general defence

---

11   Ibid.
12   Ibid., p. 160.
13   Here I list: (i) *Friends*: J. Kekes, 'Essentially Contested Concepts: A Reconsideration' (1977) 10 *Philosophy and Rhetoric*, pp. 71 - 89; W. Connolly, *The Terms of Political Discourse*, revised 2nd edition (Oxford: Martin Robertson 1983); W.B. Gallie, *Philosophy and the Historical Understanding* (London: Chatto and Windus, 1964) chapter 8; S. Lukes, *Essays in Social Theory* (London: MacMillan, 1977) chapters 8 and 6 and his 'Under-determination of Theory by Data', *P.A.S. Supp.* Vol. L 11 (1978) (though note that he there invokes the thesis in an elliptical way which owes more to Habermas than Gallie: see pp. 97-9 - the first reason stated therein (p. 97, last paragraph) is the only one which Lukes connects with the thesis: ibid. p. 100); and (ii) *Ambivalent Friends* - E. Gellner, 'The Concept of a Story' (1967) IX *Ratio* pp. 49-66; J. Gray, 'Liberty, Liberalism and Essential Contestability' (1978) 8 *British Journal of Political Studies* 385-402.

of the thesis for that would take me even further away from the issue of children's rights. The application of the thesis to rights discourse does, however, presuppose that such a defence is available.

Second, having used the terms 'right' and 'rights' above, and going on to use them a good deal below, it needs to be pointed out that by them I mean to refer to both institutional and non-institutional rights. The difference is that the former must arise under some institutional practice, of whatever level of formality, whereas the latter need not. Unless otherwise stated, or manifest absurdity results, all of what is said in this essay is applicable to both kinds of rights.

The final preliminary point consists of an explicit statement of the structure of the essay. In Section I I seek to state the core claim of the thesis and demonstrate its applicability to the concept of a right. Section II takes up 'the what question', which demands a statement of what essentially contested concepts (hereinafter 'ECCs') look like in general terms. I state their marks and seek to show that the concept of a right manifests them. The 'why question' asks why some concepts are essentially contested and Section III labours toward a plausible answer. As will be evident from Sections II and III, I do not assume that the answers offered to the what and why questions must be completely distinct; rather, I suggest they overlap in an important way. Finally, some concluding remarks are offered in Section IV.

I. The core claim

The core claim of the thesis is one which no one from amongst its friends has sought to reject completely (the reason for the 'completely' qualification will become apparent in Section III). It is Gallie's claim that there are concepts which 'essentially involve endless disputes about their proper uses on the part of their users.'[14] Two strategies are used in order to demonstrate that the core claim is applicable to theories of rights. First, the historical longevity of the dispute between will and interest theories illustrates that the controversy is seemingly endless and thus suggests that it is rationally irresolvable.[15] For to deny this demands an heroic scepticism about

14   Gallie, ibid., p. 158.
15   See R. Tuck, *Natural Rights Theories* (Cambridge: University Press, 1979) chapter 1.

•
the rational capabilities of those historically and presently involved in
the dispute. Second, we can focus on a modern episode of the dispute
- that between Hart and MacCormick and their followers[16] - and
examine the arguments they use. Such an examination will testify to
the inconclusive nature of the dispute. And that, I assume, is at least
prima facie evidence that the dispute is rationally irresolvable.

I examine, in a rather cursory way, only three arguments from
this contemporary episode; a more thorough examination would take
up the remainder of this essay and would not strengthen the point I
am making. The first argument is the 'range' argument. It consists of
a determination of which, if any, of the two theories of rights covers
in a felicitous way all our rights language (i.e. the Hohfeldian
scheme). Neither do, but both fail for very different reasons. The
'will' theory can account for the first three types of Hohfeldian 'right
talk' very well - this much is conceded by MacCormick.[17] So it tells
us, as already noted, that the important point about rights language is
that it protects agents' options or powers of waiver over the
enforcement of a duty. The fourth type of Hohfeldian right - an
immunity right - does not fit well with the will theory, although this
may be so because the interest theorists' point here[18] raises the
argument about inalienability and waiver of rights to which the will
theory may be able to respond, an issue I take up below.

That this weakness of the will theory cannot lead to the
inference that the interest theory better satisfies the range argument
can be seen from the following. As the will theory with its emphasis
on choice fits the Hohfeldian scheme well, the interest theory must
claim that choices are protected because they are important interests.

---

16   The principal sources of this debate are: H. L. A. Hart, *Essays on Bentham*
      (Oxford: Clarendon, 1982) Chapter 7 (referred to as *Essays* hereinafter); N.
      MacCormick, 'Rights in Legislation' (hereinafter *Rights*) in P. M. S.
      Hacker and J. Raz (eds), *Law, Morality and Society* (Oxford: Clarendon,
      1977) and his *Children's Rights,* ibid., n. 3; N. E. Simmonds, *Central
      Issues,* supra note 5, Chapter 8 and book review (1983) 3 *Legal Studies,* pp.
      337-40. A more recent contribution to the debate, which adopts the interest
      theory for reasons which are far from compelling, is found in J. Waldron,
      The Right to Private Property (Oxford: Clarendon, 1988) chapter 3, esp.
      pp. 79 - 102.
17   MacCormick, *Rights,* pp. 192 - 5.
18   Ibid.

Yet this move brings with it the problem of determining when something is in someone's interest. If we use a simple 'agent relative' answer here, which is that X is in A's interest when A says it is, there arises the problem of a person who denies that what we regard as their rights (e.g. a right to vote) are in their interest at all. If to circumvent this problem the interest theory invokes an account of a person's 'real' interests which is not relative to that person's own views, then it must be morally and methodologically acceptable. While this is not in principle impossible (and I raise the issue again in Section III, part b (iii)) it raises a problem equal in stature for the interest theory to the problem of immunities for the will theory.

A second non-conclusive argument used in the dispute between will and interest theories concerns the existence of inalienable rights. If such rights exist, and MacCormick suggests they do,[19] they appear to be counter-examples to the will theory for the following reason. That theory tells us that rights protect agents' options or powers of waiver over the enforcement of a duty. Inalienable rights apparently refute this claim once it is recognised that an agent may choose to alienate his/her inalienable rights. And that, of course, cannot be done; hence we have some rights which are immune to the choices (options or powers) of the right holder. If we accept the will theory we are compelled to say, paradoxically, that inalienability reduces agents rights 'by restricting the scope of the power of waiver,'[20] rather than *strengthens* those rights; thus MacCormick's observation 'the more they are inalienable the less they are rights'.[21]

However, further consideration of the type of inalienable right which MacCormick has in mind will demonstrate the plausibility of one reply to this argument.[22] Some statutory provisions impose duties upon employers to provide their employees with safe conditions of work, the employees being unable to contract out of that

19   MacCormick, *Rights*, pp. 197-8.
20   Simmonds, *Central Issues*, p. 137.
21   MacCormick, *Rights*, p. 199.
22   Made by Simmonds, *Central Issues*, pp. 137-8; Simmonds, n. 16, p. 339.

protection.[23] Now on its face this example seems to fit MacCormick's argument perfectly. Yet it does so only on the assumption that the employees' right includes *only* the power to demand that the employer performs his/her obligations. There is no compelling reason to make this assumption and will theorists do not, holding that the right *also* includes the power to sue or not as the employee chooses. Hence 'MacCormick ... confuses the power of waiver over the enforcement of the duty (which, according to the will theory, is the essence of a right) with the power to alienate the right'.[24] And while the latter power is lacking in MacCormick's example the former is not. Nor will the standard interest theorists response to this point (which MacCormick also offers)[25] help: for the counter claim that the will theorists argument here confuses the right with the supposed remedy for breach is insufficiently rigorous. That is, until it is shown that the distinction it proposes between right and remedy is one which cannot be deconstructed and reconstructed with considerable leeway, the counter claim lacks force.

We seem then to have a position of stalemate: the interest theorists argument that will theorists offer a paradoxical account of inalienable rights is rebutted. It could still be maintained by the interest theorist, however, that the very existence of inalienable rights pose a counter example to the will theory. For the mere fact that they are inalienable seems to fit ill with the spirit of the will theory. That this argument is weak is obvious, especially if we bear in mind the essence of the will theorists response: inalienable rights are not necessarily incompatible with the power of waiver over the enforcement of a duty. And this claim is the only one will theorists must make.

23   It is in fact difficult to find statutory provisions which fit MacCormick's and Simmonds' hypotheticals; The Health and Safety at Work Act 1974 lays down duties upon employers to maintain safe places of work: ss 2 - 8. However, these duties are not the basis of civil actions by those injured as a result of breach: s. 47. The duties are enforced by the Health and Safety Inspectorate and the ultimate sanction is criminal prosecution. There are restrictions on contracting out of the provisions of the Employment Protection (Consolidation) Act 1978: s. 140(1). However, these restrictions are of limited range: s. 140(2). See I. Smith and J. Wood, *Industrial Law* (London: Butterworths, 4th edn., 1989) chapter 11.

24   Simmonds, *Central Issues*, p. 138, and n. 16, p. 339.

25   MacCormick, *Children's Rights*, p. 158.

The third argument in fact consists of two 'red herrings'. The first is the correlativity thesis which has been used by proponents of each rights theory against defenders of each. Thus Hart claims that the interest theory embraces the correlativity thesis, which holds that claim rights must necessarily correlate with duties, and because of this it is open to the argument that it makes rights language redundant.[26] That is so because a rights statement, if the correlativity thesis holds, is merely a reflex or mirror image of a duty statement. Now Bentham's version of the interest theory does invoke correlativity - but the interest theory need not necessarily do so, as MacCormick points out. Moreover, in MacCormick's version of the interest theory not only is correlativity denied but the redundancy argument which is based upon it is thereby neutralised.[27] Yet this does not alert MacCormick to the point that the will theory also need not necessarily be committed to correlativity, though Hart's version is. When this is realised MacCormick's efforts to find counter-examples to the correlativity thesis are without purpose. As neither theory of rights must necessarily embrace correlativity the argument from it is a *non-sequitur*.[28]

The second red herring is the third party beneficiary argument. This argument is a failure when used by both parties to the dispute. Proponents of the will theory like Hart have used it to embarrass the interest theory[29] only to discover that it can be equally an embarrassment to them.[30] Thus the argument serves no role in the dispute.

Further examination of the arguments used in this modern episode would serve to reinforce the point that the core claim is

---

26 Hart, *Essays*, pp. 181 - 2.
27 MacCormick, *Children's Rights*, pp. 159-63, see also J. Waldron's response to this issue in 'The Right to Private Property', n. 16.
28 For argument that the will theory need not accept correlatively see Simmonds, n. 16, p. 338.
29 Hart, *Essays*, pp. 187-8.
30 MacCormick, *Rights*, pp. 208-9.

applicable to rights theories.[31]   Yet if disputes to which the thesis
applies are indeed long term and seemingly endless, the natural
assumption is that there is not in fact any genuine disagreement here.
Thus it may be assumed that parties to the rights dispute are merely
using one word with different and incompatible meanings, just talking
past one another.   I offer, in Section III, reasons why such an
assumption ought not to be made.   Before doing that, however, the
'what' question must be answered.

II The 'what' question

This question is answered by stating the identifying marks of ECCs
which the friends do or would agree upon.   There are at least five.

First, ECCs refer to what Kekes calls voluntary goal directed
activity: '[t]hus ECCs do not refer to individual instances of such
activities [as rationality, democracy, etc.] but to the class comprising
them'.[32] This mark of the thesis is not one which any of the friends
other than Kekes explicitly state.   It is, however, probably implicit in
all they say and for that reason is unlikely to be questioned by them.
For there is nothing at stake in doing so if all this first mark does is to
make plain what all have unproblematically assumed.   And it is
difficult to interpret this mark in any other way.   For the concept of a
right to be essentially contested there must be no absurdity - and there
is not - in saying that in its general sense the concept refers to the
voluntary goal - directed activity of making rights claims.   The
concept therefore seeks to identify what holds that practice together
and marks it out from other practices; it need not refer to any
particular instance of that practice.

The second mark is one which all friends of the thesis
explicitly state, the only difference between them being one of
emphasis.   It is that ECCs are evaluative: the voluntary goal directed

31   One argument between interest and will theorists not mentioned here seems
        to favour the will theory.   It is the argument about compossibility made
        initially by H. Steiner, 'The Structure of a Set of Compossible Rights'
        (1977) 74 *Journal of Philosophy*, pp. 767-75.   An interest theorist's
        response, which is not entirely convincing, can be found in J. Waldron,
        'Rights in Conflict' (1989) 99 *Ethics*, pp. 503 - 19.
32   Kekes, n. 13, p. 74.

activity to which they refer is a valued state of affairs, the value consisting in the goal and the activity which leads to it. Moreover, the value of the state of affairs is assumed to be of a particular type. Friends of the thesis do not suggest that democracy, justice or rights are good in a purely prudential or instrumental sense, so that their value does not rest solely in the fact that they allow particular individuals or groups to achieve their ends (self interested or otherwise). Rather, the state of affairs referred to by ECCs is morally valuable. That some additional argument must be offered to show that the state of affairs referred to by the essentially contested concept of a right is morally valuable, by contrast with the same claim about justice or democracy, is clear from the criticism made of the practice of having and claiming rights by, *inter alia*, Bentham and Marx.[33] A common theme to their criticism is that rights lead to moral impoverishment - to the replacement of genuine moral concern by self-interested egoism. Nevertheless, such additional argument is available[34] and establishes an at least presumptive case for the claim that having rights is morally valuable.

Now the moral value of the state of affairs to which ECCs refer will have a number of criteria. To these evaluative criteria we need add criteria of application which, though not necessarily completely distinct from the former, provide a means of determining whether or not the state of affairs in question is covered by the ECC. The existence of both sets of criteria illustrate the third mark of ECCs, their internal complexity. Hence reference needs be made to a large number of criteria in order to determine whether or not the state of affairs in question is an instantiation of the concept and whether or not it has the value the concept normally has. That this is true of the concept of a right can be seen if we ask what needs be determined in order to decide whether or not A has a right to X in a particular situation. The first group of questions to ask and answer involve what we have just called evaluative criteria and draw upon our foundational theory: we need to know whether or not A is covered by it, whether or not it generates the right in question and what its

---

33   See K. Marx, 'On the Jewish Question', and J. Bentham, 'Anarchial Fallacies', in J. Waldron (ed.), *Nonsense Upon Stilts* (London: Methuen, 1987) chapters 5 and 3.
34   Waldron, ibid., chapter 6.

specific ambit and weight is. Of course all this presupposes some general strategy of justification for rights which our foundational theory must provide.

The second distinct series of questions to ask and answer invokes criteria of application and involves determining whether or not A's claimed right actually fits our rights language (the Hohfeldian scheme). If it does not, the assumption, which can be rebutted by showing that the Hohfeldian account of our rights language is wrong, is that A has no such right. The third question falls within the range of the will and interest theories: to be a right A's claim must either protect a choice or an interest A has. If it does not, A has no right.

The fourth mark of the thesis holds that criteria for the application and evaluation of ECCs are relatively open. Thus both sets of criteria, if distinct, can be ranked differently on different occasions. Think, for example, of criteria for the non-moral evaluation of a particular car: the list would be large and quite possibly ranked differently by different persons depending on their requirements. Nevertheless, we could probably fix a list which mentioned all the criteria everyone would use, though we could not fix a list specifying the weight everyone would give to each criteria. Similarly, we can imagine asking X and Y why a morally important concept like, for example, justice, is of moral value. The reply we may receive (assuming that neither X nor Y are followers of G. E. Moore)[35] could well contain a number of criteria of evaluation of the form 'justice is valuable because - '. Now X may well fill in the blank with criteria ranked differently to Y, although they both may use the same list of criteria. And this possibly of differential ranking or weighting of the criteria for the evaluation or application of a concept manifests the fourth mark of ECCs. It is well captured by Lively's statement of ambiguous concepts which, though they share this feature with ECCs, lack marks two and five. He says of such concepts that (i) there are no particular criteria within *an agreed range* which 'are regarded as necessary and sufficient . . . [and (ii)] . . . . the degree to which particular criteria need be satisfied is unclear

---

35   Who would reply, I suppose, that justice is a non-natural quality and cannot be further analysed.

[and (iii)] . . . there are problems about what real world phenomena fit the criteria.'[36]

To return to the concept of a right we can illustrate the relative openness of the criteria for the evaluation and application of the concept if we bear in mind the questions and answers raised in the discussion of the third mark of ECCs. Now the answers to these questions and our attitude to them - for example, our emphasis on fit with rights language and the inference to draw in its absence - are open. They can be and are revised in the light of the foundational theory we adopt and changes in that theory will often lead to changes in our answers to the other questions.[37] It is in this way that the criteria for the application and evaluation of the concept of a right are open. And while this may not be so obvious in the case of uncontroversial institutional rights such as some legal rights - where we are tempted to think that whether or not A has a legal right to do X is merely a matter of looking at the legal record, be it statute or precedent - once such rights become controversial, once questions are raised as to their ambit or applicability in a particular situation, all the questions we have noted are raised in order to find an answer.[38] Moreover, previous partially relevant answers to these questions, if there be such, are often open to reinterpretation though rarely explicitly rejected.

The final mark of an ECC is that different formulations of it are used aggressively and defensively by participants to a dispute. One use or application of the concept is urged as being superior to others and insulated against criticism. That this is true of the argument between competing theories of rights needs no elaboration: the few arguments from the contemporary dispute between will and interest theorists stated in Section I suffice to illustrate the point. Now we can explain how competing uses or application of an ECC are possible in a rather unsatisfactory way by pointing to the openness

---

36   J. Lively, 'Essentially Contested Concepts: A Re-appraisal' (Unpublished, delivered by Professor Lively, of the University of Warwick, Department of Politics, as a seminar at the Department of Government, University of Manchester).

37   For what looks like recognition of the overlap between conceptual and foundational issues in rights discourse see L. W. Sumner and N. E. Simmonds, n. 8.

38   Simmonds, ibid., offers a similar account at pp. 6-8.

and complexity of the criteria for application and evaluation. But there are, no doubt, many concepts which are open and complex in just this way and yet are not essentially contested. Hence we are led to ask why the openness and complexity of ECCs must lead to essential contestedness; this is the why question and an answer to it must now be offered.

III The 'why' question

I here gesture towards a plausible answer to the question 'why are some concepts essentially contested?' which gives sense to the core claim. The discussion of that answer takes three steps: first, I offer a preliminary point; second, I rule out an often made but unacceptable answer to the why question, which I call the Babel argument; and third, I seek to sort the wheat from the chaff in a range of related answers to the why question which are referred to as the incommensurability arguments. It is one of these arguments which I claim provides a plausible answer to the why question.

The preliminary point concerns a claim made above (p. 217) that there are no obvious reasons to assume that our answer to the why question must be incompatible with the answer to the what question. It is therefore appropriate to determine what overlap, if any, exists between the marks of ECCs identified in the answer to the what question, on the one hand, and a plausible answer to the why question, on the other.

Although a detailed examination of each mark of ECCs cannot be carried out in order to determine this issue, I offer a brief argument to show that marks one, three (in a limited sense) and five do not furnish part of an answer to the why question. That each mark is true of a concept which is not essentially contested can be seen from the following example: the concept 'football' refers to goal [*sic*] directed voluntary conduct, the concept being internally complex and used aggressively and defensively (as when one team's tactics or style of play is attacked), yet it is not essentially contested. Thus marks two, four and three (again in a limited sense) are the only potential answers to the why question. We need determine, then, what it is about these marks which compel us to conclude that ECCs are essentially contested. Suffice it to say that these three marks are often assumed to connect with some or other incommensurability claim. I identify three such claims below, one of which, I argue, is the best way of justifying the thesis and also of connecting the marks in question to a compelling answer to the why question. Before doing that the Babel argument must be dealt with.

a. The Babel argument

This argument is a more complete restatement of a *prima facie* response to the core claim of the thesis. As stated above (p. 222), that response holds that if some disputes about concepts are rationally irresolvable the disputants cannot be talking about the same thing, they must be using the same word with a (completely) different meaning. This explanation can be offered of any essentially contested dispute including that between proponents of competing theories of rights. Two points about this explanation need be noted. First, it is a response to the why question which friends of the thesis cannot accept without rendering the thesis trivial and uninteresting. For the thrust of the explanation is this: any essentially contested dispute is equivalent to silly arguments about, for example,[39] the number of banks in the UK, when one disputant means river banks and the other means savings banks. Thus the disputants are just talking past one another. A response such as this to the why question could only be adopted if it were the case, which I argue it is not, that no more compelling response could be offered. The second point to note is that this explanation comes with a theory of meaning attached, holding that the words and concepts we use are used and meaningful only if there are shared criteria for their application and - if appropriate - evaluation. Genuine disagreement can therefore only arise (i) about whether or not the shared criteria are satisfied - and on the fourth mark the criteria for an ECC are open - and (ii) under the fact of open texture;[40] critics assume that disagreement about ECCs does not fall completely under either of these heads.

    This picture of meaning and disagreement may be dubious for

---

39   The example is R. Dworkin's, *Law's Empire* (London: Fontana, 1986) p. 44.

40   F. Waisman, 'Verifiability', in A. Flew (ed.), *Essays on Logic and Language, First Series* (Oxford: Blackwell, 1951) pp. 120-1.

a number of reasons[41] and friends of the thesis may do well to reject it.[42] However, both they and the critics assume its truth, even though it seems to cause problems for the thesis. It only seems to do so because I argue here that even in terms of this dubious picture the thesis can be defended against the Babel argument. Adherence to this theory of meaning demands that friends of the thesis show, in any dispute over an ECC, that there is an agreed concept over which the dispute takes place. Critics suggest that in such disputes there is no single concept but a number of them; hence they deny that there are any shared criteria between disputants.[43]

This last point contradicts one clearly made in our statement of the marks of the thesis: that there is agreement on a list of shared criteria for an ECC but no agreement on how to rank them. And agreement on the list of criteria satisfies the theory of meaning which both friends and critics assume. Moreover, agreement on the list of criteria for the concept allows us to state the concept in a sufficiently general and abstract way so that it begs no questions between competing conceptions, understood as different and competing interpretations of the concept.[44] Such conceptions are different and compete because they involve differential rankings of the criteria of the concept. On this account, then, the concept is the common core of agreement in a dispute about ECCs: 'Contests ... are after all, contests over something: essentially contested concepts must have some common core; otherwise, how could we justifiably claim that the contests were about the same concept?'[45]

Three points need be made about the concept/conception strategy. First, the statement of the concept about which an essentially contested dispute takes place must (i) be sufficiently abstract and general to cover all the criteria of the concept and (ii) beg no substantive questions between competing conceptions (thus it must

41   For another picture see R. Dworkin, n. 39, chapters 1 and 2.
42   Both J. Grey and E. Gellner, n. 13, may be committed to doing this as they employ no reply to the Babel argument.
43   For a good example of this criticism see Keekok Lee, *A New Basis for Moral Philosophy* (London: RKP, 1985) pp. 21-3.
44   Invoked by S. Lukes, *Power: A Radical View* (London: MacMillan, 1974) p. 27; R. Dworkin, n. 39, pp. 70-3; J. Rawls, *A Theory of Justice* (Oxford: Clarendon, 1971) pp. 5-6.
45   Lukes, n. 13, chapter 8, p. 187.

not prejudice the argument in favour of a particular conception). Second, evidence of agreement about the list of criteria for a concept can be sought from the participants to the dispute and from the contours of the practice of disputing the concept in question. Taking rights and justice as our examples we can, by reference to the 'testimony of intelligent participants [to the] debate',[46] and by reference to the contours of its traditional forms, 'distinguish conceptions of justice [and rights participants] reject, even deplore, from positions [they] would not count as conceptions of justice [or rights] at all even if ... presented under that title'.[47] Hence we are able to say why claims such as 'abstract art is unjust'[48] and 'shoes have rights' are silly. And being able to say this gives us a toe-hold towards stating what those concepts involve.

The characterisation of the concept of a right I recommend, which is both sufficiently abstract to cover all the criteria of the concept and begs no questions between the will and interest theories, holds that a right be understood as an entitlement. Thus what 'one has a right to do is what one is entitled to, and that in virtue of which one has a right, the ground of the right, is what entitles one'.[49] The conceptual controversy between the will and interest theories is best understood as a contest between competing conceptions of that concept. Yet for such a claim to be defended it needs be shown that the suggested concept of a right fits the arguments which participants in the dispute use; and to do that would require a discriminating examination of the whole dispute. Thus for present purposes I assume rather than show that this claim can be made out.

The third point about the concept/conception strategy is one of emphasis. For it serves to remind us that if the two requirements of the first point are not satisfied then there cannot be a dispute about *one* ECC. That is so because the first point constitutes a contingently necessary condition for a dispute about ECCs. While space does not permit a detailed statement of reasons for this last claim it nevertheless needs defence on two fronts. First, against arguments which recommend other strategies as guarantees of the fact that

46   Kekes, n. 13, p. 76.
47   Dworkin, n. 39, p. 75.
48   Ibid.
49   A. R White, *Rights* (Oxford: Clarendon, 1984) p. 72.

essentially contested disputes are about one concept; and, second, against arguments directed specifically at this concept/conception strategy. The other strategies which have been recommended include Gallie's appeals to exemplars and 'a number of historically independent but sufficiently similar traditions'.[50] The largest problem which these strategies have is that examples can be found of disputes about ECCs such as, for example, democracy, where neither condition is present but our suggested contingently necessary condition is. Unlike some[51] I do not reject Gallie's exemplar strategy by invoking the genetic fallacy because to do so involves interpreting that strategy in a logically necessary way - such an interpretation lacks interpretive charity and is not obviously in the text; it is therefore unsatisfactory.

I turn now to the second kind of argument, an initial example being provided by Swanton.[52] Against the claim that there are shared criteria for a particular contested concept, the dispute being between competing conceptions of the concept, she *alleges* that in some such disputes (about rights and freedom) there is no agreed concept, and actually argues that this is true of the dispute about justice. Her argument about justice does not succeed, however, because it mistakenly takes conceptions of justice (those offered by Rawls, Nozick and Miller) to be competing concepts of justice. Thus she ignores the point made above and by other users of the concept/conception distinction, namely, that the statement of the disputed concept must beg no substantive questions between rival conceptions. Using these rival conceptions of justice as competing concepts does just that. Moreover, Swanton's allegation about the rights dispute is even less convincing for it is simply an unsubstantiated allegation; no argument is offered to support it and we have already stated a *prima facie* argument against it. Therefore it cannot be taken seriously.

A second argument used by Swanton[53] and Lively[54] against the concept/conception strategy is seemingly more powerful. It

50   Gallie, n. 13, p. 180.
51   Gellner, n. 42.
52   C. Swanton, 'On the "Essential Contentedness" of Political Concepts' (1985) 95 *Ethics,* pp. 811-27, at pp. 816-18.
53   Ibid., p. 816.
54   Lively, n. 36, pp. 20-1.

alleges that adoption of this strategy, when combined with other claims of the thesis, means that the thesis 'rests on two contradictory premises - that such concepts involve essential contestation of the meaning of the concepts and that such concepts rest on essential agreement on the meaning of such concepts'.[55] Now a contradiction in this context would involve affirming P (the proposition that the concept which an essentially contested dispute is about has a shared meaning) and its exact or equivalent negation not-P (the proposition that the concept which an essentially contested dispute is about has no shared meaning). Do or must the friends of the thesis affirm both P and not-P if they maintain the concept/conception strategy?

One argument that they do not and must not holds that in using this strategy friends of the thesis are not affirming both P and its exact negation not-P. Rather, they are affirming P and P1, P1 holding that conceptions of concepts do not have a shared meaning; the meaning of the competing conceptions is indeterminate in the sense that each offers a particular and different ranking of the criteria which taken together give the concept determinate meaning. *Prima facie*, we are not faced with a contradiction here unless it can now be argued that P1 is exactly equivalent to not-P. And it is difficult to envisage how such an argument would progress; certainly, Lively does not provide one. In fact his statement of ambiguous concepts (p. 224 above) provides an argument which is structurally the same as that urged by friends of the thesis (i.e. the conjunction of P and P1). Therefore he cannot seek to establish that P1 is equivalent to not-P without refuting his own argument. That argument holds that there can be agreement on the list of criteria for ambiguous concepts, hence they have meaning in that sense,[56] while their meaning (in a wider sense) remains indeterminate for reasons stated in the quotation above. Lively therefore offers an argument which is structurally the same as the conjunction of P and P1. The only difference between this argument and the thesis is a point of detail: each argument has a different explanation for indeterminacy. I turn now to examine other explanations for indeterminacy which are put forward to answer the why question.

55   Ibid., p. 21.
56   Ibid., p. 9, last paragraph.

b. The incommensurability arguments.

Here I state three incommensurability claims which are offered as answers to the why question and criticise the first two. We are left with only one plausible answer and I briefly both offer some reasons in its favour and sketch its applicability to theories of rights.

(i) Theoretical incommensurability (hereinafter 'TI') holds that competing theories cannot be compared one with another because the 'meanings of all the fundamental terms in each theory differ' and/or 'there is no way of showing that the fundamental terms of each theory mean the same thing'.[57] Insofar as TI can properly be extended from natural scientific theories to social scientific theories, and insofar as it is true of the former,[58] it must hold, when invoked to support the ECC, that concepts about which there are essentially contested disputes are equivalent to fundamental theoretical terms. Disputes about the correct meaning of ECCs cannot be resolved because each competing conception is articulated within different theoretical frameworks across which we cannot communicate. Thus this version of TI must embrace the claim that meaning is incommensurable. If it does so it apparently overlaps with the Babel argument. For the latter holds that where there are no established and shared criteria for the meaning of words and concepts there can be no genuine disagreement about them; so too does TI where the words and concepts are fundamental theoretical terms.

There are two reasons against accepting TI. The first is merely a restatement of the reply to the Babel argument. Insofar as TI entails the Babel argument, and to the degree that the latter cannot be accepted by friends of the thesis, then, *a fortiori*, TI cannot be accepted by the friends. The second reason is independent of the thesis and consists of a demonstration that proponents of TI are caught up in a contradiction.[59] The contradiction takes the form of affirming the proposition (let us call it P) which holds that truth is an

---

57   Swanton, p. 822.
58   I have severe reservations about both points.
59   Thanks to my colleague Stuart Toddington who put this argument to me
      with his customary wit and vigour; it is his and appears in fuller form in his
      Ph.D. dissertation: 'Towards an Integrated Theory of Natural Law',
      (submitted to the Centre for Criminological and Socio-Legal Studies,
      University of Sheffield, 1989) chapter 3.

inter-systemic/theoretic notion, while also affirming its exact negation, not-P, which holds that truth is an intra-systemic/theoretic notion. That opponents of TI must affirm P can be seen from the following. If the claim that fundamental theoretical terms are incommensurable is to be intelligible proponents of TI must hold that (i) there are at least two incompatible (incommensurable) theories and (ii) there is a proposition (M) which is true in one theory and false in the other. M is true in theory 1 and false in theory 2 because the fundamental theoretical terms in theory 1 are defined by reference to an incommensurable background theory which make those terms true. Hence if M is a proposition about mass[60] it could tell us that mass = R and this would be true in Newtonian mechanics but false in relativistic mechanics. Thus the fundamental theoretical term mass is incommensurable because the background theories which give it meaning are incommensurable.

How, then, does the affirmation of P lead proponents of TI to affirm its exact negation, not-P? Consider again proposition M. Proponents of TI can make the following statement of M: it is true in theory 1 but false in theory 2. Yet this statement contradicts P because it shows that truth is not *inter* but *intra* systemic. For the statement proponents of TI make about M is indeed intra-systemic; being able to make it shows that 'there are conditions of truth [and perhaps also] rules of logic, and criteria of rationality which are universal and fundamental';[61] these rules, conditions and criteria are *a priori* requirements for translation and understanding to be possible.[62] This, then, is the contradiction into which proponents of TI fall.

If this argument against TI is correct it is therefore odd that Swanton claims TI is the answer Lukes must give to the why question. For the ascription to Lukes of TI can only be defensible if there is no contradiction between affirming cognitive realism, the view that there are 'conditions of truth [etc.] which are universal and

---

60   I steal this example from I. Hacking, *Representing and Intervening* (Cambridge: University Press, 1983) p. 73. Neither he nor I use it for anything more than expository purposes.

61   Lukes, n. 13, p. 159.

62   This argument is put in compelling form by M. Hollis, 'Reason and Ritual', in B. Wilson (ed.), *Rationality* (London: Blackwell, 1979) p. 216.

fundamental' - a view which Lukes does indeed affirm - and affirming TI. But, of course, there is a contradiction, as we have already demonstrated. Hence TI cannot be ascribed to Lukes without assuming, uncharitably, that he has recognised the contradiction and then gone on to ignore it. Swanton is misled into assuming TI is Lukes' answer to the why question because of his curious statement that competing moral theories are incommensurable in the 'Kuhnian sense'.[63] The only plausible explanation of this phrase which fits Lukes rejection of cognitive relativism/TI is stated in (iii) below.

(ii) Metaphysical incommensurability (MI) is the answer offered to the why question by Gray. He holds that 'differing uses of essentially contested concepts hinge upon opposed metaphysical commitments about mind and action and so about the nature of human nature and society'.[64] Now insofar as this claim is equivalent to TI it must be rejected for the reasons stated above. Also, if it is equivalent to TI disputes about ECCs cannot, as Gray suggests they might,[65] be rationally resolvable.

To the extent that MI is not equivalent to TI then it is of little interest in relation to the core claim of the thesis. This is so because whatever the ultimate structure of the argument for MI (Gray has only ever stated it *en passant*), it will hold that ECC disputes are rationally resolvable. And that, obviously, is a rejection of the core claim of the thesis - hence the qualification in the statement of it above (p. 217). Therefore I turn to another version of incommensurability which, I argue, can maintain the core claim, make sense of Lukes curious statement, link up the three marks of ECCs with a plausible answer to the why question, and cover the dispute between competing theories of rights.

(iii) Value incommensurability (VI) holds that as between two moral values it is possible that there exists no neutral metric which can comparatively value them. Thus the relationship between two or more moral values, if they are incommensurable, is not a transitive one. A transitive relation between values would look like this: if A is more valuable than B, and B is more valuable than C, then A is more

---

63   Lukes, n. 13, p. 165.
64   Gray, n. 13, p. 394.
65   Ibid., p. 395. Kekes, n. 13, also makes this claim.

valuable than C. If the values in question are incommensurable we have no warrant for making that kind of claim. Hence if we are confronted with a choice between two incommensurable values we cannot make it by reference to compelling reasons one way or the other: '[i]ncommensurability speaks not of what does escape reason but of what must elude it'.[66]

Before determining how VI can be a plausible answer to the why question it is important to show that it is defensible in general terms. There are at least three arguments that it is not. The first claims that at a common sense level the denial of transitivity is counter intuitive. A compelling reply to this is to provide plausible examples of a failure of transitivity between moral values.[67] This reply may be thought unsatisfactory, and the first argument strengthened, by reference to the second which claims that the relationship of transitivity between all propositions (including moral propositions) must be necessarily true. This argument is not persuasive simply because it is difficult to imagine how it could ever be made out. That is not to say, however, that it cannot. It is to say that until such time as it is VI need not be threatened by it.

The third argument that VI is indefensible begins from the rejection of logical positivism and its ethical-cum-metaphysical limb, non-cognitivism. Insofar as non-cognitivism entails logical positivism it is to be rejected because the latter must be (because, e.g., the verification principle is neither analytic nor synthetic/empirical, cannot be protected by Russellian set theory because that theory begs too many questions, and rules out too many 'meaningful' statements). Now because the reasons for the rejection of logical positivism - which I have only hinted at - are compelling it is unlikely that any of the friends of the thesis would want to embrace it. That, however, adds power to the next step in the third argument which consists of the claim that VI is equivalent to non-cognitivism. Thus friends who seek to offer VI as an answer to the why question are in the position of, I assume, denying logical positivism while affirming VI, itself equivalent to non-cognitivism which entails logical positivism.

---

66   J. Raz, *The Morality of Freedom* (Oxford: Clarendon, 1986) p. 334.
67   Ibid., pp. 335 - 53.

Now there are many ways of replying to this argument. The reply suggested here denies that VI and non-cognitivism are equivalent, on two grounds.

The first is that non-cognitivism is a far broader claim than VI holding that at least *all* moral statements are meaningless and/or reports of speakers feelings.[68] VI, by contrast, holds that only *some* moral values *may* be incommensurable: those of which transitivity does not hold. Moreover, incommensurability is silent about the meaning of moral statements/values. Thus there is no contradiction between affirming both that two moral values are incommensurable and that they (or the propositions in which they are expressed) have more than emotive meaning. This is the second ground of the denial.

It therefore remains briefly to state both why VI is an improvement upon other answers to the why question and that it explains the dispute between competing theories of rights. Clearly it ties marks two, three and four into the answer it provides in the following way. Those marks are either completely or partially evaluative. Dispute about them will be endless insofar as the criteria of evaluation for ECCs invoke incommensurable values. Thus ECCs can have meaning at the level of claims about *the* disputed concept, that meaning being indeterminate at the level of claims about the best conception of the concept insofar as such conceptions rank the criteria of the concept differently on the basis of incommensurable values.

VI also allows us to make sense of Lukes' misleading claim. All he can mean by his reference to moral theories being incommensurable in the Kuhnian sense is VI. If he means more than that he runs the risk of contradicting himself. Needless to say, there is nothing in VI which compels us to accept TI as stated above. However, VI can in a sense entail a very thin version of TI which would hold that competing theories are incommensurable if both (i) those theories are inescapably evaluative/moral and (ii) the moral values they invoke are incommensurable (i.e. there is a failure of transitivity).

To demonstrate that VI explains the dispute between competing theories of rights requires a statement of potential

---

68   A standard source of this view is A. J. Ayer, *Language, Truth and Logic* (Harmonsworth: Pelican, 1971) pp. 110-11.

candidates for the status of incommensurable values underlying the competing theories. My nominations are the values of liberty/autonomy, on the one hand, and utility/welfare, on the other. I assume a very close relationship between each value in each pair. If that assumption is a defensible one I need only show that the will theory is in some way related to, based upon, or tracks, liberty or autonomy and that the same is true of the interest theory and welfare/utility.

Before attempting to make a presumptive case for the claim that the will theory tracks liberty/autonomy and the interest theory utility, account must be taken of Coleman's cryptic remarks.[69] Their thrust is that an analysis of the 'logical form' of rights is independent of any foundational theory. Now this claim is unproblematic provided that the process of offering an account of the 'logical form' or syntax of rights is not synonymous with the will and interest theories. Yet if we assume, as Coleman does, that will and interest theories offer competing accounts of logical form, and assume that his independence claim is true, we have a block to the application of the thesis to theories of rights.

This block can be circumvented by denying Coleman's first assumption: we deny that will and interest theories offer an account of logical form or syntax. This denial is plausible for the following two reasons. First, it is implausible to assume that such controversy, in the context of rights discourse, could have been caused merely by competing analyses of the logical *form* of a right. Second, if we consider what an examination into the logical form or syntax of a concept should offer our answer would be something like: an account of the general characteristics of the concept which hold across all institutions of it. (Thus our (philosophical) dictionary definitions of the notions of logical form or syntax stress generality). If this is a correct view of what Coleman has in mind when he uses the phrases 'logical form' and 'syntax' then the following inference is warranted: our analysis of the concept of a right in terms of an entitlement provides the logical form or syntax of that concept. And the will and interest theories are competing conceptions of that concept: they are

---

69   J. Coleman, *Markets, Morals and the Law* (Cambridge: University Press, 1988) p. 34 and n. 10 on p. 347.

concerned to present it and work out its implications in the best possible way.

The presumptive case for the claim that competing theories of rights invoke incommensurable values is established in two ways. First, a tension in the claim that the interest theory tracks liberty/autonomy will be noted.[70] An initial manifestation of this tension arises between a non-agent relative account of real interests, on the one hand, and an assumption made by many accounts of liberty/autonomy, on the other. For the question an interest theorist must answer is this: which interests, out of the range available, actually generate rights? An initial filter on the range of interests which have this power is the requirement that an agent's own assessments of his interests do not count. This requirement does not, however, lead to the characterisation of a list of interests so generated as being 'real' interests, for there are available agent - relative accounts of 'real' interests, as we shall see below. Thus in this context 'real' must be taken in a very vague way as referring to interests which are not expressed by existing agents here and now. The conflict which arises between this non-agent relative account of real interests and liberty/autonomy flows from the assumption that to have liberty is to be free to, *inter alia*, make one's own choices; and self rule, as part of an interpretation of autonomy, consists of the same freedom.[71] The tension, which verges on contradiction, is between agent relative and non-agent relative determinations of an individual's good.

Now it might be thought that an agent relative account of real interests would resolve this tension. This would be a mistake because the tension we have highlighted exists here also. This much is clear from the accounts of Lukes and Connolly.[72] Both offer agent relative accounts of real interests: agent relative in that agent's choices are determinative of what their interests are, real in the sense that these choices are not ones which agents make here and now. As Connolly puts it 'policy X is more in A's real interest than policy Y if A, were

70   A claim made by, *inter alia*, T. D. Campbell, 'Philosophy, Ideology and Rights' (1985) 5 *Legal Studies*, pp. 10 - 20 at p. 13.
71   J. S. Mill is one who makes this assumption; see his account of interests in *On Liberty*, in *Utilitarianism, Liberty and Representative Government* (London: Dent, Dutton, 1972) p. 133.
72   Lukes, n. 44, at p. 33; W. B. Connolly, n.13.

he to experience the results of both X and Y, would choose X as a result he would rather have for himself'.[73] That an account such as this is an improvement upon a non-agent relative account, from the point of view of the proponent of liberty/autonomy, is obvious. However, though it can be characterised as an agent relative account of interests it is still insufficiently agent-relative to satisfy the assumption at the root of some accounts of liberty/autonomy we are imagining. Conflict arises between that assumption and the Lukes-Connolly account of interests because, although the latter 'accord[s] to actors the status of *ultimate* arbiters as to their own interests . . . [it] . . . provisionally withhold[s] the status of *immediate* arbiters'.[74] Moreover, these ultimate choices are not ones which are in fact made by real agents - they are made by the observer on the basis of an agent's imagined response to a hypothetical choice situation. Also, it is the observer and not a real agent who chooses one of a range of hypothetical choice situations to serve as a privileged forum for determining an individual's real interests.[75] Hence the choices which form the basis of an assessment of an individual's real interests are distant from that individual and this distance is incompatible with the root assumption our imagined liberal accepts.

A further difficulty for the interest theorist who takes up the Lukes-Connolly account of interests is apparent if we make two large and so far unwarranted suppositions, namely, that the conflict we have discussed can be resolved and that such an account of interests can generate and individuate[76] interests which are also rights. For the invocation of the Lukes-Connolly strategy by an interest theorist leaves him/her open to the reply of redundancy. It can be pointed out that this account of real interests is one which determines interests on the basis of an agent's choices. And the question which immediately arises is 'why bother with the interest theory in the first place?'. It merely makes the same claim as the will theory but at a higher level of abstraction. For the interest theorist rights are interests protected

73   W. Connolly, n. 13, p. 64.
74   T. Benton, 'Realism, Power and Objective Interests', in K. Graham (ed.), *Contemporary Political Philosophy* (Cambridge: University Press, 1982) p. 24.
75   Both arguments are offered by T. Benton, ibid.
76   A point well dealt with by N.E. Simmonds, n. 8, p. 5.

by the imposition of a duty. To the question 'which interests are so protected?' the answer that we have assumed would be offered is this: those interests which are the agent's real interests - that is, those things the agent would choose in a hypothetical choice situation. So rights are interests and interests are choices. So, rhetorically, what advantages does the interest theory have over the will theory, why should we bother with it?

The conclusion we have reached is this: a liberty/autonomy foundational theory is incompatible with the interest theory of rights insofar as the latter invokes an account of real interests. In order to avoid this conflict interest theorists could take up an account of interests which relies upon agent's present choices or preferences. This strategy does not avoid the redundancy argument and indeed generates other problems. One of these, which has already been hinted at in the discussion of accounts of real interests, is the problem of individuation: of determining which interests, out of the vast range of interests which can be generated in this way, create rights. It would be absurd of the interest theorist to suggest that all such interests generate rights and self defeating to say none do. In order to give an answer which falls between these extremes the interest theorist needs to formulate a principle of distinction which is both consistent with her other theoretical claims and non-arbitrary. It is by no means obvious that this can be done.

The second way of making out the presumptive case consists of noting a similar tension between the will theory and a foundational strategy which invokes welfare/utility. The tension comes in this form: the will theory taken independently of the utility/welfare foundational strategy can accommodate an important feature of rights language whereas in conjunction with that foundational strategy it cannot. Thus we have a tension between the will theory's pretensions to fit the dimensions of rights language and the block to such fit presented by the utility/welfare strategy. Moreover such a block is not present when the will theory is conjoined with the liberty/autonomy foundational strategy.

The feature of rights language which the will theory fits well is the importance attached to rights by those who argue about them; moreover, a criteria if importance is permanence. Thus we hold that the right to liberty in Article 3 of the Universal Declaration of Human Rights is not a right which can be changed as and when anyone wishes: in both an institutional and non-institutional sense we assume that it has permanence and that is usually guaranteed by our foundational strategy. Of Article 3 the will theory tells us that the right to liberty is, at least, a protected sphere of choice which we all have regardless of how much we benefit, actually or potentially, from it.

Yet when the will theory is conjoined with the welfare/utility foundational strategy the latter frustrates the former's attempts to fit our rights language in the following way. For such a conjunction will tell us of Article 3 that we have that right, which is a protected sphere of choice, insofar as it contributes to individual welfare and/or group utility. Now if it be established that either such a sphere of choice does not actually contribute to my welfare (because, e.g., I chose to do harmful things to myself like smoke, etc . . .) or reduces group utility, then this foundational strategy must deny me that right.[77] This point could conceivably be generalised across a range of supposed rights with the consequence that such 'rights' lack the permanence we assume all important rights (institutional and non-institutional) have. And the insight in the claim that rights are trumps must be that they are insulated against such contingencies.

Conclusion

The argument I have sought to make out, although rather tentative, is simple. I have tried to show that controversy about particular rights claims should be understood in the light of the deep structure of controversy about the nature of rights in general. To do that I suggested that the concept of a right is essentially contested, displaying all the features such concepts are said to have. Moreover, I offered an account of why that concept is essentially contested which could equally apply to other essentially contested concepts. In the course of developing these points many incidental issues were tackled, albeit in a rather superficial way, in order to ensure that the argument is as compelling as it could be within these confines. That is not to say that more cannot be done; it can, but not here.

---

77   For attempts to square utility and rights see, e.g., L. W. Sumner and J. Griffin in R. G. Frey (ed.) *Utility and Rights* (Minneapolis: University of Minnesota Press, 1984).

What, then, is the point of the argument and how does it affect those specifically concerned with Children's Rights? Again the answer is simple. The argument offers one potential explanation of why rights claims generate so much seemingly endless dispute. One who would deny that rights claims are controversial in this way would be making a very curious point indeed; a point, it would appear, which ignores the features of much political, moral and legal argument, for rights claims do indeed seem to have become an infatuation of contemporary discourse. Clearly those who seek to make, defend and adjudicate particular rights claims must appreciate the true complexity of the subject matter with which they are dealing. And it is just that which I have sought to illustrate.

10

The Changing Face of Wardship

M. L. Parry

Hugh Bevan's career at the University of Hull spanned almost four decades starting in 1950. That period witnessed an unprecedented expansion in the law relating to children,[1] both in terms of statutory development and case law. The subject of this essay is one particular aspect of that expansion, namely the wardship jurisdiction. Being an inherent jurisdiction it retained a considerable degree of flexibility which enabled it to adapt to changing social needs and attitudes whilst not being circumscribed by the statutory constraints associated with other areas of child law. That flexibility came to be tempered by a variety of judicial and statutory limitations upon the exercise of the jurisdiction, but none on the scale of those enacted at the end of the period under review in the Children Act 1989. That Act reforms both the private and the public law relating to children to an extent not previously seen in a single statute. As a consequence there would have been a reduced need to rely on wardship had no limitations been imposed. In one particular context, however, wardship had become

---

1   A testimony to which are H. K. Bevan, *The Law Relating to Children* (London: Butterworths, 1973) 522 pp. and *Child Law* (London: Butterworths, 1989) 856 pp.

the victim of its own flexibility, namely its use by local authorities in the context of child protection. Hence specific restrictions have been introduced regarding the use of wardship to place a child in the care or under the supervision of a local authority. Not only has wardship had to pay the price for its flexibility but so also, it may be argued, have those for whose benefit the jurisdiction exists. There is likely to be a marked decline in the use of wardship in view of the high proportion of applications in which local authorities are the plaintiff[2] and a concentration of the courts' resources upon other uses of the jurisdiction, in so far as they still exist.

The 1950s

This review of forty years of wardship begins,[3] as it will end, with a consideration of the impact of statutory regulation of the jurisdiction. The year before Hugh Bevan's appointment saw the enactment of the Law Reform (Miscellaneous Provisions) Act 1949, prior to which there was no set wardship procedure. A child became a ward of court if an action relating to the child's person or property was commenced in the Chancery Division of the High Court whether or not wardship was sought. Thus in some cases a child became a ward of court where wardship was neither necessary nor desirable, whilst in those cases where it was desired to make a child a ward of court it was not possible to make a simple application to that effect. It was necessary to settle a sum of money on the child and then commence an action to administer the trusts of the settlement.[4] After the 1949 Act no child could be made a ward of court except by virtue of an order to that effect made by the High Court.[5] These changes were more than procedural in consequence. They laid the foundation of a greater use of the jurisdiction and a greater emphasis being placed upon the welfare of the child, with the result that the jurisdiction was to become increasingly significant in the context of child protection. At the same time increased responsibility was being placed upon local

2   See below, p. 256.
3   For the pre 1950 development see N. V. Lowe, and R. A. H. White, *Wards of Court* (London: Barry Rose, 2nd edn 1986) paras 1-1 to 1-6 and 4-1 and references there cited.
4   See e.g. *Re X's Settlement* [1945] Ch 44.
5   s. 9(1), see now Supreme Court Act 1981, s. 41.

authorities in that field, consequent upon the passing of the Children Act 1948.

The availability of wardship was enhanced at this time as a result of the Legal Aid and Advice Act 1949 which removed some of the financial constraints upon the jurisdiction's use. The impact of this, and the other reforms, was not immediate however and throughout the fifties wardship continued to be little used. In 1950, 62 originating summonses in wardship were filed, and by 1956 the number had only risen to 86. As the reported case law[6] testifies, the issue of jurisdiction featured prominently. Wardship was the main jurisdiction in cases of kidnapping. It was still used occasionally as a means of restraint, as for example in *Re Elwes (No 1)* [7] where an order was made that the applicant and the ward be restrained from intermarrying. The applicant was duly committed to prison for disobedience of the order. Religious upbringing too still occasionally exercised judicial attention.[8]

One statutory reform at the end of the decade which was of relevance indirectly, was made by the Legitimacy Act 1959[9], with the extension to the father of an illegitimate child of the right to apply for custody or access. Before that date he was limited to a claim by way of habeas corpus or, more appropriately, in wardship. Wardship was to remain as an alternative jurisdiction but it became less attractive than the statutory jurisdiction in terms of convenience, cost and the available orders.

The 1960s

The second decade under review saw a gradual increase in the number of originating summonses issued from 258 in 1961 to 444 in

6   *McKee* v *McKee* [1951] AC 352 (weight to be attached to a foreign order); *Re C (an infant) The Times*, 14 Dec. 1956 (foreign child physically present in the jurisdiction); *Harben* v *Harben* [1957] 1 WLR 261 (jurisdiction over child a British subject irrespective of child's whereabouts); *Re Chrysanthou* [1957] CLY 1748 (court accepted jurisdiction but declined to make an order against a foreign resident on grounds of enforceability); *Re C (an infant)* [1959] 1 Ch 363 (diplomatic immunity).

7   [1958] CLY 1618 and 1620.

8   *Re A (an infant)* [1955] 2 All ER 202.

9   s. 3 amending the Guardianship of Infants Act 1885.

1966.[10] This increase was reflected in the varied nature of applications. Whilst issues of jurisdiction and kidnapping still featured prominently, they ceased to dominate to the same extent. The protection of the child's welfare was being seen in a wider context, it being made clear that once the jurisdiction was invoked no important step in the child's life could be taken without the court's consent.[11] Moreover in cases of emergency, where, for example, there was an imminent danger of the child being removed from the jurisdiction, it was held possible to obtain an injunction under the court's inherent jurisdiction, preliminary to the issue of the originating summons.[12]

Issues of restraint of a ward and of preventing undesirable marriages, whilst still a feature,[13] were out of line with the liberated attitudes of that time, witnessed in part by the lowering of the age of majority from 21 to 18 by the Family Law Reform Act 1969, which implemented the recommendation to that effect in the 'Latey Report'.[14] That emancipation served to reduce the likelihood of the misuse of wardship which occurred in Re Dunhill,[15] where a night-club owner made a model a ward of court for publicity purposes. The Family Law Reform Act 1969 also gave effect to two proposals of the Latey Report specifically relating to wards of court. The first concerned their maintenance. It had been doubted whether the Chancery courts, which then had exclusive jurisdiction in wardship, were empowered to make maintenance orders under the inherent jurisdiction and so the cumbersome and expensive practice had developed of coupling wardship applications with an application under the guardianship legislation. Section 6 was thus enacted to avoid such duplication by conferring statutory power upon courts in the exercise of the wardship jurisdiction to order parents[16] to provide

10	See S. M. Cretney, *Principles of Family Law* (London: Sweet & Maxwell, 1974) p. 289.
11	*Re S (infants)* [1967] 1 WLR 396.
12	*Re N (infants)* [1969] Ch 512.
13	*Re Crump (an infant)* (1963) 107 Sol Jo 682.
14	*Report of the Committee on the Age of Majority*, 1967, Cmnd 3342.
15	(1967) 111 Sol Jo 113. See also *Practice Direction* [1967] 1 WLR 623 which required the applicant to state his relationship to the ward.
16	In its original form the legislation was limited to parents of legitimate children.

maintenance. The second proposal related to the belief that the Chancery courts' inherent powers did not extend to placing a ward in the care or under the supervision of a local authority. Hence s. 7 was enacted to confer such powers upon the wardship court in 'exceptional circumstances'. The section was to prove a further statutory impetus to the use of wardship, in particular as a palliative available to local authorities in overcoming the inadequacies of the Children and Young Persons Act enacted in the same year. The nature and scope of s. 7 was to be a matter of some uncertainty during the ensuing twenty years leading to its repeal by the Children Act 1989.

The increased and varied use of wardship raised the general issue of principle of the jurisdiction's perimeters. In particular its scope as a challenge to the exercise of statutory powers vested in others came in for clarification and limitation. Thus in *Re Mohamed Arif (an infant): Re Nirbhai Singh (an infant)* [17] the Court of Appeal held that, so long as the immigration authorities exercised their powers honestly and fairly, wardship was not to be used to prevent the implementation of an order for the removal of a child from the jurisdiction. Similarly a distinction was drawn between the unacceptability of wardship being used by a party who was dissatisfied with the way in which effect was being given to a custody order,[18] compared with the acceptability of wardship where the relief sought was outside the jurisdiction of the court which made the order.[19]

The issue of principle involved had already been established in the context of the inter-relationship between wardship and local authorities' exercise of their statutory powers over children in care. The Court of Appeal in *Re M (an infant)* [20] accepted that 'the ancient prerogative will not be held by the courts, to be ousted or restricted by any statute, unless the statute in question does so expressly or by clear implication of its terms'.[21] In the absence, however, of any

---

17   [1968] Ch 643.

18   *Re K (KJS) (an infant)* [1966] 1 WLR 1241; *Re P (AJ) (an infant)* [1968] 1 WLR 1976.

19   *Re H (GJ) (an infant)* [1966] 1 WLR 706; *Re P (infants)* [1967] 1 WLR 818.

20   [1961] Ch 328.

21   At 338.

challenge as to the propriety, rather than the wisdom, of the local authority's actions, the matter of judging what was in the child's best interests was held to have been placed by Parliament in the exclusive jurisdiction of the local authority. The accepted view was that expressed by Pearson L.J. in *Re B (infants)* [22] that 'in the absence of special circumstances, the court ought not to exercise its power of control in a sphere of activity which has been entrusted by statute to a local authority'. The manner in which it had been entrusted, however, was regarded as significant so that where the child had been received into so called voluntary care, rather taken into compulsory care, the wardship jurisdiction was not ousted because of the tenuous nature, as then perceived, of the local authority's care of the child. [23] The fact of local authority care had not yet become accepted as a sufficient restriction by itself upon the use of wardship.

The increased use of wardship also resulted in a clarification of the role of the Official Solicitor. Consistent with the principle that any important step in a ward's life required the court's consent, it was made clear that the Official Solicitor did not have custody of the child so as to confer upon him an unfettered discretion, [24] any major decisions had to be referred to the court. If called upon to act, his duty was identified as being to represent the ward's interests, which extended not only to the conduct of the proceedings but could, if the circumstances justified, go beyond the hearing. [25] In carrying out his responsibility of placing before the court the evidence which he considered to be material on the ward's behalf, it had become the practice to submit a statement of facts and a confidential report. It was held by the House of Lords in *Official Solicitor v K*, [26] however, that the submission of a confidential report was justified only in exceptional circumstances, where the Official Solicitor believed disclosure might be harmful to the child, the court having a discretion to refuse to disclose to the parties the contents of the report. The case was significant also in relation to hearsay evidence, because of the view expressed by Lord Devlin 'that an inflexible rule against

---

22   [1962] Ch. 201 at 223. See also *Re C(A) (an infant)* [1966] 1 WLR 415.
23   *Re S (an infant)* [1965] 1 WLR 483.
24   *Re L (an infant)* [1968] P 119.
25   *Re R (PM) (an infant)* 1 WLR 385.
26   [1965] AC 201.

hearsay is quite unsuited to the exercise of a parental and administrative jurisdiction'. The prevailing consideration was the paramountcy of the child's welfare.

Towards the end of the decade a landmark in relation to the importance to be attached to the child's welfare was the decision in *J* v *C*,[27] in which the House of Lords, after a comprehensive review, established beyond doubt that the paramountcy principle applied to disputes not only between parents but also between parents and strangers, and strangers and strangers. In applying that principle, the rights and wishes of the parents had to be assessed and weighed for their bearing on the welfare of the child, in conjunction with all other relevant factors. In the words of Lord Guest:

> the law administered by the Chancery Court as representing the Queen as *parens patriae* never required that the father's wishes should prevail over the welfare of the infant. The dominant consideration has always been the welfare of the infant.[28]

The decision thus served to clarify the meaning of the principle as well as its scope. The child's welfare had to prevail over all other considerations, including the claims of the natural parents. The scene was set for wardship's continued expansion.

The 1970s

It was not until the 1970s that the increase in the use of wardship became significant, setting a trend which was to continue into the next decade. A major reason for this increase was the transfer of jurisdiction in 1971 from the Chancery Division to the Family Division of the High Court[29] and the extension of wardship to District Registries. In that year there were 622 originating summonses issued which by the end of the decade had risen to 1685, of which 913 were issued out of the Principal Registry and 772 out of District Registries. This transfer and extension of jurisdiction can be

27   [1970] AC 668.
28   At 697.
29   Administration of Justice Act 1970, s. 1(2) and Schedule 1.

linked also with an increase in the issue of Practice Directions from that time, as a means of clarifying and elaborating upon the procedural niceties of wardship.

Lowe and White in the first edition of their major work, *Wards of Court* [30] published in 1979, identified four major factors which contributed to the further growth after the procedural changes in 1971.[31] First, the change in social attitudes resulting in the recognition that the future well-being of society lay in the welfare of children, the achievement of which required that children be regarded as separate beings whose welfare was not always best served by having those interests treated as one with the parents. It is submitted, however, that this change had already come about in the previous decade and that the procedural changes consequent upon the Administration of Justice Act 1970 allowed for further acknowledgment to be given to this change. A good example of the child's interests being severed from those of the parents was provided by *Re D (a minor) (wardship: sterilisation)* [32], where the proposed sterilisation of a mentally backward girl aged eleven, with her mother's consent, was prevented by the application in wardship of a local authority educational psychologist. A distinction came to be drawn, however, between those proceedings which related to the custody and upbringing of the ward or the administration of his property and those which did not. Only in the former was the child's welfare regarded as paramount.[33] In the latter due regard had to be paid to the interests of others. Thus in *Re X (a minor) (wardship: jurisdiction)* [34] the Court of Appeal drew a distinction between direct and indirect interference with a ward and held that custody or upbringing did not cover the issue of restraining publication of a book containing an account of the ward's father's depraved sexual activities. Notwithstanding that some harm to the ward might be foreseen, some interest, in particular the public interest,[35] might outweigh the ward's interest. In view of the differing emphasis to be

---

30   (London: Butterworths, 1979).
31   See p. 10.
32   [1976] Fam 185.
33   See e.g. *Re K (minors) (children: care and control)* [1977] Fam 179.
34   [1975] Fam 47.
35   See also *Re R (MJ) (publication of transcript)* [1975] Fam 89.

placed upon the ward's welfare, it became necessary to determine whether or not particular proceedings related sufficiently directly to the ward's custody, upbringing or property for the paramountcy principle to apply. Lowe and White drew a distinction between the 'custodial jurisdiction' and the 'protective jurisdiction' which was seen as going to the very function of the court:[36]

> Under the custodial jurisdiction the court must act in the ward's best interests and because the ward's welfare is the first and paramount consideration, other interests can only be considered incidentally and only in so far as they reflect on the ward's welfare. Under the protective jurisdiction, on the other hand, the court's concern is to protect the child from harm, but because the child's welfare is not accorded overriding significance, other interests assume a much greater importance. In such cases the court will be forced to make a policy decision as to which interest to protect.

In *Re D* the court, although seeking to protect the child from harm, was doing so, it is submitted, in relation to her upbringing and hence was exercising its custodial jurisdiction and the paramountcy principle applied, whereas in *Re X* the court was exercising its protective jurisdiction and so the paramountcy principle was inapplicable.

The second factor identified by Lowe and White as contributing to the expansion in use was the appreciation by local authorities that wardship could be used to avoid 'the restrictions and difficulties presented by legislative provisions'.[37] This practice was to receive judicial approval as a further palliative to the inadequacies of the Children and Young Persons Act 1969 and it can be seen as directly linked with the learned authors' third factor,[38] for the local authorities' increased reliance upon wardship was due in no small part to the courts being 'far more prepared to act in a supervisory

---

36   p. 124.
37   p. 10.
38   Lowe and White acknowledge that both factors were related to the greater concern for the interests of the child.

capacity and review the decisions of other courts or local authorities'. Thus in *Re D (a minor) (justices' decision: review)*[39] Dunn J. concluded that:

> Far from local authorities being discouraged from applying to the court in wardship . . . they should be encouraged to do so, because in many of these cases it is the only way in which orders can be made in the interests of the child untramelled by the statutory provisions of the Children and Young Persons Act 1969'.

Thus wardship came to serve as an additional and wider means of child protection, where, for example, the local authority was unable to prove one of the conditions in s. 1 of the 1969 Act, yet applying the paramountcy principle the wardship court considered it to be in the child's best interests to be in the care of the local authority, or where, as in *Re D,* the local authority wished to challenge the discharge of a care order.

This supervisory use of wardship was itself distinguishable between the decisions of other courts and the decisions of local authorities. In the context of the former, it came to be used essentially by local authorities as a 'supplementary jurisdiction', whereas in relation to the latter there were attempts to use it against local authorities as a 'review jurisdiction'. As a supplementary jurisdiction the principle in issue was again the inter-relationship between the wardship jurisdiction and the lower courts' statutory jurisdiction. It was seen as an acceptable use of the jurisdiction where the relief sought was outside the statutory jurisdiction of the court which made the order. The reluctance to sanction the use of wardship as a review jurisdiction was not surprising, however, in view of the restrictive principle in *Re M.*[40] That principle was applied in *Re T (AJJ) (an infant)* [41] to the case of a child in care under the Children and Young Persons legislation, in a like manner to a child subject to a 'parental rights' resolution under the Children Act

39   [1977] Fam 158.
40   [1961] Ch 328, see above p. 247.
41   [1970] Ch 688.

1948, on the basis that in both cases the local authority was 'firmly in the saddle'.[42] If a local authority wanted the court's assistance[43] then the wardship jurisdiction was exercised sparingly, as a supplementary rather than a review jurisdiction, in a way similar to its being exercised to supplement the powers of the lower courts. Otherwise the courts consistently refused to interfere with a local authority's statutory care of a child unless it was alleged that there had been some impropriety on the authority's part, such as occurred in *Re L (AC) (an infant)* [44] where the statutory procedure had not been adhered to. The more flexible approach, based on the child's best interests, adopted in the context of supplementing the lower courts' powers, was not generally adopted to review the local authorities' exercise of their statutory powers. The case of *Re H (a minor) (wardship: jurisdiction)* [45] did serve as an exception however, the Court of Appeal drawing the questionable distinction between, on the one hand, challenging the exercise of a discretionary power, for which the court would not use its wardship jurisdiction, and, on the other hand, challenging the source of that power, for which the use of wardship was seen as legitimate, where the circumstances were sufficiently unusual to justify its intervention. That decision was to be the high water mark of the supervisory exercise of wardship based upon principles of flexibility and furtherance of the child's best interests. The distinction drawn in that case between the position, as there, of a natural parent applicant and that of a foster parent applicant, as in *Re M* and *Re T (AJJ)*, was not seen as significant in *Re W (minors) (wardship: jurisdiction)* [46] where a natural parent of a child subject to a care order was held to have no right to challenge the merits of a local authority decision. The retreat from *Re H* was continued by Sir George Baker P in *M v Humberside County Council*,[47] when he held that the High Court would only assume jurisdiction in three situations. First, if the powers of the lower court were inadequate and needed to be supplemented, second if there had

42   Per Russell LJ at p. 694.
43   See e.g. *Re B (a minor) (wardship: child in care)* [1975] Fam 36.
44   [1971] 3 All E.R. 743. See also *Re D (a minor)* (1978) 122 Sol Jo 193.
45   [1978] Fam 65.
46   [1980] Fam 60.
47   [1979] Fam 114.

been some irregularity or excess in the local authority's exercise of its powers or third there was something exceptional about the case. In the ensuing decade the first situation was to receive considerable qualification, the second was to be rejected in favour of judicial review, whilst the third was to receive unqualified rejection. These judicial limitations were to prove insufficient to prevent eventual emasculation of wardship.

The final of Lowe and White's four factors was the greater mobility in the population and the consequent increase in kidnapping of children from one jurisdiction to another, for which at that time wardship was the best solution. A significant impetus to the jurisdiction's use was the change in judicial approach in *Re L (minors) (wardship: jurisdiction)* [48] which became 'the *locus classicus*'[49] in such cases until the enactment, some ten years later, of legislation to deal specifically with the issue of child abduction. Before *Re L*, if wardship proceedings were instituted promptly, the court would make a summary order for the return of the child, unless it could be shown that such an order was against the child's interests.[50] The courts regarded it as their duty to ensure that a party doing wrong by kidnapping did not gain advantage by that wrongdoing. That principle operated in favour of the party from whom the child had been kidnapped, because the kidnapper had to show that a summary order would have caused harm to the child. In *Re L* the Court of Appeal applied the paramountcy principle and held that the court had a discretion either to investigate the merits of the case, or to make a summary order for the return of the child so that the foreign court could investigate the merits.[51] That discretion was to be exercised on the basis of the paramountcy of the child's welfare and whether or not there existed an order of the foreign court. That principle favoured the kidnapper because it was for the other party to show that a summary order was in the child's best interests.[52]

---

48   [1974] 1 WLR 250.
49   See *Re C (minors) (wardship: jurisdiction)* [1978] Fam 105.
50   *Re H (infants)* [1966] 1 WLR 381.
51   See *Re M-R (a minor)* [1975] 5 Fam Law 55.
52   See *Re NC, JC and AC (minors)* (1977) 7 Fam Law 240.

Legislative reform of child law in the 1970s centred upon the Children Act 1975,[53] and did not, it is submitted, play a significant part in relation to wardship. The most noteworthy reform was the availability to certain qualified applicants with whom the child had his home, other than the child's mother and father, of the right to become custodian of the child. There was, however, to be a ten year delay before custodianship was implemented and demand for it was not to be great. Statutory reforms were to be of far greater significance in the ensuing decade.

The 1980s

As the following figures[54] show, the use of wardship continued to increase during this decade, in both the Principal Registry and District Registries.

Year	Principal Registry	District Registries	Total
1980	925	1037	1962
1981	822	1081	1903
1982	875	1426	2301
1983	802	1338	2140
1984	952	1456	2408
1985	965	1850	2815
1986	1149	2250	3399
1987	1105	2500	3605
1988	1068	2636	3704

Notwithstanding the increase, the period was noticeable for the limitations imposed by the courts on the circumstances in which they were prepared to exercise their powers. The increase itself was due largely to wardship's popularity with local authorities. Thus, whereas

53   Others included the Guardianship of Minors Act 1971 and the Guardianship Act 1973, the former being of a consolidating nature and the latter was primarily directed at achieving equality of parental rights in the absence of proceedings. Other consolidating Acts included the Adoption Act 1976 and the Legitimacy Act 1976.

54   Showing the number of originating summonses issued, see *Judicial Statistics* Annual Reports.

only 2.5% of cases in 1971 involved local authorities, this had risen to 30% by 1981, at least 40% by 1985[55] and in 1988 local authorities issued 61% of all summonses. As was to be expected, following on from the judicial encouragement given to local authorities during the previous decade and the restrictions placed upon the use of wardship against them, they were rarely involved as defendants. Two decisions of the House of Lords restricted further the use of wardship against local authorities. First in *A v Liverpool City Council*[56] the House confined the use of wardship as a means of review to the legality of administrative decisions. The courts had no jurisdiction to challenge a local authority's exercise of its discretionary powers. Secondly, in *Re W (a minor)* [57] the House rejected the argument put forward by relatives that there was a residual category of exceptional cases which justified the intervention of the High Court, for example where there was an alleged *lacuna* in the legislation.[58] The cases which contained *dicta* to the contrary, such as *M v Humberside County Council*,[59] although rightly decided on their facts, were a false guide to the true principle of law. Moreover, that principle applied not only to cases where parental rights and duties were vested in a local authority (whether under a care order, by virtue of a 'parental rights' resolution, or where the care of the child had been committed to a local authority in guardianship, matrimonial or divorce proceedings),[60] but also where an authority had physical care but not parental rights.[61] It applied also where the local authority intended to take care proceedings but had not had an opportunity to do so before the parent applied in wardship.[62] Thus the availability to a local authority of statutory powers, rather than the exercise of those powers, became the justification for denying the use of wardship. The 'supplementary jurisdiction' was in effect restricted to cases where the application

---

55   See Law Commission Working Paper No. 101, *Wards of Court*, para. 3.3.
56   [1982] AC 363.
57   [1985] AC 791.
58   See also *Re M (a minor)* [1985] Fam 60.
59   [1979] Fam 114, see above, p. 253.
60   *J v Devon County Council* [1986] 1 FLR 597.
61   *Re E (minors)* [1983] 1 WLR 541; *Liddle v Sunderland Borough Council* (1983) 13 Fam Law 250; *W v Nottinghamshire County Council* [1986] 1 FLR 565.
62   *W v Shropshire County Council* [1986] 1 FLR 359.

was made by or with the support of the local authority,[63] so where a local authority felt that its powers were inadequate to protect the child, the court was justified in exercising wardship.[64] Local authorities continued to be encouraged to invoke the jurisdiction 'in cases of difficulty, complexity, possible notoriety or where a stalemate had been reached'.[65] The position of local authorities was further enhanced by the Court of Appeal decision in *Re CB (a minor)*[66] that, contrary to the view which led the Latey Report to recommend the enactment of s. 7 of the Family Law Reform Act 1969, the section did not apply if the local authority were the plaintiff. In that situation the court had an unfettered inherent jurisdiction to decide the question of care and control according to the paramount interests of the child. This enabled the court in *Re SW (a minor) (wardship: jurisdiction)* [67] to place a ward aged seventeen in the care of a local authority notwithstanding that the statutory power was limited to minors below the age of seventeen. Where, however, a local authority did not consider itself inhibited in seeking to protect the child, third parties could neither seek a review of the local authority's exercise of its statutory responsibility nor seek to supplement the powers of the lower courts. Thus in *Re T (minors)* [68] the Court of Appeal held that the guardian *ad litem* of four children of one family, who were the subject of two sets of care proceedings brought by two local authorities in different juvenile courts, did not have *locus standi* to issue a wardship summons so that the cases of all the children could be heard before one court.

The use of wardship against local authorities was further curtailed by the decision of the Court of Appeal, in *Re DM (a minor) (wardship): jurisdiction),*[69] that judicial review and not wardship was

63   *Re C (a minor) (wardship: surrogacy)* [1985] FLR 846; *A v B and Hereford and Worcester County Council* [1986] 1 FLR 289, *Re JT (a minor) (wardship: committal to care)* [1986] 2 FLR 207.

64   *Re W (a minor) (justices' decision; review)* (1981) 2 FLR 62; *Re W (wardship proceedings)* (1981) 3 FLR 129; *Re R (a minor) (discharge of care order: wardship)* [1987] 2 FLR 400.

65   *Re LH (a minor) (wardship: jurisdiction)* [1968] 2 FLR 306; *Re M (a minor) (access application)* [1988] 1 FLR 35 at 42 per Sheldon J.

66   [1981] 1 WLR 379.

67   [1986] 1 FLR 24. See also *Salford City Council v C* (1981) 3 FLR 153.

68   [1989] 2 WLR 954.

69   [1986] 2 FLR 122.

the appropriate remedy where it was alleged that action taken by a local authority was outside its statutory powers or there had been some impropriety or irregularity by the local authority in the exercise of its discretion. This further restriction was, it is submitted, a regrettable one in view of the narrow procedural nature of judicial review. Attempts were made at first instance to ameliorate the effects of the decision, by the courts, when granting leave to apply for judicial review, being encouraged to recommend that wardship proceedings be instituted.[70]

The limitations being imposed upon wardship at this time were not confined to the jurisdiction's inter-relationship with the powers and responsibilities of local authorities. In *Re F (in utero)*,[71] a local authority sought to ward an unborn child so as to exercise control over the child's mother who had a history of mental illness and drug abuse. The Court of Appeal held that there was no jurisdiction because of the undesirable conflict between the legal interests of the mother and those of the unborn child and the insuperable difficulties of enforcing any order in respect of an unborn child against its mother.

In protecting the child's welfare the courts continued to distinguish between proceedings directly related to the ward's custody or upbringing and those affecting rights of third parties, hence in *Re JS (a minor)*[72] there was held to be no power in wardship to grant a bare declaration of paternity. A further limitation was that whilst the court in wardship had the power to grant a non-molestation order, if such was in the child's interests, there was no power to attach a power of arrest to such an order.[73]

The 1980s also saw the introduction of legislation to deal specifically with child abduction, which reduced to some extent the need to invoke wardship in cases of kidnapping. Thus the Child Abduction Act 1984 created two criminal offences of child abduction. In the context of civil remedies the Child Abduction and Custody Act 1985, Part I gave effect to the Hague Convention of 1980 on the Civil Aspects of International Child Abduction, which provided for the

---

70   See *R* v *London Borough of Newham, ex. p. McL* [1988] 1 FLR 416.
71   [1988] Fam 122.
72   [1981] Fam 22.
73   *Re G (wardship)* (1982) 4 FLR 538.

return to the country of his or her habitual residence of a child under the age of sixteen who had been wrongfully removed to, or retained in, another Contracting State. Part II of the Act gave effect to the European Convention of 1980 on Recognition and Enforcement of Decisions concerning Custody of Children and on the Restoration of Custody of Children. Cases in which there was a conflict of jurisdiction within the United Kingdom were not dealt with by the 1985 Act but by the Family Law Act 1986, Part I Chapter V of which provided for the recognition and enforcement throughout the United Kingdom of custody orders made in another part of the United Kingdom.

The Family Law Act 1986 also introduced new jurisdictional rules in wardship depending upon the basis upon which jurisdiction was exercised. This dichotomy arose because of a desire to ensure that jurisdiction throughout the United Kingdom was based on common grounds, whilst retaining the English courts' jurisdiction to make orders which did not fall within the 1986 Act's definition of 'custody orders'.[74] In so far as orders in wardship fell within that definition they came within the Act's scheme of uniform rules of jurisdiction, whereas orders other than 'custody orders' remained based on the inherent jurisdictional test of allegiance. The complex statutory rules were more limited than the inherent ones in requiring a greater *nexus,* based primarily but not exclusively on habitual residence, between the child and the forum. This jurisdictional division left the law in an unsatisfactorily complicated state, which it was accepted warranted further consideration.[75] Of note also in the jurisdictional context was the introduction of[76] (again complex) rules of transfer and re-transfer of the whole or part of proceedings between the High Court and county court. It remained the case, however, that an application for an order that a child be made, or cease to be, a ward of court had to be made to the High Court and it was doubted whether many cases would be transferred.[77]

---

74 For example an order relating to a child of whom care or care and control was, immediately after the order, vested in the local authority was not a custody order.
75 See Law Commission Report, 'Custody of Children - Jurisdiction and Enforcement within the United Kingdom', Law Com No. 138 para. 1.27.
76 By the Matrimonial and Family Proceedings Act 1984, sections 32 and 38.
77 Lowe and White, 2nd edn, para. 4-22.

Notwithstanding that the underlying trend behind the developments during the 1980s can be identified as one of containment, wardship's strength continued to be its flexibility. In the words of Lord Scarman:[78]

> a court exercising jurisdiction over its ward must never lose sight of a fundamental feature of the jurisdiction that it is exercising, namely that it is exercising a wardship, not an adversarial jurisdiction. Its duty is not limited to the dispute between the parties: on the contrary, its duty is to act in the way best suited in its judgment to serve the true interest and welfare of the ward. In exercising wardship jurisdiction the court is a true family court. Its paramount concern is the welfare of its ward.

For that reason the scope of the court's responsibility extended beyond that of a parent. Thus, for example, notwithstanding the decision of the House of Lords in *Gillick* v *West Norfolk and Wisbech Area Health Authority*[79] that, in certain circumstances,[80] a doctor had a discretion to give contraceptive advice or treatment to a girl under sixteen without her parents' consent, it is submitted that if the girl was a ward of court then applying the principle that no important step can be taken in a ward's life without the court's consent, the provision of such advice or treatment would be subject also to that consent, otherwise the doctor would be in contempt of court.

In view of the special nature of the wardship jurisdiction, it was not surprising that the courts were asked increasingly to exercise their powers in relation to medical treatment of children. In *Re B (a minor) (wardship: medical treatment)* [81] on the application of a local authority, the Court of Appeal authorised a life-saving operation for a child suffering from Down's syndrome, against the considered wishes of the parents. For those wishes were subordinate to the child's best interests. Certain treatment, in particular any sterilisation of a girl

---

78   In *Re E (SA) (a minor) (wardship)* [1984] 1 WLR 156 at 158.
79   [1986] AC 112.
80   See Lord Fraser at 147.
81   [1981] 1 WLR 1421.

under eighteen, was seen as justified only with the leave of a judge in wardship after a full and informed investigation.[82] That issue related directly to the child's upbringing and hence in accordance with the court's exercise of its custodial jurisdiction was properly determined on the basis of the paramountcy of the child's welfare.

In one important respect wardship could be said not to have afforded the protection that might reasonably have been expected, namely in relation to the publication of information identifying the ward. The relevant legislation[83] was aimed at prohibiting publication of information relating to wardship proceedings before any court sitting in private and not information relating to the ward. Thus in *Re W (wards) (publication of information)* [84] it was held not to be a breach of the automatic restrictions imposed by wardship proceedings in private, to publish the name and address of the ward or to identify him, or the fact that wardship proceedings were or had been taking place. If publication of the ward's identity was to be prevented there had to be an order of the court to that effect,[85] which could extend to the prohibition of any publication which could identify persons connected with the ward, for example the ward's parents or carers.[86] In deciding whether or not to exercise that power the court was regarded as exercising, what Lowe and White identified as, its protective jurisdiction, which required the court to balance the need to protect the ward from harm, against the importance of maintaining freedom of the press. It is a sad comment upon this limit upon the automatic protection in wardship that, in the words of the Report of the Inquiry into Child Abuse in Cleveland 1987:[87] 'The restrictions imposed automatically on the media in the Juvenile Court . . . affords greater automatic privacy to the child than the High Court in wardship proceedings'. The Inquiry's view[88] that 'at the very least . . . there

---

82   Per Lord Templeman in *Re B (a minor) (wardship: sterilisation)* [1988] AC 199.

83   Administration of Justice Act 1960, s. 12.

84   [1989] 1 FLR 246.

85   *Re L (a minor) (wardship: freedom of publication)* [1988] 1 All ER 418.

86   *X County Council v A* [1984] 1 WLR 1422; *Re C (a minor) (wardship: medical treatment)* [1989] 3 WLR 240; *Re C (a minor) (No. 2) (wardship: medical treatment)* [1989] 3 WLR 252.

87   Cm 412 para. 16.50.

88   Para. 16.51.

should be automatic restriction upon the publication of the names, addresses, photographs and identification of children, who are the subject of civil proceedings' did not receive the attention it deserved.

Where there were criminal investigations and, for example, the police wished to interview a ward there was a clearer need for the court to balance the ward's interest against the public interest that the wardship jurisdiction should not be extended so as to give protection to criminal offenders.[89] The court had to perform a balancing exercise weighing the potential damage to the ward against the public interest and in reaching that decision the ward's interest was not necessarily the first and paramount consideration. Moreover, a distinction was drawn between, on the one hand, the situation where a child had been warded before any criminal proceedings, in which case the court's leave had to be sought for the police to interview the ward,[90] and on the other hand the situation where the prosecution process had been set in train before the wardship proceedings began, in which case it was not appropriate for the court to exercise wardship.

By way of conclusion to this review of the limitations which came to be imposed upon wardship during this decade, it is noteworthy that in *Re F (minors) (wardship: jurisdiction)*[91] the Court of Appeal, by a majority, held that the very wide discretion of the wardship jurisdiction had to be exercised on the basis of some significant evidence upon which to find a concern sufficient to justify that exercise. In *Re F*, one of the cases of suspected child abuse in Cleveland in 1987, where the local authority took wardship proceedings to protect the children, there was no significant evidence at the hearing to support the allegation of sexual abuse and the Court of Appeal dewarded the children and ordered their return to their parents.

---

89   *Re S (minors) (wardship: police investigation)* [1987] Fam 199; *Re F (minors) (wardship: police investigation)* [1988] Fam 18.
90   Provided the ward had not attained the age of 17, see *Re B (a minor) The Times*, 20 Dec. 1989.
91   [1988] 2 FLR 13.

The movement for reform

The pace of change so far discussed made wardship ripe for review. So, in 1984[92] when the Law Commission embarked upon a review of the private law relating to the upbringing of children, wardship was included. In a Working Paper[93] the Commission suggested a four-fold classification of the functions of the wardship jurisdiction: as an alternative jurisdiction to achieve a result which could equally be achieved under the statutory codes; as an independent jurisdiction to achieve an object which could not be achieved under the statutory codes; as a supportive jurisdiction to achieve more effectively a result which could be achieved under the statutory codes and as a review or appellate jurisdiction to challenge a decision which had been taken under the statutory codes. The Commission then went on to put forward three main approaches to reform.[94] Option A: retain wardship as a separate jurisdiction, perhaps with some specific reforms, but retaining its four functions. Option B: make wardship a residuary jurisdiction so as to make good deficiencies in the statutory codes. As such it would retain its supportive function and, in so far as this was not inconsistent with the statutory codes, its independent function; but not its alternative or appellate jurisdiction, at least where rights of appeal exist. Option C: end wardship as a separate jurisdiction and incorporate some of its features within the statutory codes. In reply it is submitted that however careful the consideration that has been given to the framing of the statutory codes, it is not possible to legislate for every eventuality in which a child might require the court's protection. In view of its adaptability to deal with cases of an unusual or complex nature, wardship should have a place as an independent jurisdiction, at least where such a jurisdiction is not inconsistent with the statutory codes.

The response to the Working Paper indicated considerable support for some reform,[95] but only after the reform of the private

---

92 In the same year the *Report of the Select Committee on Children in Care* suggested wardship should be limited to rare and exceptional cases, 1983-4, HC 360 para. 82.

93 No. 101, para. 3.53.

94 Paras 4.6-4.25.

95 See The Law Commission, *Family Law, Review of Child Law, Guardianship and Custody*, Law Com. No. 172, para. 1.4.

and public statutory procedures. So, in its Report on the *Review of Child Law* published in July 1988, the Commission postponed making any substantial recommendations for the reform of wardship, the aim being to incorporate the most valuable features of wardship into the new statutory system:

> this should reduce the need to resort to wardship proceedings save in the most unusual and complex cases. It will also enable the true scope for a residual power for the courts to assume guardianship over certain children to be determined.[96]

In the same month as the publication of the Law Commission's Report, support for the continued use of wardship was forthcoming from the *Inquiry into Child Abuse in Cleveland*:[97]

> There is no doubt that the wardship jurisdiction came to the rescue of an otherwise overburdened Juvenile Court. It has proved in Cleveland to be an invaluable procedure to enable extremely difficult, complex and emotive issues to be fully considered and adjudicated upon. Wardship has an ethos which is recognised by those who use and are engaged in the jurisdiction. We see wardship having a role to play in care proceedings in the future.

The Inquiry went further,[98] however, in identifying as an injustice the ability of a local authority to issue wardship proceedings whilst the parents were denied that right, such as to warrant reconsideration of the decision in *A v Liverpool City Council*.[99] The Children Act 1989[100] met that injustice not by removing the restriction on the parental use of wardship but by imposing restrictions on local authority use of the jurisdiction so that wardship is not to be used by

---

96 Law Com. No. 172, para. 1.4.
97 Para. 16.37.
98 Para. 16.65.
99 [1982] AC 363, see above p. 256.
100 Not anticipated to be fully in force until Autumn 1991.

local authorities to circumvent the requirements of the Act. Hence s. 100 (2) provides that:

> No court shall exercise the High Court's inherent jurisdiction with respect to children -
>
> (a) so as to require a child to be placed in the care, or put under the supervision, of a local authority;
> (b) so as to require a child to be accommodated by or on behalf of a local authority;
> (c) so as to make a child who is the subject of a care order a ward of court; or
> (d) for the purpose of conferring on any local authority power to determine any question which has arisen, or which may arise, in connection with any aspect of parental responsibility for a child.

As a child who is the subject of a care order cannot be warded, a local authority will not be able to seek, or agree to a third party seeking, the supplementary assistance of the wardship court in relation to such a child under the rule in *A* v *Liverpool City Council*.

The power in s. 7 of the Family Law Reform Act 1969 to place a ward in the care or under the supervision of a local authority is abolished.[101] Wardship proceedings are family proceedings within the meaning of the Children Act[102] and so, in line with the power available in such proceedings, if it appears to a wardship court that it may be appropriate for a care or supervision order to be made, the court may direct a local authority to undertake an investigation of the child's circumstances.[103] The decision whether or not to apply for a

---

101 s. 100(1).
102 s. 8(3)(a).
103 s. 37(1).

care order or a supervision order is then a matter for the local authority.[104] The making of a care order in respect of a ward of court terminates the wardship.[105] Where the wardship court gives a direction to a local authority to undertake an investigation it may make an interim care order or an interim supervision order provided it is satisfied that there are reasonable grounds for believing that the statutory conditions for making such an order[106] are satisfied.

The court's inherent jurisdiction, which includes but is not limited to wardship,[107] may only be invoked on the application of a local authority, with leave of the court.[108] So, although a child who is in care cannot be warded,[109] he could be the subject of an application under the inherent jurisdiction independent of wardship. The circumstances justifying such an application are, however, severely limited. The court's leave to the making of an application by a local authority for any exercise of the court's inherent jurisdiction with respect to children may only be granted if the court is satisfied that the local authority's desired result could not be achieved through the making of any order other than under the inherent jurisdiction[110] and there is reasonable cause to believe that if the inherent jurisdiction is not exercised the child is likely to suffer significant harm. Hence if the child can be equally protected by the local authority's use of its statutory powers, the inherent jurisdiction may not be invoked.

The overall effect is that consequent upon the reforms of the statutory code relating to children in care, wardship has ceased to be available to local authorities as an alternative jurisdiction, a supportive jurisdiction and a review or appellate jurisdiction. In so far as the wider inherent jurisdiction has a use by local authorities it is as an independent jurisdiction where this is not inconsistent with the statutory code and only then with leave of the court.

---

104   If the local authority decide not to apply for an order, they must inform the court of their reasons, any service or assistance which they have provided or intend to provide and any other action taken or proposed, see s. 37 (3).

105   s. 91(4).

106   s. 38(1) and (2).

107   See e.g. Jacob, 'The Inherent Jurisdiction of the Court' (1970) 23 CLP 23.

108   s. 100(3).

109   s. 100(2)(c).

110   s. 100(4) and (5).

Further reform of wardship is likely to depend upon how the Children Act 1989 works. The availability under the Act of new procedures will, however, provide an alternative to wardship and serve to reduce further the need to rely upon that jurisdiction. In the context of private individuals, relatives have been a major user, for wardship provided the only means of seeking an order relating to a child's upbringing until the introduction of custodianship, with the implementation in 1985 of Part II of the Children Act 1975. These custodianship provisions are repealed by the Children Act 1989[111] and replaced with power to make a 'residence order' or 'contact order'[112] on the application of a person who is entitled to apply for such an order or who has obtained the leave of the court to make such an application. The Act has also introduced 'specific issue' and 'prohibited steps' orders, relating to particular aspects of upbringing, which are derived from similar orders in wardship.[113] Entitlement to apply is more limited than in the case of 'residence and contact orders',[114] but an application may also be made with leave of the court. This latter general availability, subject to leave, is of particular significance in opening up access to the courts. In the words of the Law Commission:[115]

> The object of this scheme is to enable anyone with a genuine interest in a child's welfare to make applications relating to his upbringing, as can at present be done by making a child a ward of court . . . The requirement of leave is intended as a filter to protect the child and his family against unwarranted interference in their comfort and security, while ensuring that the child's interests are properly respected.

Wardship will, however, continue to play its part in those contexts where the court's parental role is warranted, for example in relation to kidnapping, in so far as the child abduction legislation

111   Sch. 15.
112   s. 10.
113   See Law Commission Working Paper No. 101, para. 4.23 (iv).
114   See s. 10(4) and (5).
115   Law Com. No. 172, para. 4.41.

does not provide a remedy, and in cases of an unusual or complex nature not otherwise catered for. It will continue to have the advantage of preserving the *status quo* pending the hearing of the application and as a means of securing continuing responsibility of the court in those limited cases where it is really needed. In this way the court's limited resources will be better utilised. Whilst the forty year period here reviewed may serve to testify how wardship outgrew itself, it does not testify that it has outlived itself.

11

Child Maintenance Problems in New Zealand when a non-Custodial Parent is denied Access by a Custodial Parent

P. R. H. Webb

The problem for discussion is narrow but controversial: may a New Zealand Family Court Judge properly refuse a child maintenance order to a custodial parent[1] who, apparently deliberately, declines to allow the non-custodial parent to have access to the relevant child or

This article is prompted by the decision of Hollis J in the English case, *Foot* v *Foot* [1987] FCR 62; [1987] Fam Law 13, that the court cannot properly make a discount in the child maintenance payments which might have been ordered in the normal course because the parent with custody has refused the non-custodial parent reasonable access to the relevant children. They were aged between six and thirteen in that case.

1   'Custody' means 'the right to possession and care of a child:' see Guardianship Act 1968, s. 2.
     'Guardianship' is a wider concept, meaning 'the custody of a child (except in the case of a testamentary guardian and subject to any custody order made by the Court) and the right of control over the upbringing of a child, and includes all rights, powers and duties in respect of the person and upbringing of a child that were at the commencement of this Act vested by

children?[2] The governing legislation in New Zealand is the Family
Proceedings Act 1980. S. 75 of that Act gives Family Courts
jurisdiction to hear and determine child maintenance applications.
The provisions of the Act which principally bear on this problem read
as follows:

s. 72 Maintenance of children
(1) Each parent of a child is liable to maintain the child -
   (a) Until the child attains the age of 16 years; and
   (b) Where it appears to the Court to be in the best
        interests of a child who has attained or will shortly
        attain the age of 16 years, until the child attains
        the age of 18 years or such earlier age as the Court
        directs; and

any enactment or rule of law in the sole guardian of a child, and "guardian"
has a corresponding meaning.' s. 3 of the 1968 Act.
'Upbringing' is defined by s. 2 as including education and religion. As to
who is a child's guardian, see ss 6-8.
Thus *both* parents should consult, even after divorce, as to where their
children should go to school: see, e.g. *Seabrook* v *Seabrook* [1971] NZLR
947 (CA).
See also the decision of Hardie Boys J in *Johnston* v *Johnston* (1984) 3
NZFLR 311 and that of Williamson J in *W* v *D* (1986) 4 NZFLR 85.
While the court may remove a guardian under s. 10 of the 1968 Act, the
unilateral act of one parent cannot take away the rights of the other co-
guardian parent.
Under s. 20A(1) of the 1968 Act, every person commits an offence and is
liable on summary conviction to a fine not exceeding NZ $1,000 who,
without reasonable excuse and with intent to prevent an order for access to
a child from being complied with, hinders or prevents access to a child by a
person who is entitled under the order to access to the child. By subs (2)
nothing in the section is to limit the power of a Court to punish a person for
contempt of court.

2   It has been held that nothing in the Family Proceedings Act 1980 requires
maintenance for a child to be paid to the custodial parent as a contribution
to that parent's general funds: *Klasema* v *Klasema* (1987) 4 NZFLR 458,
discussed below. 'Maintenance' in respect of a child is defined by s. 2 of
the Family Proceedings Act 1980 as meaning 'the provision of money,
property and services' including 'provision for the child's education and
training to the extent of the child's ability and talents.'

(c)   Where it appears to the Court that the child is or will be engaged, after attaining the age of 16 years, in a course of full-time education or training and it is expedient that the child should continue to be maintained, until the child attains the age of 20 years or such earlier age as the Court directs.

(2)   In determining the amount that is payable by a parent for the maintenance of a child, the Court shall have regard to all relevant circumstances affecting the welfare of the child, including -

(a)   The reasonable needs of the child; and

(b)   The manner in which the child is being educated or trained, and the expectations of each parent as to the child's education or training.

(3)   In determining the amount that is payable by a parent for the maintenance of a child, the Court shall also have regard to the following circumstances:

(a)   The means, including the potential earning capacity, of each parent:

(b)   The reasonable needs of each parent:

(c)   The fact that either parent is supporting any other person:

(d)   The contribution (whether in the form of oversight, services, money payments, or otherwise) of either parent in respect of the care of that or any other child of the marriage:

(e)   The financial and other responsibilities of each parent:

(f)   Where the person against whom the order is sought is not a natural or adoptive parent of the child -

(i)   The extent (if at all) to which that person has assumed responsibility for the maintenance of the child, the basis on which that person has assumed that responsibility, and the length of time during which that person has discharged that responsibility; and

(ii)   Whether that person assumed or discharged any responsibility for the maintenance of the child knowing that that person was not a natural parent of the child; and

(iii)   The liability of any other person to maintain the child:

(g)   Any property and income of the child:

(h)   Where the child has attained the age of 16 years, any earning capacity of the child.

* * *

s. 74 Applications for maintenance orders in respect of children

An application for a maintenance order in respect of a child may be made only -

(a)   By a parent against another parent; or

(b)   By a person who has lawful care of the child, or by a Social Worker, against a parent or parents of the child

* * *

s. 76 Maintenance orders in respect of children

(1) on hearing an application under section 74 of this Act, a Family Court may, subject to subsections (2) and (9) of this section, make any one or more of the following orders:

(a)   An order directing the respondent to pay such periodical sum towards the future maintenance of the child as the Court thinks fit:

(b)   An order directing the respondent to pay such lump sum towards the future maintenance of the child as the Court thinks fit:

(c)   An order directing the respondent to pay such lump sum towards the past maintenance of the child as the Court thinks fit.

It will be noticed that none of these sections refers at all to the conduct of the paying parent or to that of the recipient parent.[3] Nor does any section mention the reasonableness or otherwise of making a child maintenance order or allow regard to be paid to 'any other circumstances that the Court thinks relevant.'[4] Nor does any section permit the child to apply for his or her own maintenance.[5]

A cognate problem also arises in the context of s. 99(1) and (2) of the 1980 Act. These provide that the court 'may' make order discharging, varying or suspending (*inter alia*) child maintenance orders and registered maintenance agreements covering children. In each case, however, the court must be satisfied that it 'ought' to take such step 'having regard to the principles of maintenance set out in,' *inter alia*, s. 72 of the Act. s. 99(6) provides that the court 'may' remit all arrears due under a maintenance order or registered maintenance agreement or suspend payment thereof. There is no express requirement that the court should refer back to s. 72 at all. The problem in this context, then, becomes: may the Judge properly refuse to discharge, vary or suspend a child maintenance order because, for instance, the wife with custody of the children has, without justification, refused to allow her husband (or, for that matter, her former husband) to see them? And, if the husband has deliberately allowed arrears to accrue because of her attitude, will the Court allow any remission of them?

The rival approaches

The knub of the problem comes down to this: can s. 76(1) be taken to indicate that a Family Court has a residual discretion whether or not to make a child maintenance order and is free to take into account factors not specifically listed in s. 72(2) and (3)? Or does s. 76(1) only constitute a machinery provision affording it no more than a discretion to choose which of the three permitted forms of order it will make?

3   Cf. s. 66 of the Family Proceedings Act 1980 in the context of spousal maintenance.
4   Cf. the now repealed Domestic Proceedings Act 1968, ss 35 and 36.
5   *Klasema* v *Klasema* (1987) 4 NZFLR 458.

Sinclair J, in *Shrimski* v *Shrimski*,[6] clearly favoured the latter alternative. The wife left her husband and departed with their two children, born in 1972 and 1974, for Melbourne, where her parents lived. An Australian Family Court granted her custody of them, allowing the husband access to their boy. The husband, in later New Zealand proceedings, sought access in respect of their girl. He was frustrated by the wife's attitude. Ultimately, the wife initiated child maintenance proceedings in New Zealand in respect of both children. The Family Court Judge decided that the wife had unilaterally removed the children to Australia, thus putting the possibility of access virtually out of the husband's reach. The Judge thought the wife had taken on to herself the rights and duties of parenthood to the effective exclusion of the husband to the degree where he could not be asked to make further financial contribution. It was accordingly held, in the light of decisions not pinpointed by Sinclair J but very probably some of those to be discussed below, that the conduct of the wife disentitled her to any child maintenance order and, in purported exercise of the discretion thought to exist under s.76(1), the Court declined the application outright. On the wife's appeal to the High Court, Sinclair J agreed that the lower court had been justified in criticising the mother but considered that the dominant consideration under s. 72(2) was the children's welfare. The reference there to 'all relevant circumstances affecting the welfare of the child' was held to rule out, by implication, consideration of other circumstances. Hence the mother's conduct had no bearing on the children's entitlement to maintenance or on the liability of either parent to maintain their children. There was no discretion, in the opinion of Sinclair J, of the kind thought to exist by the court below. He remitted the case for determination of the quantum of maintenance in the light of the judgment he had given. The wish of the learned Judge not to punish

---

6   (1985) 3 NZFLR 707. The decision will be seen to accord not only with *Foot* v *Foot* [1987] FCR 62; [1987] Fam Law 13 but also with *PN* v *PN* (1984) 3 NZFLR 277 in the context of s. 99(2) of the 1980 Act. And see *Smith* v *Smith* (1982) FLN 54.

the children by visiting upon them the conduct of their mother is perfectly understandable.[7]

There were, however, as already observed, certain earlier decisions in which access-denying custodial parents were involved in child maintenance proceedings. In *Stone* v *Maintenance Officer*,[8] a husband had been convicted for default[9] in paying maintenance in respect of two children of whom the wife had custody. The husband had been granted access to them. The wife had, without notice, taken them to Australia. The conviction was quashed on appeal to what was then the Supreme Court. The wife was seen as desirous of enforcing the maintenance order while in breach of the access order. It was accepted that maintenance and access were distinct matters but had a common link in that both were for the benefit of the children. The father was viewed as having no way of knowing whether their maintenance was being applied for that purpose or, even, whether they were with their mother at all. A caution was voiced by the court against the father's thinking that the mother's failure to allow access as ordered was, of itself, 'reasonable cause' for non-payment of maintenance by the father.

In *Denby* v *Croucher*,[10] another case predating the 1980 Act, it was stated *obiter* by Chilwell J in the High Court that, where a child maintenance agreement had been entered into as part of an overall settlement after divorce, which settlement included access rights, and where the mother had, as there, ignored her obligations under it and had flouted Supreme Court orders requiring her to permit access, and where the father had faithfully observed all his obligations, these factors were relevant in deciding whether the amount payable under the agreement should be increased on the mother's application.

7   See especially (1985) 3 NZFLR at 710-712. It is suggested, at 712, that the non-custodial parent should seek an attachment order against the unco-operative custodial parent.

        There cannot have been any prior consultation between the parents, or any approach to any New Zealand court, as to whether the children were to reside in Australia. See *W* v *W* (1984) 2 NZFLR 335 (CA).

8   [1979] NZ Recent Law 175.

9   Under s. 107(1) of the former Domestic Proceedings Act 1968. See now s. 124 of the 1980 Act.

10   [1979] NZ Recent Law 141.

In contrast, in a case[11] just post-dating the coming into force of the 1980 Act, the Family Court found that the mother never attempted to hinder access but that the relevant children had merely refused to see their father or to discuss access with counsel or with the psychologist. It was held that the father could not decline to pay child maintenance. In short, access had simply failed.

In another case,[12] it was said by Speight J on an appeal that, where there was evidence that children might be disadvantaged by lack of funds from their father, it was doubtful whether his mere inability to see them would be taken into account in deciding whether to vary or cancel a child maintenance order in respect of them. In the special circumstances of the case, the court stated that the father's money would be better applied to the purpose of saving for visits. The order was cancelled. The children were seen as having been deprived by their mother of contact with their father, which they needed to maintain. Their mother had taken them to Australia after she and the father had separated and orders had been made for maintenance and access. She had, moreover, remarried there into very comfortable circumstances.

In *Hamer* v *Colthorpe*[13] it was posited *obiter* by Judge Inglis QC that there might be cases where arrears of child maintenance could justifiably be remitted because of the unwarranted exclusion of the liable parent from access to the children. A parent who, by depriving the other parent of access, elected to assume *de facto* guardianship might, it was put, properly be regarded as having assumed sole responsibility for their maintenance.

To make out such a case could, however, prove to be no easy task. In *Gilmer* v *Gilmer*[14] the wife resorted to deliberate deceit to remove the parties' child to Australia for a year on one occasion and, on another, she took the child there again for a like period - without informing the husband. Judge Mahony (who is now the Principal Family Court Judge) regarded the case as lacking that element of aggravation and persistence to justify his remitting all maintenance

---

11   *Boxall* v *Boxall* (1981) FLN 37.
12   *Fletcher* v *Fletcher* (1981) FLN 47. See also *McLaren* v *SSC* [1983] NZ
       Recent Law 166.
13   (1983) FLN 140 (2d).
14   [1984] NZ Recent Law 99.

arrears arising in respect of those two periods - during which, of course, access had been effectively denied to the father.[15] It was observed that the rights vested in children to be maintained by their parents and for access by the non-custodial parent were distinct, and created separate and distinct obligations which were not normally interrelated. Breach of one order by one parent did not, in itself, excuse the breach of the other order by the other parent. Breach of an access order did not, *per se*, relieve the other from the obligation to maintain the child. Conversely, where a non-custodial parent fell into arrears, the custodial parent was not thereby relieved of an obligation to permit access. The case was thus not to be viewed as one where the refusal of access had been of such a kind and degree as effectively to shut out the father from the child's life.

In a contemporary case, *Payne* v *Payne*,[16] the wife chose to stay in Australia, where she had relatives, having decided to separate from her husband. She had their two children with her. The husband sought variation or discharge of the child maintenance order on the ground that the children were in Australia against his will and that he could not exercise his guardianship rights effectively. Judge Inglis QC held that the case was not one of access being denied by the wife but as simply having been made more difficult by the force of circumstances. The husband should not be wholly relieved of his obligation to support his children, it was said, but he should be allowed a temporary relief until he could resume payment in full. The wife was considered not to have moved to Australia motivated by any

15   One fifth of the arrears was remitted as the father had contributed to the child's return air-fare at the end of the second period.

          Cf. *W* v *SSC* (1986) 4 NZFLR 321, especially at 325, per Judge Carruthers. He there distinguished the *Shrimski* case but he was dealing with the Liable Parent Contribution scheme and not, strictly speaking, with 'private' maintenance.

          The first wife's unjustified denial of access at every point to the former husband had led directly to grave financial and health problems for him. This was held to be one of many good reasons for holding, with reference to s. 72(2), that he was not liable at all to contribute under this Scheme towards the cost of the domestic purposes benefit being paid to his former wife in respect of her care of these children.

16   (1984) 3 NZFLR 305.

desire to cut the husband off from his children. Nor had she placed obstacles in the way of his seeing them or communicating with them. Indeed, he had visited them in Australia and he had seen them briefly when they visited New Zealand. Clearly, this wife could not be said to have usurped her position as guardian.

In *DY* v *DY*,[17] however, the position was markedly different. The husband sought to enforce an access order in respect of his children aged twelve, ten and eight and to have cancelled the child maintenance orders that had been made against him. The wife sought the upward variation of the latter. The children had lived with her since 1979, when the husband left. He had seen but little of them since. The case was the culmination of over five years' interparental litigation. The absence of access was primarily due to the mother's bitterness towards the father and her success in capturing the children's souls to the extent that they were united in their resistance to him. In these unfortunate circumstances Judge Ryan understandably cancelled the maintenance order because of the total and complete denial of access brought about solely by the mother's attitude towards her husband.[18] He thought no useful purpose would be served by further attempts at access, which was a dead letter. The access order was discharged.

In *Nilsen* v *Sands*[19] the mother of a boy born in 1976 sought the cancellation of a child maintenance order made against her in 1979. The parties had separated, the mother worked full time and it was accepted by them that the father should have the principal charge of the child in the week and that the mother should have weekend access. Difficulties over access were quick to arise. Eventually the mother 'gave up' altogether. There were discussions in 1982 about her right to see the boy. The father, who did not defend the application, had evidently told her that he had told the child that he did not have a mother and had generally made it clear to the mother that she was no longer seen as part of the child's life. She now had

---

17   (1985) 3 NZFLR 446.
18   See at p. 448.
19   [1985] NZ Recent Law 401.

another child of her own to care for and had no income. Judge Inglis QC held that the situation could be placed 'squarely in the category of the exceptional class of case where the parent who has *de facto* custody of the child has assumed exclusively the role of *de facto* guardian and has deliberately set out to exclude the other parent from rights of guardianship.' Sole responsibility to maintain the child thus rested with the father at his own choice. The order was cancelled and all arrears were remitted.[20]

Judge Inglis QC was not prepared to adopt this approach in *Kearns* v *Kearns*.[21] The father, who had remarried and had a second family to support, sought the reduction of a child maintenance order, made by consent in 1981, in respect of the parties' two children. He pleaded that he could not afford to meet it. His former wife, who had custody of the children by agreement, did not seek an increase. Her sensitivity to the situation was such that she was willing to accept the agreed figure. It was found that the father could regulate his affairs so as to provide for the children without hardship to his second family. In furtherance of his case, he had sought to say that the mother had, without consulting him,[22] moved - with the children - to be near her parents in comparatively distant parts of New Zealand and, ultimately, to Brisbane, Australia. He had not, however, made any attempt to prevent these moves. Indeed, it was considered that he had let himself be discouraged too early and too easily from obtaining as much access as he wanted and that he would have got it had he pressed more firmly. If he wished to maintain his effectiveness as co-guardian, he should, the court considered, have adopted a less passive stance. The 'exceptional' cases showed that there had always been a history of strenuous efforts by the non-custodial parent to assert his or her role as guardian and determined opposition to that by the

---

20   Judge Inglis QC had, in fact, already taken the same stance in the unreported case of *Dawick* v *Dawick* (Family Court, Napier; 23 May 1983; No. FP 041/206/77).

21   [1986] NZ Recent Law 95.

22   It seems she had received legal advice that she need not consult - wrong, of course, in view of *Seabrook* v *Seabrook* [1971] NZLR 947 (CA) and *W* v *W* (1984) 2 NZFLR 335 (CA).

custodial parent. In any case, the former wife had stated sincerely that she did not oppose access. There was no reason to suppose that she would not use the maintenance for the children's benefit, and the father could afford to provide a 'reasonable fund to enable him to have access to the children of his first marriage if he wishes to do so.' Although the court declined to decrease the quantum of maintenance, it was prepared to set the parties 'off to a fresh start' by suspending the accumulated arrears of maintenance while the father regularly and faithfully paid the current maintenance.

Undoubtedly factors beyond those set out in s.72(2) and (3) were again taken into account here, but it had recently been stated by Tompkins J in *Woolley* v *Carmichael*[23] that the matters specifically set out in those subsections were not exhaustive in that the court could, in the exercise of its discretion, have regard to matters other than those expressly stated. Later on in his judgment he opined that s.72 left with the court a full discretion to determine the amount payable by a parent for the maintenance of a child and that, although the section specified matters to be taken into account, those matters were not exhaustive and there remained an overall discretion in the court to make what, in all the circumstances, it regards as an appropriate order.[24]

Judge Inglis QC was ready to regard *Comrie* v *Therkleson*[25] as 'exceptional'. The father sought variation of a maintenance order in respect of his three children. Their mother, his former wife, had remarried and she and her second husband were comfortably off. She had departed, with these children, on 14 February 1985 without any prior consultation with their father. He first heard of the intended departure on the evening of 13 February. The children were then nearing the end of a long stay with their father's mother. The children's mother collected them on the morning of 14 February and the father had never heard of them since then. He thought that his former wife and her second husband had sold their New Zealand

23   (1984) 2 NZFLR 426, at 429.
24   At 431. Arguably both these statements are *obiter*.
25   [1986] NZ Recent Law 136.

home and taken their furniture to Australia. Inquiries as to the children's whereabouts proving fruitless, the father informed the Department of Social Welfare that he was ceasing to pay maintenance and was putting money into a savings account as a fund for the children if and when he learned of their whereabouts. The court accepted that maintenance should not be withheld as a punishment for denial of access but pointed out that the mother had not been entitled to take the children out of the country without the father's express consent as parent and guardian. Accordingly the mother's actions had to be regarded as an acceptance by her of sole responsibility for the children's maintenance. The maintenance order was suspended until further order as from 14 February 1985. Any maintenance paid after that date should be refunded. The mother was ordered to pay NZ $150 towards the father's costs.

In *Green* v *Green*[26] the wife initiated child maintenance proceedings in respect of the parties' three daughters aged fifteen, twelve and eight. They had been in her *de facto* custody since the parties' separation in March 1984 and were being supported by the wife's *de facto* husband. Difficulties about the husband's seeing his children appear to have been occasioned by his extreme religious views - he was a member of the Worldwide Church of God and the wife was an Anglican - and their having been frightened by events occurring before the separation. The wife admitted that she did her best to try to protect the children against their father. She in particular had failed to appreciate the distinction between guardianship and custody, for she never consulted her husband about where the children were to go to school or about their religious upbringing. The husband did not press any earlier claim for definition of access, though he had thought of doing so. He realised that the access question must be central to the question of child maintenance now being raised by the wife.

Though no access order had actually been flouted by the wife here, the case verges on the 'exceptional' in that, though the father did see the middle child until nine months previously, the mother thought

26   (1986) 2 FRNZ 21.

damage had been done thereby and she intended to discourage further contact between the children and their father. Various of the cases already mentioned[27] were considered by the court, which concluded that it could not see, 'how the subsequent withholding of maintenance in respect of the child by the non-custodial parent with Court approval can be said to be having regard to the welfare of the child. It would seem in that situation that the child not only is affected by the refusal of access but is in addition affected by the denial of maintenance.'[28]

The court was also of the view that the list of criteria in s.72(3) was exclusive and that Parliament would have expressly included the right of the child to access in the list had it required that matter to be considered. Judge McAloon held that he must decline to refuse to make a maintenance order. He made an order in respect of all three children.[29] The eldest was attending a Presbyterian boarding school.

27   Viz., *Stone* v *Maintenance Officer* [1979] NZ Recent Law 175; *Denby* v *Croucher* [1979] NZ Recent Law 141; *Dawick* v *Dawick* (unreported); *Comrie* v *Therkleson* [1986] NZ Recent Law 136 and *Blake* v *Rhodes* (1983) 2 NZFLR 117.
      In this last case Judge Inglis QC held that a step-father was not, in the circumstances, liable to contribute towards the boarding-school fees of his step-son in the custody of his former wife. She had applied solely because funds were running short for this purpose. He was able to arrive at this decision in the light of s. 72 and 76(2). The latter subsection is beyond the scope of this article, but it is clear that the learned Judge considered that s. 76(1) gave him a discretion whether or not to make a maintenance order and that he would have exercised it against making one. See especially at pp. 121, 124. Reference may also be made to *Jones* v *Jones* [1983] NZ Recent Law 329, *H* v *C* (1985) 3 NZFLR 749 and *Clarke* v *Clarke* (1988) 5 NZFLR 33. Judge McAloon did not make an express finding that there had been an abuse of guardianship or wilful refusal of access: see at p. 24.
28   At 23.
29   See at p. 24. The *Shrimski* case, which had not then been reported, evidently came to Judge McAloon's attention after he had dictated his judgment. It, of course, vindicated his decision. In an addendum to his judgment (at 24) he pointed out that Mr Green must understand that a High Court decision bound the Family Court.

The post-*Shrimski* decisions

After the decision of Sinclair J had become known, *Pearce* v *Fitzgerald*[30] came before Judge Inglis QC. It cannot strictly be described as one of his 'exceptional' cases. It was found that the mother's course of conduct had led the father to believe that his child maintenance obligations would not be enforced; that she had acquiesced in his non-culpable failure to contribute to his children's support; that the father had altered his position and undertaken new responsibilities in reliance on the mother's course of conduct and acquiescence with the result that he could not meet payments of past maintenance without serious hardship to his new family, and that it had not been established that his failure to contribute to the children's support had prejudiced their welfare. The *Shrimski* decision would, of course, mean that this approach was unacceptable. Judge Inglis QC confined that case to its own facts and declined an order for past child maintenance (and, indeed, for future maintenance). Parliament could never, he thought, have intended maintenance to be assessed by an inflexible process.[31]

Early in 1987, two cases, *Klasema* v *Klasema* and *Ray* v *Ray*,[32] were heard on the same day by Judge Inglis QC. They were classic 'exceptional' cases. The fathers sought variation, suspension or discharge of child maintenance orders and remission of arrears. They each had access orders in their favour. They now objected to paying child maintenance subsidising their former wives' household expenses. The court was satisfied that the mothers, who had custody of the children, had deliberately denied access and guardianship rights to the fathers and had excluded them from the children's lives. None of the children would suffer, it was found, if child maintenance were not paid to the mothers, who were in any case unlikely to change their attitudes. Very much more detailed and wide-ranging submissions were made by counsel than had been made in the *Shrimski* and *Green*

---

30   (1986) 4 NZFLR 178.
31   At p. 182. The court relied heavily on the decision of Chilwell J in *Caron* v *Caruana* [1975] 2 NZLR 372 which could not possibly be concerned with the 1980 Act.
32.   (1987) 4 NZFLR 458.

cases. The salient points made in the long judgment of the court were as follows:[33]

(a) As a matter of public policy, a non-custodial parent has a right to participate in the guardianship of his or her children regardless of separation or divorce.

(b) As a matter of public policy, a child has a right to the continuing influence and company and control of both parents.

(c) A child cannot claim maintenance under s. 72 or enforce a maintenance order or seek its variation. In terms of the Act, child maintenance proceedings are between parent and parent. The child is not a party to them. The order requires the payer to pay the custodial parent a contribution to his or her household expenses, the child being a member of that household. How the money was used was the payee's decision and there might, or might not, be a direct benefit to the child.

(d) In terms of s. 72(1), the parental obligation is to the child. If that obligation - which is to provide 'money, property, and services' - is converted solely into a money obligation by means of a child maintenance order, it becomes an obligation to the custodial parent, enforceable by that parent and payable to that parent. To recognise an obligation to 'maintain' a child is one thing; to convert it into an obligation to the custodial parent is fundamentally different. A child's right to maintenance is not the same thing as a custodial parent's right to claim a money contribution towards the child's maintenance, especially in cases such as the present.

(e) The word 'payable' in s. 72(2) and (3) meant 'to be provided' and a maintenance order was not the only way by which maintenance could be defined and enforced. Hence a custodial parent's choice to seek an order does not necessarily mean that the court will grant one once liability had been established in terms of s. 72.

---

33   The judgment extends from p. 459 to p. 475.

(f) An order can only be expressed in terms of money, but s. 72 does not impose an obligation to pay money alone. The section does not direct how the obligation to maintain should be discharged or enforced. While a legal obligation may exist, the court may decline to allow its enforcement in a particular way. The court does have a discretion to consider whether or not an order is appropriate to express the general obligation imposed by s. 72. Hence the power to make an order under s. 76(1) must be discretionary.

(g) There is a residual discretion under s. 99(1). s. 99(6) was unfettered by any express provision.

(h) The mothers here must be left to apply afresh when they were prepared to obey the access orders and recognise the fathers' rights as co-guardians. It would be entirely speculative to attempt to assess the children's needs in relation to their fathers' positions. The cases were not ones of the fathers' showing their first real interest in their children when it served their purpose to use access denial as a reason for wanting not to pay child maintenance or of delegation by them of their guardianship rights to the mothers.

In the case of Mrs Ray, her child maintenance order was suspended and all arrears were remitted, Mr Ray having established that he had no present ability to pay. In the case of Mrs Klasema, the same order was made, but a condition was imposed on Mr Klasema, who had the present ability to pay. It was that he set up a fund for his daughter, now aged sixteen, he and she being now in contact again. He was to pay NZ $80 per month into the fund and report to the Registrar every sixth month on the state of it.[34]

34   In *Jones* v *Jones* (1986) 4 NZFLR 106 the parties' marriage broke down and they had separated. Their two daughters, aged fourteen and ten, were in their mother's care but maintaining a good relationship with the father. The father had been unable to accept the separation and felt resentful at the idea of paying their mother anything. The interparental bitterness was likely to poison the children's lives. Judge Inglis QC sympathetically and ingeniously solved the *impasse* by making a child maintenance order against the husband

Those who support this approach will naturally accept that the mothers were in contempt (which they had not purged) and that the fathers had no means of controlling their children's standard of living, their education and the amount to be spent on each, and their expectations in life - all matters that ought to be jointly decided, as s. 72(2) presupposes, by the parents as co-guardians, failing which by the court. They will also accept that a child maintenance order does not automatically benefit the child as is commonly assumed, and that the obligation to maintain a child is an obligation of guardianship, as envisaged by s. 72(2). Doubtless, if it came to the point, they would argue in favour of amendment of s. 72 so as to allow maintenance orders to require that the money be paid to the child or be used only for the child's benefit, and of s. 76(1) so as to make clear that the Court does have a discretion whether or not to make an order and may go beyond the realms of s. 72(2) and (3).

Conclusion

It is obvious from the conflicting cases recounted above that the last word on this vexed issue has yet to be said. One cannot but sympathise with the sterling attempts to temper the statutory rules with fairness to the access-denied parent in the 'exceptional' cases and in situations such as that of Mr DY. One cannot but also concur with the insistence of Sinclair J that the child should not be punished by deprivation of maintenance, that the dominant feature of s. 72 is the welfare of the child and that a parent's liability to maintain his or her child should, as a rule, be regarded as 'absolute'. It may very well

for NZ $25 per child per week and suspending it under s. 99(1) so long as the husband opened a savings account for each girl and paid the weekly sum into it by direct credit: see at pp. 108-109. See also his decision in *Tristram* v *Department of Social Welfare* (1988) 5 NZFLR 289, at 290.

Although Sinclair J described the liability of a parent to maintain his or her child as 'absolute' (at 712), he accepted that there were certain cases where this was not the case: see at p. 710 and especially at 712, where he states that there could be cases where sufficient provision had been made for children other than by money, that they could be dealt with under s. 72(2) and that a Court could properly hold that child maintenance should not be ordered.

be that, if there is to be a discretion in this context, it should be limited to the Court's making no order at all - or only a reduced one - only in those cases where the relevant children are being maintained in some satisfactory and sufficient but nevertheless alternative manner, e.g. by being clothed and provided with accommodation at the expense of the access-denied parent, or are themselves in receipt of the maintenance money from that parent. In short, the position should be that the court is under a duty to ensure that the access-denied parent meets his or her substantive liability under s. 72 though it should have a discretion confined, and confined strictly, to the manner in which that parent is performing his or her obligation under that section.

12

The United Nations Convention on the Rights of the Child

David Freestone

The text of the United Nations Convention on the Rights of the Child was adopted by acclamation without a vote by the UN General Assembly on 20 November 1989.[1] The Convention is now open for signature and will come into force thirty days after it has been ratified by twenty states.[2] The text is the culmination of ten years of negotiations which were given particular urgency in the latter stages by the wish to finalise the text on the thirtieth anniversary of the adoption by the General Assembly of the Declaration of the Rights of the Child on 20 November 1959.[3]

1   UNGA Doc. A/RES/44/25 of 5 December 1989. The Resolution with annexed Convention text is reproduced in 28 ILM 1448 (1989), with an Introductory Note by Cynthia Price Cohen.
2   Article 49, the full text of the Convention is at pp. 294 ff, below.
3   UNGA Resolution 1386 (XIV). Reproduced in I. Brownlie, *Basic Documents on Human Rights* (Oxford: University Press, 2nd ed. 1981) p. 108.

The Convention is the most recent of a number of international instruments designed to secure the rights of children. In 1923 Eglantine Jebb, founder of the Save the Children International Fund, drafted a Declaration on the Rights of the Child, which was adopted by the League of Nations in 1924.[4] This formed the basis for the 1959 United Nations Declaration on the Rights of the Child, itself the starting point for the negotiation of the present Convention. In fact, it was Poland that initiated the ten year negotiation by putting forward a model text in the International Year of the Child in 1979,[5] but, as Cohen reports, its original proposal of twenty rights was expanded 'to a comprehensive treaty containing more than forty rights and covering the full spectrum of human rights protection'.[6] The process of negotiation itself is worthy of comment; in addition to the traditional Working Group of Experts procedure established in 1979, the texts developed and negotiated by the biannual meetings of the Working Group were, after 1983, subjected to detailed scrutiny by a Non-Governmental Organisation Ad Hoc Group on the Drafting of the Convention on the Rights of the Child composed of representatives of some thirty NGOs with UN consultative status. Many of the recommendations made by this NGO Group are reported to have been adopted by the Working Group and to have contributed to the formation of consensus.[7]

The acceptance of the text of the Convention without opposition within the General Assembly represents an important negotiating achievement, given the cultural diversity and the widely different legal systems and traditions of the States represented there. In particular, the negotiations managed to reconcile the traditional preference of western states for the enumeration of civil and political rights with that of 'eastern bloc' (to the extent that this is still a valid term to use in international affairs) and developing states for social

4   League of Nations, *Official Journal, Special Supplement No. 21*, October 1924, p. 43.
5   UN ESCOR Supp. (No. 16), UN Doc. E/CN.4/1349 (1979).
6   Cohen, n. 1, p. 1450.
7   Ibid., p. 1449. She describes this as 'a unique model of international legislative drafting' and reports that a number of rights can be traced directly to NGO recommendations, including Article 24(3) on protection against harmful 'traditional practices' (eg. female circumcision); Articles 34-6 on sexual exploitation; Articles 17(d), 29(d) and 30 on protection of rights of indigenous children.

and economic rights. Inevitably many of the articles concerned with the latter rights are expressed in aspirational or hortatory language, rather than imposing precise legal obligations, and many of the provisions dealing with the former types of rights still allow significant margins of discretion or appreciation to states in their implementation. These provisions themselves often reflect difficult compromises; for example, for the purposes of the Convention a 'child' is defined by Article 1 as 'every human being below the age of eighteen years unless, under the law applicable to the child, majority is attained earlier.' In addition to the obvious explicit discretion which this provides at the upper end of the age range, Davidson points out that the 'opaque terminology' of 'human being' avoids the sensitive issue of when a foetus becomes a human being.[8] *Prima facie* this is still a matter for each State's national law to determine.

Some delegations argued that a specific convention on the rights of the child was unnecessary, given the fact that children are human beings protected by existing human rights conventions. However as the negotiations progressed it became clear that there were a number of specific rights which could be identified as exclusively children's rights. As Cohen points out, one of the most unusual of these is the right to 'identity' in Article 8. This article, sponsored by Argentina, arose from Argentina's experience with children who 'disappeared' during the 'Dirty War'.[9] As a reading of the Convention will reveal, other articles demonstrate the way that general human rights are to be applied in relation to children.[10] This

---

8   J. S. Davidson, 'The United National Convention on the Rights of the Child' (1990) *New Zealand Family Law Bulletin*. He points out that Article 4 of the American Convention on Human Rights, which provides a right to life from the moment of conception, has been one of the reasons the US has not become a party to that Convention. See also P. Alston, 'The unborn child and abortion under the Draft Convention on the Rights of the Child' (1990) 12 *Human Rights Quarterly* 156-78.

9   Cohen, n. 1, p. 1451. And see Davidson, n. 7, who reports that children of *desesperados* were given to childless supporters of the military junta.

10   T. Hammarburg, 'The UN Convention on the Rights of the Child - and how to make it work' (1990) 12 *Human Rights Quarterly* 97-105 has suggested that the substantive rights protected by the Convention may be divided into three groups which he terms the 'three Ps': Provision (food, clothing, health care, etc.), Protection (from commercial and sexual exploitation, mental or physical abuse, use in warfare, etc.) and Participation (right to participate in decisions affecting his/her life and to express opinions).

in itself more than justifies the work devoted to the task, but the Convention has an additional juridical advantage. From the point of view of the development of the international law of human rights in general terms, the formal repetition of rights and standards in this way plays an important role in their adoption and recognition as a part of customary law. The acceptance of rights under customary law makes them binding not simply on parties to human rights conventions, but on all states except those that specifically object - and significantly the Convention text was adopted without dissent.

Apart from the definition itself, other controversial areas were the right to foster care and adoption, freedom of religion and the minimum age for participation in armed combat. The first two areas posed problems for Islamic countries, for Islamic law does not recognise adoption, nor does it accept a child's freedom to choose or change his or her religion. The Islamic concept of *Kafalah* permits orphaned or abandoned children to be cared for within a family unit, but without acquiring rights to use the family name or to inherit property. Consequently the texts of Articles 14 (on freedom of religion) and 20 and 21 (on adoption) are the results of 'very difficult and delicate' negotiations.[11] The 'recruitment' of children into the armed forces was given topicality by numerous reports that child-soldiers were being used in the Iran-Iraq war. The overwhelming majority of the Working Group were in favour of establishing eighteen as the minimum age for participation in armed conflict. Interestingly it was reported to be the United States which stood out against this, arguing that the 1977 Geneva Protocols accepted the age of fifteen as a minimum and that the Working Group was 'not a proper forum to alter existing standards of international humanitarian law'.[12]

The implementation of the Convention is to be governed by the principle of the 'best interests of the child'.[13] When it comes into force, the Convention will establish a ten-member Committee on the Rights of the Child to supervise the implementation of the Convention by States Parties. The members of the Committee will be 'experts of high moral standing and recognized competence in the field' and

11   Cohen, n. 1, p. 1451. See further Davidson, n. 8.
12   Cohen, ibid.
13   Article 3.

although elected from among nationals of States Parties will serve in their personal capacity.[14] In line with the procedure of other human rights conventions, States Parties must submit written reports to the Committee 'on the measures they have adopted which give effect to the rights recognized herein, and on the progress made on the enjoyment of those rights'.[15] The initial national report must be submitted within two years of becoming a Party, and thereafter at five yearly intervals. As Davidson comments, the Convention is silent on whether these reports may ultimately be discussed by the General Assembly but, by analogy with other such conventions, it seems likely that they will be, for:

> the discussion of an unfavourable report before the General Assembly, the plenary organ of the UN, and the attendant publicity is one of the few effective 'sanctions' available in the field of human rights law.[16]

In fact, the emphasis of the Committee procedure is on assisting the States Parties to meet their obligations under the Convention rather than on penalising non-compliance; specific provisions permit reference of requests for technical assistance directly to specialised agencies, UNICEF and 'other competent bodies', and, in another unusual development, such agencies and bodies are also given a direct input into the Committee's monitoring process.[17]

It has been argued that the rush to complete the Convention by 1989 meant that some important proposals could not be incorporated in the text - notably the idea of an International Ombudsman for the Rights of the Child, proposals for national monitoring committees, and mechanisms for reviewing complaints by individual children of violation of the rights contained in the Convention.[18] Nevertheless, the ten years of negotiation have clearly changed the original conception of the treaty beyond recognition and

---

14   Article 43.
15   Article 44.
16   Davidson, n. 8.
17   Article 45.
18   Cohen, n. 1, p. 1452.

the 1989 deadline seems to have provided an important impetus for agreement. Such criticisms as can legitimately be made of the text should not detract from the significant achievement of approving a text acceptable to all UN members which will undoubtedly provide an important benchmark for the basic standards of treatment of children by members of the international community.

The Text of
the United Nations Convention on
the Rights of the Child

PREAMBLE

The States Parties to the present Convention,

Considering that in accordance with the principles proclaimed in the Charter of the United Nations, recognition of the inherent dignity and of the equal and inalienable rights of all members of the human family is the foundation of freedom, justice and peace in the world,

Bearing in mind that the peoples of the United Nations have, in the Charter, reaffirmed their faith in fundamental human rights and in the dignity and worth of the human person, and have determined to promote social progress and better standards of life in larger freedom,

Recognizing that the United Nations has, in the Universal Declaration of Human Rights[1] and in the International Covenants on Human Rights,[2] proclaimed and agreed that everyone is entitled to all the rights and freedoms set forth therein, without distinction of any kind, such as race, colour, sex, language, religion, political or other opinion, national or social origin, property, birth or other status,

---

1   UNGA Resolution 217 A (III).
2   see UNGA Resolution 2200 A (XXI), annex.

Recalling that, in the Universal Declaration of Human Rights, the United Nations has proclaimed that childhood is entitled to special care and assistance,

Convinced that the family, as the fundamental group of society and the natural environment for the growth and well-being of all its members and particularly children, should be afforded the necessary protection and assistance so that it can fully assume its responsibilities within the community,

Recognizing that the child, for the full and harmonious development of his or her personality, should grow up in a family environment, in an atmosphere of happiness, love and understanding,

Considering that the child should be fully prepared to live an individual life in society, and brought up in the spirit of the ideals proclaimed in the Charter of the United Nations, and in particular in the spirit of peace, dignity, tolerance, freedom, equality and solidarity,

Bearing in mind that the need to extend particular care to the child has been stated in the Geneva Declaration on the Rights of the Child of 1924[3] and in the Declaration of the Rights of the Child adopted by the General Assembly on 20 November 1959[4] and recognized in the Universal Declaration of Human Rights, in the International Covenant on Civil and Political Rights (in particular in articles 23 and 24),[5] in the International Covenant on Economic, Social and Cultural Rights (in particular in article 10)[6] and in the statutes and relevant instruments of specialized agencies and international organizations concerned with the welfare of children,

3	See League of Nations, *Official Journal, Special Supplement No. 21*, October 1924, p. 43.
4	UNGA Resolution 1386 (XIV).
5	see UNGA Resolution 2200 A (XXI), annex.
6	Ibid.

Bearing in mind that, as indicated in the Declaration of the Rights of the Child, 'the child, by reason of his physical and mental immaturity, needs special safeguards and care, including appropriate legal protection, before as well as after birth',[7]

Recalling the provisions of the Declaration on Social and Legal Principles relating to the Protection and Welfare of Children, with Special Reference to Foster Placement and Adoption Nationally and Internationally[8] the United Nations Standard Minimum Rules for the Administration of Juvenile Justice (The Beijing Rules)[9] and the Declaration on the Protection of Women and Children in Emergency and Armed Conflict,[10]

Recognizing that, in all countries in the world, there are children living in exceptionally difficult conditions, and that such children need special consideration,

Taking due account of the importance of the traditions and cultural values of each people for the protection and harmonious development of the child,

Recognizing the importance of international cooperation for improving the living conditions of children in every country, in particular in the developing countries,

Have agreed as follows:

PART 1

Article 1

For the purposes of the present Convention, a child means every human being below the age of eighteen years unless, under the law applicable to the child, majority is attained earlier.

---

7   UNGA Resolution 1386 (XIV), third preambular paragraph.
8   UNGA Resolution 41/85, annex.
9   UNGA Resolution 40/33, annex.
10   UNGA Resolution 3318 (XXIX).

Article 2

1.   States Parties to the present Convention shall respect and ensure the rights set forth in this Convention to each child within their jurisdiction without discrimination of any kind, irrespective of the child's or his or her parent's or legal guardian's race, colour, sex, language, religion, political or other opinion, national, ethnic or social origin, property, disability, birth or other status.

2.   States Parties shall take all appropriate measures to ensure that the child is protected against all forms of discrimination or punishment on the basis of the status, activities, expressed opinions, or beliefs of the child's parents, legal guardians, or family members.

Article 3

1.   In all actions concerning children, whether undertaken by public or private social welfare institutions, courts of law, administrative authorities or legislative bodies, the best interests of the child shall be a primary consideration.

2.   States Parties undertake to ensure the child such protection and care as is necessary for his or her well-being, taking into account the rights and duties of his or her parents, legal guardians, or other individuals legally responsible for him or her, and, to this end, shall take all appropriate legislative and administrative measures.

3.   States Parties shall ensure that the institutions, services and facilities responsible for the care or protection of children shall conform with the standards established by competent authorities, particularly in the areas of safety, health, in the number and suitability of their staff as well as competent supervision.

Article 4

States Parties shall undertake all appropriate legislative, administrative, and other measures for the implementation of the rights recognized in the present Convention. With regard to economic, social and cultural rights, States Parties shall undertake such measures to the maximum extent of their available resources and, where needed, within the framework of international co-operation.

Article 5

States Parties shall respect the responsibilities, rights and duties of parents or, where applicable, the members of the extended family or community as provided for by the local custom, legal guardians or other persons legally responsible for the child, to provide, in a manner consistent with the evolving capacities of the child, appropriate direction and guidance in the exercise by the child of the rights recognized in the present Convention.

Article 6

1.   States Parties recognize that every child has the inherent right to life.
2.   States Parties shall ensure to the maximum extent possible the survival and development of the child.

Article 7

1.   The child shall be registered immediately after birth and shall have the right from birth to a name, the right to acquire a nationality, and, as far as possible, the right to know and be cared for by his or her parents.

2.   States Parties shall ensure the implementation of these rights in accordance with their national law and their obligations under the relevant international instruments in this field, in particular where the child would otherwise be stateless.

Article 8

1.   States Parties undertake to respect the right of the child to preserve his or her identity, including nationality, name and family relations as recognized by law without unlawful interference.

2.   Where a child is illegally deprived of some or all of the elements of his or her identity, States Parties shall provide appropriate assistance and protection, with a view to speedily reestablishing his or her identity.

Article 9

1.   States Parties shall ensure that a child shall not be separated from his or her parents against their will, except when competent authorities subject to judicial review determine, in accordance with applicable law and procedures, that such separation is necessary for the best interests of the child. Such determination may be necessary in a particular case such as one involving abuse or neglect of the child by the parents, or one where the parents are living separately and a decision must be made as to the child's place of residence.

2.   In any proceedings pursuant to paragraph 1 of the present article, all interested parties shall be given an opportunity to participate in the proceedings and make their views known.

3.   States Parties shall respect the right of the child who is separated from one or both parents to maintain personal relations and direct contact with both parents on a regular basis, except if it is contrary to the child's best interests.

4.   Where such separation results from any action initiated by a State Party, such as the detention, imprisonment, exile, deportation or death (including death arising from any cause while the person is in the custody of the State) of one or both parents or of the child, that State Party shall, upon request, provide the parents, the child or, if appropriate, another member of the family with the essential information concerning the whereabouts of the absent member(s) of the family unless the provision of the information would be detrimental to the well-being of the child. States Parties shall further ensure that the submission of such a request shall of itself entail no adverse consequences for the person(s) concerned.

Article 10

1.   In accordance with the obligation of States Parties under article 9, paragraph 1, applications by a child or his or her parents to enter or leave a State Party for the purpose of family reunification shall be dealt with by States Parties in a positive, humane and expeditious manner. States Parties shall further ensure that the submission of such a request shall entail no adverse consequences for the applicants and for the members of their family.

2.   A child whose parents reside in different States shall have the right to maintain on a regular basis, save in exceptional circumstances, personal relations and direct contacts with both parents. Towards that end and in accordance with the obligation of States Parties under article 9, paragraph 2, States Parties shall respect the right of the child and his or her parents to leave any country, including their own, and to enter their own country. The right to leave any country shall be subject only to such restrictions as are prescribed by law and which are necessary to protect the national security, public order (*ordre public*), public health or morals or the rights and freedoms of others and are consistent with the other rights recognized in the present Convention.

Article 11

1.   States Parties shall take measures to combat the illicit transfer and non-return of children abroad.

2.   To this end, States Parties shall promote the conclusion of bilateral or multilateral agreements or accession to existing agreements.

Article 12

1.   States Parties shall assure to the child who is capable of forming his or her own views the right to express those views freely in all matters affecting the child, the views of the child being given due weight in accordance with the age and maturity of the child.

2.   For this purpose, the child shall in particular be provided the opportunity to be heard in any judicial and administrative proceedings affecting the child, either directly, or through a representative or an appropriate body, in a manner consistent with the procedural rules of national law.

Article 13

1.   The child shall have the right to freedom of expression; this right shall include freedom to seek, receive and impart information and ideas of all kinds, regardless of frontiers, either orally, in writing or in print, in the form of art, or through any other media of the child's choice.

2.   The exercise of this right may be subject to certain restrictions, but these shall only be such as are provided by law and are necessary:

    (a)   for respect of the rights or reputations of others; or

    (b)   for the protection of national security or of public order (*ordre public*), or of public health or morals.

Article 14

1.   States Parties shall respect the right of the child to freedom of thought, conscience and religion.

2.   States Parties shall respect the rights and duties of the parents and, when applicable, legal guardians, to provide direction to the child in the exercise of his or her right in a manner consistent with the evolving capacities of the child.

3.   Freedom to manifest one's religion or beliefs may be subject only to such limitations as are prescribed by law and are necessary to protect public safety, order, health or morals, or the fundamental rights and freedoms of others.

Article 15

1.   States Parties recognize the rights of the child to freedom of association and to freedom of peaceful assembly.

2.   No restrictions may be placed on the exercise of these rights other than those imposed in conformity with the law and which are necessary in a democratic society in the interests of national security or public safety, public order (*ordre public*), the protection of public health or morals or the protection of the rights and freedoms of others.

Article 16

1.   No child shall be subjected to arbitrary or unlawful interference with his or her privacy, family, home or correspondence, nor to unlawful attacks on his or her honour and reputation.

2.   The child has the right to the protection of the law against such interference or attacks.

Article 17

States Parties recognize the important function performed by the mass media and shall ensure that the child has access to information and material from a diversity of national and international sources, especially those aimed at the promotion of his or her social, spiritual and moral well-being and physical and mental health. To this end, States Parties shall:

   (a)   Encourage the mass media to disseminate information and material of social and cultural benefit to the child and in accordance with the spirit of article 29;

   (b)   Encourage international co-operation in the production, exchange and dissemination of such information and material from a diversity of cultural, national and international sources;

(c)   Encourage the production and dissemination of children's books;

(d)   Encourage the mass media to have particular regard to the linguistic needs of the child who belongs to a minority group or who is indigenous;

(e)   Encourage the development of appropriate guidelines for the protection of the child from information and material injurious to his or her well-being, bearing in mind the provisions of articles 13 and 18.

Article 18

1.   States Parties shall use their best efforts to ensure recognition of the principle that both parents have common responsibilities for the upbringing and development of the child. Parents or, as the case may be, legal guardians, have the primary responsibility for the upbringing and development of the child. The best interests of the child will be their basic concern.

2.   For the purpose of guaranteeing and promoting the rights set forth in the present Convention, States Parties shall render appropriate assistance to parents and legal guardians in the performance of their child-rearing responsibilities and shall ensure the development of institutions, facilities and services for the care of children.

3.   States Parties shall take all appropriate measures to ensure that children of working parents have the right to benefit from child-care services and facilities for which they are eligible.

Article 19

1.   States Parties shall take all appropriate legislative, administrative, social and educational measures to protect the child from all forms of physical or mental violence, injury or abuse, neglect or negligent treatment, maltreatment or exploitation, including sexual

abuse, while in the care of parent(s), legal guardian(s) or any other person who has the care of the child.

2.   Such protective measures should, as appropriate, include effective procedures for the establishment of social programmes to provide necessary support for the child and for those who have the care of the child, as well as for other forms of prevention and for identification, reporting, referral, investigation, treatment and follow-up of instances of child maltreatment described heretofore, and, as appropriate, for judicial involvement.

Article 20

1.   A child temporarily or permanently deprived of his or her family environment, or in whose own best interests cannot be allowed to remain in that environment, shall be entitled to special protection and assistance provided by the State.

2.   States Parties shall in accordance with their national laws ensure alternative care for such a child.

3.   Such care could include, *inter alia*, foster placement, *kafala* of Islamic law, adoption or if necessary placement in suitable institutions for the care of children. When considering solutions, due regard shall be paid to the desirability of continuity in a child's upbringing and to the child's ethnic, religious, cultural and linguistic background.

Article 21

States Parties that recognize and/or permit the system of adoption shall ensure that the best interests of the child shall be the paramount consideration and they shall:

    (a)   ensure the adoption of a child is authorized only by competent authorities who determine, in accordance with applicable law and procedures and on the basis of all pertinent and reliable information, that the adoption is permissible in view of the child's status concerning parents, relatives and legal guardians and that, if required, the persons concerned have given their informed consent to the adoption on the basis of such counselling as may be necessary;

(b)   recognise that inter-country adoption may be considered as an alternative means of child's care, if the child cannot be placed in a foster or an adoptive family or cannot in any suitable manner be cared for in the child's country of origin;

(c)   ensure that the child concerned by inter-country adoption enjoys safeguards and standards equivalent to those existing in the case of national adoption;

(d)   take all appropriate measures to ensure that, in inter-country adoption, the placement does not result in improper financial gain for those involved in it;

(e)   promote, where appropriate, the objectives of this article by concluding bilateral or multilateral arrangements or agreements, and endeavour, within this framework, to ensure that the placement of the child in another country is carried out by competent authorities or organs.

Article 22

1.   States Parties shall take appropriate measures to ensure that a child who is seeking refugee status or who is considered a refugee in accordance with applicable international or domestic law and procedures shall, whether unaccompanied or accompanied by his or her parents or by any other person, receive appropriate protection and humanitarian assistance in the enjoyment of applicable rights set forth in this Convention and in other international human rights or humanitarian instruments to which the said States are Parties.

2.   For this purpose, States Parties shall provide, as they consider appropriate, co-operation in any efforts by the United Nations and other competent intergovernmental organizations or non-governmental organizations co-operating with the United Nations to protect and assist such a child and to trace the parents or other members of the family of any refugee child in order to obtain information necessary for reunification with his or her family. In cases where no parents or other members of the family can be found, the child shall be accorded the same protection as any other child permanently or temporarily deprived of his or her family environment for any reason, as set forth in the present Convention.

Article 23

1.   States Parties recognize that a mentally or physically disabled child should enjoy a full and decent life, in conditions which ensure dignity, promote self-reliance and facilitate the child's active participation in the community.

2.   States Parties recognize the right of the disabled child to special care and shall encourage and ensure the extension, subject to available resources, to the eligible child and those responsible for his or her care, of assistance for which application is made and which is appropriate to the child's condition and to the circumstances of the parents or others caring for the child.

3.   Recognizing the special needs of a disabled child, assistance extended in accordance with paragraph 2 of the present article shall be provided free of charge, whenever possible, taking into account the financial resources of the parents or others caring for the child, and shall be designed to ensure that the disabled child has effective access to and receives education, training, health care services, rehabilitation services, preparation for employment and recreation opportunities in a manner conducive to the child's achieving the fullest possible social integration and individual development, including his or her cultural and spiritual development.

4.   States Parties shall promote, in the spirit of international co-operation, the exchange of appropriate information in the field of

preventive health care and of medical, psychological and functional treatment of disabled children, including dissemination of and access to information concerning methods of rehabilitation, education and vocational services, with the aim of enabling States Parties to improve their capabilities and skills and to widen their experience in these areas. In this regard, particular account shall be taken of the needs of developing countries.

Article 24

1.   States Parties recognize the right of the child to the enjoyment of the highest attainable standard of health and to facilities for the treatment of illness and rehabilitation of health. States Parties shall strive to ensure that no child is deprived of his or her right of access to such health care services.

2.   States Parties shall pursue full implementation of this right and, in particular, shall take appropriate measures:

(a)   to diminish infant and child mortality;

(b)   to ensure the provision of necessary medical assistance and health care to all children with emphasis on the development of primary health care;

(c)   to combat disease and malnutrition, including within the framework of primary health care, through, *inter alia,* the application of readily available technology and through the provision of adequate nutritious foods and clean drinking water, taking into consideration the dangers and risks of environmental pollution;

(d)   to ensure appropriate pre-natal and post-natal health care for mothers;

(e)   to ensure that all segments of society, in particular parents and children, are informed, have access to education and are supported in the use of basic knowledge of child health and nutrition, the advantages of breast-feeding, hygiene and environmental sanitation and the prevention of accidents;

(f)   to develop preventive health care, guidance for parents and family planning education and services.

3.   States Parties shall take all effective and appropriate measures with a view to abolishing traditional practices prejudicial to the health of children.

4.   States Parties undertake to promote and encourage international co-operation with a view to achieving progressively the full realization of the right recognized in the present article. In this regard, particular account shall be taken of the needs of developing countries.

Article 25

States Parties recognize the right of a child who has been placed by the competent authorities for the purposes of care, protection or treatment or his or her physical or mental health, to a periodic review of the treatment provided to the child and all other circumstances relevant to his or her placement.

Article 26

1.   States Parties shall recognize for every child the right to benefit from social security, including social insurance, and shall take the necessary measures to achieve the full realization of this right in accordance with their national law.

2.   The benefits should, where appropriate, be granted, taking into account the resources and the circumstances of the child and persons having responsibility for the maintenance of the child, as well as any other consideration relevant to an application for benefits made by or on behalf of the child.

Article 27

1.   States Parties recognize the right of every child to a standard of living adequate for the child's physical, mental, spiritual, moral and social development.

2.   The parent(s) or others responsible for the child have the primary responsibility to secure, within their abilities and financial capacities, the conditions of living necessary for the child's development.

3.   States Parties in accordance with national conditions and within their means shall take appropriate measures to assist parents and others responsible for the child to implement this right and shall in case of need provide material assistance and support programmes, particularly with regard to nutrition, clothing and housing.

4.   States Parties shall take all appropriate measures to secure the recovery of maintenance for the child from the parents or other persons having financial responsibility for the child, both within the State Party and from abroad. In particular, where the person having financial responsibility for the child lives in a State different from that of the child, States Parties shall promote the accession to international agreements or the conclusion of such agreements, as well as the making of other appropriate arrangements.

Article 28

1.   States Parties recognize the right of the child to education, and with a view to achieving this right progressively and on the basis of equal opportunity, they shall, in particular:

    (a)   make primary education compulsory and available free to all;

    (b)   encourage the development of different forms of secondary education, including general and vocational education, make them available and accessible to every child, and take appropriate measures such as the introduction of free education and offering financial assistance in case of need;

(d) make higher education accessible to all on the basis of capacity by every appropriate means;

(d) make educational and vocational information and guidance available and accessible to all children;

(e) take measures to encourage regular attendance at schools and the reduction of drop-out rates.

2. States Parties shall take all appropriate measures to ensure that school discipline is administered in a manner consistent with the child's human dignity and in conformity with the present Convention.

3. States Parties shall promote and encourage international co-operation in matters relating to education, in particular with a view to contributing to the elimination of ignorance and illiteracy throughout the world and facilitating access to scientific and technical knowledge and modern teaching methods. In this regard, particular account shall be taken of the needs of developing countries.

Article 29

1. States Parties agree that the education of the child shall be directed to:

(a) the development of the child's personality, talents and mental and physical abilities to their fullest potential;

(b) the development of respect for human rights and fundamental freedoms, and for the principles enshrined in the Charter of the United Nations;

(c)   the development of respect for the child's parents, his or her own cultural identity, language and values, for the national values of the country in which the child is living, the country from which he or she may originate, and for civilizations different from his or her own;

(d)   the preparation of the child for responsible life in a free society, in the spirit of understanding, peace, tolerance, equality of sexes, and friendship among all peoples, ethnic, national and religious groups and persons of indigenous origin;

(e)   the development of respect for the natural environment.

2.   No part of the present article or article 28 shall be construed so as to interfere with the liberty of individuals and bodies to establish and direct educational institutions, subject always to the observance of the principles set forth in paragraph 1 of this article and to the requirements that the education given in such institutions shall conform to such minimum standards as may be laid down by the State.

Article 30

In those States in which ethnic, religious or linguistic minorities or persons of indigenous origin exist, a child belonging to such a minority or who is indigenous shall not be denied the right, in community with other members of his or her group, to enjoy his or her own culture, to profess and practice his or her own religion, or to use his or her own language.

Article 31

1.   States Parties recognize the right of the child to rest and leisure, to engage in play and recreational activities appropriate to the age of the child and to participate freely in cultural life and the arts.

2.   States Parties shall respect and promote the right of the child to participate fully in cultural and artistic life and shall encourage the provision of appropriate and equal opportunities for cultural, artistic, recreational and leisure activity.

Article 32

1.   States Parties recognize the right of the child to be protected from economic exploitation and from performing any work that is likely to be hazardous or to interfere with the child's education, or to be harmful to the child's health or physical, mental, spiritual, moral or social development.

2.   States Parties shall take legislative, administrative, social and educational measures to ensure the implementation of the present article. To this end, and having regard to the relevant provisions of other international instruments, States Parties shall in particular:

(a)   provide for a minimum age or minimum ages for admission to employment;

(b)   provide for appropriate regulation of the hours and conditions of employment;

(c)   provide for appropriate penalties or other sanctions to ensure the effective enforcement of the present article.

Article 33

States Parties shall take all appropriate measures, including legislative, administrative, social and educational measures, to protect children from the illicit use of narcotic drugs and psychotropic substances as defined in the relevant international treaties, and to prevent the use of children in the illicit production and trafficking of such substances.

Article 34

States Parties undertake to protect the child from all forms of sexual exploitation and sexual abuse. For these purposes, States Parties shall in particular take all appropriate national, bilateral and multilateral measures to prevent:

(a)   the inducement or coercion of a child to engage in any unlawful sexual activity;

(b)   the exploitative use of children in prostitution or other unlawful sexual practices;

(c)   the exploitative use of children in pornographic performances and materials.

Article 35

States Parties shall take all appropriate national, bilateral and multilateral measures to prevent the abduction of, the sale of or traffic in children for any purpose or in any form.

Article 36

States Parties shall protect the child against all other forms of exploitation prejudicial to any aspects of the child's welfare.

Article 37

States Parties shall ensure that:

(a)   No child shall be subjected to torture or other cruel, inhuman or degrading treatment or punishment. Neither capital punishment nor life imprisonment without possibility of release shall be imposed for offences committed by persons below eighteen years of age.

(b)   No child shall be deprived of his or her liberty unlawfully or arbitrarily. The arrest, detention or imprisonment of a child shall be in conformity with the law and shall be used only as a measure of last resort and for the shortest appropriate period of time;

(c)   Every child deprived of liberty shall be treated with humanity and respect for the inherent dignity of the human person, and in a manner which takes into account the needs of persons of his or her age. In particular every child deprived of liberty shall be separated from adults unless it is considered in the child's best interest not to do so and shall have the right to maintain contact with his or her family through correspondence and visits, save in exceptional circumstances;

(d)   Every child deprived of his or her liberty shall have the right to prompt access to legal and other appropriate assistance as well as the right to challenge the legality of the deprivation of his or her liberty before a court or other competent, independent and impartial authority and to a prompt decision on any such action.

Article 38

1.   States Parties undertake to respect and to ensure respect for rules of international humanitarian law applicable to them in armed conflicts which are relevant to the child.

2.   States Parties shall take all feasible measures to ensure that persons who have not attained the age of fifteen years do not take a direct part in hostilities.

3.   States Parties shall refrain from recruiting any person who has not attained the age of fifteen years into their armed forces. In recruiting among those persons who have attained the age of fifteen years but who have not attained the age of eighteen years, States Parties shall endeavour to give priority to those who are oldest.

4.   In accordance with their obligations under international humanitarian law to protect the civilian population in armed conflicts,

States Parties shall take all feasible measures to ensure protection and care of children who are affected by an armed conflict.

Article 39

States Parties shall take all appropriate measures to promote physical and psychological recovery and social reintegration of a child victim of: any form of neglect, exploitation, or abuse; torture or any other form of cruel, inhuman or degrading treatment or punishment; or armed conflicts. Such recovery and reintegration shall take place in an environment which fosters the health, self-respect and dignity of the child.

Article 40

1.   States Parties recognize the right of every child alleged as, accused of, or recognized as having infringed the penal law to be treated in a manner consistent with the promotion of the child's sense of dignity and worth, which reinforces the child's respect for the human rights and fundamental freedoms of others and which takes into account the child's age and the desirability of promoting the child's reintegration and the child's assuming a constructive role in society.

2.   To this end, and having regard to the relevant provisions of international instruments, States Parties shall, in particular, ensure that:

(a)   No child shall be alleged as, be accused of, or recognized as having infringed the penal law by reason of acts or omissions which were not prohibited by national or international law at the time they were committed;

(b)   Every child alleged as or accused of having infringed the penal law has at least the following guarantees:

(i)   to be presumed innocent until proven guilty according to law;

(ii)   to be informed promptly and directly of the charges against him or her, and, if appropriate, through his or her parents or legal guardians, and to have legal or other appropriate assistance in the preparation and presentation of his or her defence;

(iii)   to have the matter determined without delay by a competent, independent and impartial authority or judicial body in a fair hearing according to law, in the presence of legal or other appropriate assistance and, unless it is considered not to be in the best interest of the child, in particular, taking into account his or her age or situation, his or her parents or legal guardians;

(iv)   not to be compelled to give testimony or to confess guilt; to examine or have examined adverse witnesses and to obtain the participation and examination of witnesses on his or her behalf under conditions of equality;

(v)   if considered to have infringed the penal law, to have this decision and any measures imposed in consequence thereof reviewed by a higher competent, independent and impartial authority or judicial body according to law;

(vi)   to have the free assistance of an interpreter if the child cannot understand or speak the language used;

(vii)   to have his or her privacy fully respected at all stages of the proceedings.

3.   States Parties shall seek to promote the establishment of laws, procedures, authorities and institutions specifically applicable to children alleged as, accused of, or recognized as having infringed the penal law, and, in particular:

(a)   the establishment of a minimum age below which children shall be presumed not to have the capacity to infringe the penal law;

(b)   whenever appropriate and desirable, measures for dealing with such children without resorting to judicial proceedings, providing that human rights and legal safeguards are fully respected.

4.   A variety of dispositions, such as care, guidance and supervision orders; counselling; probation; foster care; education and vocational training programmes and other alternatives to institutional care shall be available to ensure that children are dealt with in a manner appropriate to their well-being and proportionate both to their circumstances and the offence.

Article 41

Nothing in the present Convention shall affect any provisions that are more conducive to the realization of the rights of the child and which may be contained in:

(a)   the law of a State Party; or

(b)   international law in force for that State.

PART II

Article 42

States Parties undertake to make the principles and provisions of the Convention widely known, by appropriate and active means, to adults and children alike.

Article 43

1.   For the purpose of examining the progress made by States Parties in achieving the realization of the obligations undertaken in

the present Convention, there shall be established a Committee on the Rights of the Child, which shall carry out the functions hereinafter provided.

2.   The Committee shall consist of ten experts of high moral standing and recognized competence in the field covered by this Convention. The members of the Committee shall be elected by States Parties from among their nationals and shall serve in their personal capacity, consideration being given to equitable geographical distribution as well as to the principal legal systems.

3.   The members of the Committee shall be elected by secret ballot from a list of persons nominated by States Parties. Each State Party may nominate one person from among its own nationals.

4.   The initial election to the Committee shall be held no later than six months after the date of the entry into force of the present Convention and thereafter every second year. At least four months before the date of each election, the Secretary-General of the United Nations shall address a letter to States Parties inviting them to submit their nominations within two months. The Secretary-General shall subsequently prepare a list in alphabetical order of all persons thus nominated, indicating States Parties which have nominated them, and shall submit it to the States Parties to the present Convention.

5.   The elections shall be held at meetings of States Parties convened by the Secretary-General at United Nations Headquarters. At those meetings, for which two-thirds of States Parties shall constitute a quorum, the persons elected to the Committee shall be those who obtain the largest number of votes and an absolute majority of the votes of the representatives of States Parties present and voting.

6.   The members of the Committee shall be elected for a term of four years. They shall be eligible for re-election if renominated. The term of five of the members elected at the first election shall expire at the end of two years; immediately after the first elections the names of these five members shall be chosen by lot by the Chairman of the meeting.

7.   If a member of the Committee dies or resigns or declares that for any other cause he or she can no longer perform the duties of the Committee, the State Party which nominated the member shall appoint another expert from among its nationals to serve for the remainder of the term, subject to the approval of the Committee.

8.   The Committee shall establish its own rules of procedure.

9.   The Committee shall elect its officers for a period of two years.

10.   The meetings of the Committee shall normally be held at the United Nations Headquarters or at any other convenient place as determined by the Committee. The Committee shall normally meet annually. The duration of the meetings of the Committee shall be determined, and reviewed, if necessary, by a meeting of the States Parties to the present Convention, subject to the approval of the General Assembly.

11.   The Secretary-General of the United Nations shall provide the necessary staff and facilities for the effective performance of the functions of the Committee under the present Convention.

12.   With the approval of the General Assembly, the members of the Committee established under the present Convention shall receive emoluments from the United Nations resources on such terms and conditions as the Assembly may decide.

Article 44

1.   States Parties undertake to submit to the Committee, through the Secretary-General of the United Nations, reports on the measures they have adopted which give effect to the rights recognized herein and on the progress made on the enjoyment of those rights:

(a)   within two years of the entry into force of the Convention for the State Party concerned;

(b)   thereafter every five years.

2.   Reports made under the present article shall indicate factors and difficulties, if any, affecting the degree of fulfilment of the obligations under the present Convention. Reports shall also contain sufficient information to provide the Committee with a comprehensive understanding of the implementation of the Convention in the country concerned.

3.   A State Party which has submitted a comprehensive initial report to the Committee need not, in its subsequent reports submitted in accordance with paragraph 1(b) of the present article, repeat basic information previously provided.

4.   The Committee may request from States Parties further information relevant to the implementation of the Convention.

5.   The Committee shall submit to the General Assembly, through the Economic and Social Council, every two years, reports on its activities.

6.   States Parties shall make their reports widely available to the public in their own countries.

Article 45

In order to foster the effective implementation of the Convention and to encourage international co-operation in the field covered by the Convention:

(a)   The specialized agencies, the United Nations Children's Fund and other United Nations organs shall be entitled to be represented at the consideration of the implementation of such provisions of the present Convention as fall within the scope of their mandate. The Committee may invite the specialized agencies, the United Nations Children's Fund and other competent bodies as it may consider appropriate to provide expert advice on the implementation of the Convention in areas falling within the scope of their respective mandates. The Committee may invite the specialized agencies, the

United Nations Children's Fund and other United Nations organs to submit reports on the implementation of the Convention in areas falling within the scope of their activities;

(b) The Committee shall transmit, as it may consider appropriate, to the specialized agencies, the United Nations Children's Fund and other competent bodies, any reports from States Parties that contain a request, or indicate a need, for technical advice or assistance, along with the Committee's observations and suggestions, if any, on these requests or indications;

(c) the Committee may recommend to the General Assembly to request the Secretary-General to undertake on its behalf studies on specific issues relating to the rights of the child;

(d) the Committee may make suggestions and general recommendations based on information received pursuant to articles 44 and 45 of the present Convention. Such suggestions and general recommendations shall be transmitted to any State Party concerned and reported to the General Assembly, together with comments, if any, from States Parties.

PART III

Article 46

The present Convention shall be open for signature by all States.

Article 47

The present Convention is subject to ratification. Instruments of ratification shall be deposited with the Secretary-General of the United Nations.

Article 48

The present Convention shall remain open for accession by any State. The instruments of accession shall be deposited with the Secretary-General of the United Nations.

Article 49

1.   The present Convention shall enter into force on the thirtieth day following the date of deposit with the Secretary-General of the United Nations of the twentieth instrument of ratification or accession.

2.   For each State ratifying or acceding to the Convention after the deposit of the twentieth instrument of ratification or accession, the Convention shall enter into force on the thirtieth day after the deposit by such State of its instrument of ratification or accession.

Article 50

1.   Any State Party may propose an amendment and file it with the Secretary-General of the United Nations. The Secretary-General shall thereupon communicate the proposed amendment to States Parties, with a request that they indicate whether they favour a conference of States Parties for the purpose of considering and voting upon the proposals. In the event that, within four months from the date of such communication, at least one-third of the States Parties favour such a conference, the Secretary-General shall convene the conference under the auspices of the United Nations. Any amendment adopted by a majority of States Parties present and voting at the conference shall be submitted to the General Assembly for approval.

2.   An amendment adopted in accordance with paragraph (1) of the present article shall enter into force when it has been approved by the General Assembly of the United Nations and accepted by a two-thirds majority of States Parties.

3.   When an amendment enters into force, it shall be binding on those States Parties which have accepted it, other States Parties still being bound by the provisions of the present Convention and any earlier amendments which they have accepted.

Article 51

1.   The Secretary-General of the United Nations shall receive and circulate to all States the text of reservations made by States at the time of ratification or accession.

2.   A reservation incompatible with the object and purpose of the present Convention shall not be permitted.

3.   Reservations may be withdrawn at any time by notification to that effect addressed to the Secretary-General of the United Nations, who shall then inform all States. Such notification shall take effect on the date on which it is received by the Secretary-General.

Article 52

A State Party may denounce the present Convention by written notification to the Secretary-General of the United Nations. Denunciation becomes effective one year after the date of receipt of the notification by the Secretary-General.

Article 53

The Secretary-General of the United Nations is designated as the depositary of the present Convention.

Article 54

The original of the present Convention, of which the Arabic, Chinese, English, French, Russian and Spanish texts are equally authentic, shall be deposited with the Secretary-General of the United Nations.

In witness thereof the undersigned plenipotentiaries, being duly authorized thereto by their respective governments, have signed the present Convention.

INDEX